A Recruiter's Truly Simple Guide to Stop F*cking Up When Job Searching & Interviewing

A RECRUITER'S TRULY SIMPLE GUIDE TO STOP F*CKING UP WHEN JOB SEARCHING & INTERVIEWING

Simple, as in—Everything You Need To Know, You Learned When You Were a Kid

By
Nicki Perchik

© 2023 by Nicki Perchik

All rights reserved. This book or any portion thereof may not be reproduced or used in any manner whatsoever without the express written permission of the publisher except for the use of brief quotations in a book review.

ISBN: 979-8-9884328-0-7

Dedication

This book is dedicated to my dear friend and former colleague Jennifer DeVine, who is undoubtedly smiling in heaven saying something hilarious about how long this took to complete. Jennifer was with me when I first started putting thoughts on paper and those thoughts slowly made their way into what is now this book. She and I had daily chats about everything covered here, and the laughs we shared over some of these stories are priceless memories I will forever cherish. Jennifer was a dear friend long before being a colleague and was truly remarkable in every single way. Sadly, she lost her valiant battle with cancer. To say she will be forever missed by all who knew her is an understatement!

Anyone who met Jennifer knows she lit up every room she was in. Her infectious personality, her smile, her warmth, her thoughtfulness, her loyalty, and her amazing laugh made everyone happy. While incredibly smart, polished, and extremely talented, she was, hands down, one of the funniest people you'd ever meet. Her quick wit, phenomenal sarcasm, and brilliant timing were the perfect blend. She could magically find humor in everything and I can't tell you how many times she had me doubled over laughing! Jennifer was incredibly beautiful both inside and out.

I had the great fortune to have Jennifer join me in April 2011 as my first permanent colleague. She was instrumental in helping build NLP into the business we are today. Every client and every candidate loved Jennifer! She was truly amazing at her job! She was superbly brilliant at understanding each person and every business, and I can say without hesitation that the positive impacts she made on all the lives she touched are too numerous to count and will continue to transcend time.

I was so fortunate to have Jennifer as a dear friend for twenty-plus years and equally as lucky to have her as a colleague for eight. Her strength and unwavering courage as she so bravely faced cancer head-on are a lesson to us all. She was an incredible mother, wife, daughter, sister and friend. Her contributions to this world are far too many to count, and we will never, ever forget that. Thank you, Jennifer.

And, of course, how could I not acknowledge my amazing family? My husband and boys are my biggest fans and have encouraged me every step of the way. They are my everything- I love you guys!

Introduction

I've heard many incredibly impressive executives so eloquently and articulately state that job searching "*f*cking sucks!!!*"

If you've ever had to conduct a job search, you know this is no simple task. Job searching can be a long, arduous, painstakingly brutal, humbling, and, quite frankly, thankless process that can suck the life and energy out of you on a daily basis. I mean, let's be honest, there aren't too many people I know who anxiously await the next time they get to launch a job search. In fact, I'd bet my 401(k) there are many *other* things most would prefer to do with their time: attend jury duty, get a root canal, stand in line at the DMV, or perhaps go crab fishing on the Bering Sea (have you ever seen *Deadliest Catch*? Ummm, love the show, but that shit looks scary!). Here's the great news (drumroll): job searching doesn't have to be completely dreadful. In fact, there are many ways to make this process *significantly* less painful and unbearable! There are numerous things you can do right now to dramatically and positively impact your job search, and I'm here to help. I promise what I am going to share will make job searching a lot less "*f*cking sucky.*"

But *WAIT*! What if you aren't job searching? What if you're happily employed, doing your thing, and not at all thinking about getting a new job, but out of nowhere an incredible opportunity falls into your lap? (Incredible as in you'd be a complete moron not to explore it!) Now you unexpectedly find yourself in an interview process. And what if the unthinkable happens? You thought you were really happy in your current position. You weren't even remotely looking for a new job. Yet you suddenly realize you're actually *REALLY* interested in this job! It truly is a remarkable opportunity and one you know you can't pass up. And now that you care – now that you're interested – you don't want to mess it up!

Whether you're actively job searching because you just graduated and need a first job, you're employed but hate your current job, you're unemployed...*or* you weren't actively looking at all but got a call about an amazing opportunity and found yourself suddenly thrust into an interview process, this book is for you!

I know, I know, I know—you feel like you've heard every piece of advice possible before and wonder, "What in the world can this lady tell me that I haven't heard, seen, or read before? Why is her advice special?" Trust me—I totally get it! (I'd be rolling my eyes right about now if I were you.)

Candidly, I think both job searching and interviewing are a lot like having a baby: whether or not you solicit the counsel of others, people will freely offer their own two cents (no matter how many lines they cross in the process), proclaiming their advice to be gospel. As a parent, I know how annoying this can be. I can't tell you how many times I almost popped someone right in the nose for telling me what I needed to be doing to quiet my screaming babies.

So you're likely wondering why you should listen to little old me and my "words of wisdom" when it comes to these topics. What makes me the expert, and why in the world should you take the time to read this book when you undoubtedly have little time to spare and have already read or heard a lot on this topic? Well, the answer is simple.

First, because I'm a seasoned executive recruiter with over fifteen years of experience helping thousands of people make career changes. During this time, I've seen a significant number of very impressive people f*ck things up for themselves in job searches and in interviews. Thus, whatever those aforementioned impressive people read, heard, or learned about how to properly conduct a job search and how to successfully interview wasn't enough. How do I know this? Because I told you, I see them f*ck up.

When it comes to knowing the ins and outs of how to successfully conduct a job search and / or interview process, I'm your gal. I can honestly say I've pretty much encountered it all (and much of what I've seen or heard wasn't always pretty...although, admittedly, it was, at times, rather funny!). With all the experience I've amassed, I know what professionals should be doing and, more importantly, what they should *NOT* be doing. I know the secrets to success and have a proven track record of helping innumerable top professionals navigate this tough terrain. I know what hiring managers (the decision-makers) like and don't like. I know how / why some of the most qualified people get passed over and how / why others get selected. Reading this book will supply you with key knowledge and insights, ultimately translating into far more success. And who doesn't want success?

Second, another compelling reason you should read this book is that most people who give advice are boring and dry, whereas I'm not! There's some humorous shit in here. While I can't promise you knee-slapping, peeing-in-your-pants funny, I can assure you you'll smile and have a few laughs. And we all know there are numerous studies supporting the health benefits of smiling and laughing. Like the saying goes, "Laughter is the best medicine." Although I kind of think cake is the best medicine. Ok, let's be honest…a nice glass of wine is the best medicine (and is best served with aforementioned cake!). Sorry, I know, I probably shouldn't encourage alcohol consumption…but, c'mon…many of you are nodding. Don't act like you aren't.

The third reason you should read this book is that job searching and interviewing are stressful, which inherently means you're probably feeling *stressed out*. And we all know stress is bad for you in numerous ways. In fact, I've seen (and you probably have too) studies saying stress makes people fat. Seriously? Yes, seriously! Boo! I'm sure this is a rhetorical question, but who wants to add more fat to their body? That alone contributes to even more stress! And no, I'm not fat-shaming here. I'm just being honest. The diet industry is a multigagillion-dollar industry for a reason. So adding fat to your body because of stress = more stress = bad. It's basically a vicious cycle. Get it? Got it? Good!

Getting back to lowering your stress…

How does this book lower stress, you ask? Well…this book is extremely easy to follow; rather than increase your level of stress, it will actually do the opposite. Yes, you heard me! I will help you decrease your stress (and ideally slim your waist at the same time)! How? I'll simplify things you need to know, and by doing so, your stress will surely be minimized. I don't use big fancy words and complex concepts. My perspective is too many people unnecessarily overcomplicate things. (Honestly, I think many do this just to sound smart, which really irks me. Why people need to use Ivy League vocabularies is beyond me!) I'm all about making things simple so everyone can understand, which is why I'm going to tell you what you need to know in digestible nuggets. In fact, everything I share with you, you likely learned while growing up. What I cover is really quite basic and incredibly useful. These are all commonsense points everyone knows but, as I've witnessed on a daily basis, often lose sight of. Once you start reading, you'll be able to implement changes right away, and this will help you feel more in control. When you feel more in control, stress decreases! And then—*BOOM!*—before you know it, you're less stressed out! You can thank me later.

Now, please don't get mad at me when I tell you this, and please, please, please know I am sincerely saying this with the utmost respect…but if you're currently job searching and / or interviewing and finding yourself siding with those who say this process sucks, much of the so-called suckiness could be caused by you! Yes, that's right. *You!* I'm suggesting you take a look in the mirror and realize you are often the biggest problem. You heard me. Much of the pain is often self-inflicted. (*Gasp!*)

I know this is a tough pill to swallow and I've likely ticked off a few readers.

However, many recruiters will tell you we consistently see a ridiculous number of really careless mistakes being made. And please note, these mistakes are not being made by rookies alone.

* I repeat—these mistakes are *NOT* made only by rookies.

These errors are also being made by really impressive, successful senior- and executive-level professionals. These are people who've "climbed the corporate ladder," and having done so, many naturally assume folks of this caliber would be the last ones to commit careless faux pas. Unfortunately, that's not the case. Whether someone is the CEO of a Fortune 500 company or a recent college graduate, we're all human, and no one is immune (I have a million and one stories to back this up!). So knowing even the "best of the best" make mistakes means your hands might not be clean. It's highly probable most of us have been guilty at some point. Regardless of whether you're a C-level executive or a soon-to-be college graduate, YOU need to be reading this book!

While what I cover is basic, check your ego at the door, get the eye-rolling out of your system, and know that virtually every person has made one or more of the mistakes I'll be walking you through. By the way, if I'm making you paranoid—good! You should be! Each and every professional needs to revisit these basics with me because, I promise you, the professionals who think they know it all (and who are doing the abovementioned eye-rolling as they read this) are inevitably the ones who f*ck up! So buckle your seat belt and enjoy the ride! It's going to be productive!

As mentioned, I've spent many years in the world of executive search. During my tenure, I've had the privilege of working with professionals at every level and

I've seen professionals of all levels make pretty much every single fatal error possible. Because the vast majority of these mistakes are easily avoidable, I'm often left wondering how and why so many smart and talented people mess up. Candidly, it's often the same mistakes being repeated over and over again, day in and day out. These mistakes are both big and small. Regardless of their size, though, they wreak havoc and often lead to less desirable outcomes. These errors play a significant part in why people lose out on tremendous opportunities. By committing these blunders, people become their own worst enemies and end up ruining their chances of getting great job offers they need and / or want.

On the bright side, these missteps are completely avoidable, and I'm going to help you do just that. My dad always told me, "The most important education you will ever need is one in common sense," and I'm often reminded how right he was! While I have plenty to offer throughout this book, let's start with this extremely basic tip:

When you're job searching and / or interviewing for a position, use a good dose of common sense and stop doing stupid, careless, dumbass stuff!

(By the way, I realize this is sometimes easier said than done!)

Before we get too far down the path, I should fill you in on a few things. In addition to being sarcastic, I'm someone who tends to find humor in everything. We all know how brutally tough life can be, and I'm definitely the person who can figure out a way to make almost every situation funny because laughter eases my stress. I should also acknowledge I'm one of those people who laughs at the most inappropriate moments. I have a "nervous laugh," and it gets me into a lot of trouble! I promise you, I'm a kind, caring, sweet person with a good heart. But I've been known to mess up by giggling at inopportune times. I like to find the "funny" in every situation because humor helps me put things into perspective, which helps me cope. Thus, throughout this book you'll see my personality shine through as I attempt to lighten what's often a heavy topic. So while I may poke some fun at the mistakes being made in a job search and / or interview process, the reality is it isn't all fun and games because these errors lead to lost opportunities and a much lengthier, more challenging, and frustrating job search. There's no doubt about it, and I am quite confident I don't need a scientific study to support my position: people are constantly shooting themselves in the foot. You may wonder how they're doing that. Well, by doing stupid and careless stuff.

Of course, there are some very impressive people out there who can go through an interview or job search process flawlessly. These people "get it" and are the ones who typically have shorter job searches. Why? How? Simply stated, it's because they use a lot more common sense, while the rest of us either missed that class or left those notes in our college dorm room.

Also, please know I don't mean to minimize or dismiss the challenges everyone faces in today's complex, fast-paced, high-tech world. I think it's pretty obvious how quickly the economy can change and, for anyone who's been in the professional world for a couple years, how difficult a down economy can be. For many, 2008 is a distant memory. Many of us felt déjà vu in 2020 when the COVID pandemic started. When the world shut down, it truly felt like the sky was falling yet again. Virtually overnight, we went from the lowest unemployment rate seen in fifty years to mass unemployment and fears of another Great Depression. It was scary! Things seemed to rebound fairly quickly, which was great. However, things quickly became rocky again. Layoffs, high inflation and gas prices, wars raging and many economists have had unsettling predictions. (F*ck!)

Here's the most important thing to know—economies fluctuate. Whether we're in a strong economy or a weak one, the information covered here REALLY matters! We're talking about people's careers, their lives, their ability to not only earn a living but also advance toward bigger opportunities. Now more than ever, this is extremely valuable information because if COVID taught us one thing, it's that the world can be flipped upside down in just one day.

So, pay close attention because people are making things way harder for themselves by simply failing to use good old-fashioned common sense! We always need to be aware of and focused on the fundamentals. I assure you, no executive is too senior or too smart to be above reproach. We all need to focus! A quick refresher course in common sense never hurts. And a few funny stories along the way might help!

One last disclaimer: I realize it's always easier to be the one on the sidelines—the armchair quarterback. When you're the one in any situation, it's much more difficult to see things clearly. And in a job search or interview process, people are often stressed and the competition can be fierce. People have to face the challenges of our crazy, overworked / overconnected, hectic lives every minute of every day. And with all this craziness, people have difficulty thinking clearly. While I'm not a doctor, I've read and heard enough to know that the body reacts to this enormous stress by creating hormones that make our minds fuzzy. And as mentioned earlier, these hormones can also cause an increase in belly fat—which is total BS! On top of the incredible stress, you will potentially have a fuzzy mind *and* an expanding waistline. How sad is that?!

Back to my point—when people are under crazy amounts of pressure and stress and are being pulled in eighty-five directions, it's extremely difficult to bring one's A game to the task each and every day. Unfortunately, this all adds up to common sense flying out the window, which is not a good thing!

While I can't seem to solve all of the world's problems, I'm 100 percent confident I can help people navigating the job search / interview process get on more solid footing and make things a bit easier. And again, everything covered is extremely basic! It's not rocket science. I'm not splitting atoms or curing cancer. You likely learned 99 percent of what's covered in this book during your youth. All those "basics," all those "fundamentals," all the "foundational stuff" is what this is about.

It's that simple!

But like NBA players who practice their free throws on a daily basis and still frequently miss the shot, we always need to be mindful of and go back to the fundamentals / the basics! Time and again we've heard it said that the missed free throws lost the game. As we all know, it's nearly impossible to have a perfect game, which is why athletes practice. So join me as we go back to the basics and revisit the fundamentals we learned in our youth. Here's what we're going to cover:

Slow Down	1
If You Snooze, You Lose	5
Do Good Work	9
Spelling Is Important	11
• Don't Misspell People's Names	13
• Don't Misspell a Company's Name	15
• Spell-Check Isn't the "End All, Be All"	19
Use Proper Punctuation and Grammar	21
Prepare	23
Do Your Homework	47
Don't Be a Know-It-All	51

Look Over Your Work Before You Turn It In	55
Make Your Work Look Nice	59
• Résumé	61
• Beyond the Résumé	69
Cut and Paste Carefully	71
Don't Be Lazy	75
Read with Comprehension	89
Play Nice; Treat Others the Way You Want to Be Treated	95
Tell the Truth	105
People Lie	117
Hide-and-Seek Is for Kids	123
People Don't Like Braggers	127
Mind Your Manners	129
• Remember to Say Please and Thank You	131
• Don't Eat Like a Pig	135
• Use Common Courtesy	139
• Watch Your Mouth—Don't Use Bad Words	141
No One Likes a Crybaby	143
Sometimes You Win, Sometimes You Lose, Sometimes It Rains	147
Share	153
Comb Your Hair	155
Sit Up Straight	159
Sit Still and Keep Your Hands to Yourself	161
Eat Your Fruits and Vegetables	165
Think Before You Speak	169
Choose Your Words Wisely	173
Speak Clearly	177
Stop Rambling	183
Be Specific; Get to Your Point	187
If You Don't Have Something Nice to Say, Don't Say It	193
It's Not What You Say but How You Say It	199
Look at Me When I'm Speaking to You	203
Don't Interrupt	207
Shhhhh, Stop Talking	209

Listen	211
It's a Small World	215
You Don't Know Everything	217
Everything Has a Consequence	221
You Can Be Anything You Want to Be—ish	225
Memory Is a Tough Game	229
People Aren't Mind Readers	235
Follow Directions	239
The World Doesn't Revolve All Around You	243
Use Your Head	247
You Are in Control of Your Own Actions	255
Practice Makes Perfect	261
Perfection Doesn't Exist	265
When You Fall Down, Get Back Up and Brush Yourself Off	269
Don't Be a Quitter	273
Things Break	277
People Are Busy	281
If You Did It, Admit It	283
You're NOT the Boss	287
Every Story Has an Ending	289

Slow Down

YEARS AGO (MANNNNNY YEARS AGO), I had the privilege of volunteering in my oldest son's kindergarten class. During my time there, a light bulb went off in my head (save the jokes!). It dawned on me that much of the advice and counsel I provide on a daily basis to the professionals I work with echoes what we learn as kids. Virtually all commonsense basics are taught to us during those grade-school years, when we're kids.

Within the first ten minutes of my arrival at the kindergarten classroom, I heard my son's teacher repeatedly say to those adorable five- and six-year-olds, "Careful is better than quick" (thank you, Mrs. K). "Careful is better than quick"... hmmm...so if we dummy this down, we know what Mrs. K was really saying.

She was saying:

- Slow down!
- Don't rush through what you are doing!
- Take your time!!

"Slow down": Truth be told, I've struggled with this concept my entire life. In fact, I have vivid memories of my kindergarten teacher, my first-grade teacher, and every other teacher telling me to "slow down." Unfortunately, I don't think I truly learned this lesson until I was much older (maybe I still haven't!). I was always the person who wanted my homework done as fast as possible. In college, my friends would laugh because before the semester's classes even started, I'd have each class's syllabus and would already have assignments completed. You can probably surmise I was the exact opposite of a procrastinator (is there such a thing as a "precrastinator"?). In fact, I'd rush through assignments as quickly as I possibly could just so I could check them off my to-do list. Unfortunately, in my haste, I'd make countless careless mistakes. (To this very day, I have a love / hate relationship with red ink [for the younger readers, in my day, teachers would go over / grade our work and mark mistakes, as well as make comments, in red ink].)

As Mrs. K so profoundly stated, "Careful is better than quick." While basic, it seems to be a concept many professionals forget (sometimes habitually!). Not to sound condescending, but, people, that means *PAUSE*...take a second to gather your thoughts and then be thoughtful in *every* single thing you do. It's really incredible how much more we can accomplish and how much better the quality of our output is if we just take a few extra seconds and slow down.

Now, you might be wondering why I'm spending time on such a basic concept. Well, that's easy. It's because many of the job search missteps I see can be attributed to this one incredibly important yet oh-so-simple point. In fact, you'll notice a large portion of the topics I cover throughout this book ultimately boil down to slowing down.

People + rushing = mistakes

Mistakes = bad results

People are rushing, and in their haste, they're making crucial mistakes that negatively impact a job search. Some mistakes are big (for example, typos in résumés, sending thank-you notes to the wrong person, blowing off an interview, etc.); some mistakes are small (for example, the word *and* missing from a sentence in a thank-you note). Regardless, even the slightest gaffes can ruin someone's chance of being considered. I've seen companies reject professionals for what one might deem a minor error. Thus, take a deep breath and please slow down!

Many of you know what it's like to weather tough economic times. However, some of you haven't experienced down economies before. During the less prosperous years, when unemployment goes up and companies scale back on hiring, the competition for every job opportunity becomes fierce. It's a "companys' market," meaning companies can be far more selective of who they recruit and ultimately hire. Thus, there's no room for error. It's often a catch-22 type scenario in tight job markets because professionals know the competition is tough and feel an enormous sense of urgency to be "the first applicant in line." Knowing they can't delay pursuing opportunities, people rush, and guess what? This is when mistakes happen. And these mistakes lessen one's odds of success. Regardless of the state of the economy and / or job market conditions, many professionals still rush, and mistakes happen. I see this all the time. It's not good!

Throughout each step of a job search / interview process, slow it down!

Remember, every single thing you do is being evaluated…so do every single thing to the best of your ability. Careful is better than quick! And by the way, if you speed read through this book, you'll miss key points and think this book sucks. So, slow down and pay close attention!

If You Snooze, You Lose

IF YOU SNOOZE, YOU LOSE! Most kids have heard this one before. Whenever I hear this, memories are conjured up of being little and racing out onto the playground at recess time to beat the rush and grab an open swing before they were all taken. Waiting for a swing stunk because no one got off quickly. "Last one there is a rotten egg!" You know what I'm talking about!

Whether it was being first in line for a swing or tickets or food or a ride at an amusement park, we've all learned this lesson. There's no time like the present, right? If you snooze, you lose.

Wait—I just told you to slow down! What the heck?

You're absolutely right! While I stressed how important slowing down is, there's definitely a fine line between slowing down and moving at a complete snail's pace. In a job search setting or in an interview process, you have to balance having a sense of urgency with slowing down. These are not mutually exclusive of each other. There are numerous reasons why.

First, "If you snooze, you lose" means if you're actively looking for a job, you need to be working hard at doing so. You can't drag your feet and half-ass a job search and then expect great results. Here's an oldie but goody: "You get out what you put in." How true that is. Because countless professionals may be vying for the same position, if you aren't on the ball, putting the hours in, someone might beat you to the punch by getting their application done faster than you or by getting networked into an interview process before you. Either way, you may lose out. I know a job search can become monotonous and time can feel as though it's moving as slow as molasses. However, the more time, energy, and effort you put into the search, the more you'll get out of it in a shorter period of time. Job searching is a full-time job. It's not a two-hour-a-day job. It's not a wake-up-late-watch-some-TV-work-a-few-hours-go-to-the-gym-for-three-hours-meet-friends-for-dinner-each-day job. This is an 8:00-a.m.-to-5:00-p.m.-take-a-break-8:00-p.m.-to-10:00 p.m.-type job.

Second, this means if you're interviewing for a position and you're sincerely interested in the job, make sure you follow up in a timely fashion.

For example: I've interviewed innumerable professionals who, at the time of our initial conversation, didn't have an updated résumé. When professionals express interest in the opportunity we discuss, I make it very clear their résumés need to be updated in order to advance the process forward. Most commit to updating their résumés quickly and will turn them around in a day or two. For some people, though, updating their résumé takes a back seat and is at the bottom of their priority list. For these people, I'll find myself waiting and waiting and waiting some more. Finally, a week or two later, I'll receive an updated résumé along with some lame excuse as to why their turnaround was sloth-like. Unfortunately, many times these people were too slow and, during the interim, my client started moving down the path with other candidates. Because it took these folks so long to get their résumés updated, they lost out. Sometimes clients felt they had enough highly qualified candidates in the mix. Sometimes clients were confident they'd identified their next hire. Sometimes an offer had already been made to a candidate. Regardless—what a shame! While we all want to put forth our best work, time is of the essence, and if you snooze, you could / can / might lose!

Another example: After an initial interview with a member of my search firm, we frequently send candidates what we call our "candidate profile questionnaire." We create a unique questionnaire for every search we work on to help us ensure we're examining "fit" from both angles; does this role fit what the professional is looking for, and does the professional fit what the client is looking for in this hire? These questionnaires can be extremely thorough, and, I'll admit, they can take some time to complete. I explain to professionals the importance of filling out this document and stress we can't move to the next step until we have a completed questionnaire. There are those who simply don't have a sense of urgency and end up taking days or even weeks (yikes!) to submit it back to us. By dragging their heels, they may miss the opportunity completely. (Once in a great while, there are exceptions to our process. We don't always insist on this step.) That said, candidates are always informed of what to expect, what our process looks like, and what the timeline is. Thus, there should never be a surprise. Whether someone drags their heals getting us an updated résumé or a completed questionnaire, if they're too slow, they could lose out.

Here's the gist: YOU are responsible for your follow-up items. Don't expect anyone to track you down. If you're interested in pursuing an opportunity, don't fall asleep at the wheel!

Do Good Work

YOU'RE PROBABLY THINKING..."DUHHHH! WTF is wrong with this lady? Of course one needs to do good work. I just spent money for someone to state the obvious?"

Well, I hate to be the bearer of bad news, but apparently "doing good work" isn't as self-explanatory as one would think. While this is pretty basic, it seems many professionals simply don't put forth what one would classify as "good work." Whether it's poorly crafted emails, cover letters, résumés, or thank-you notes, voice mails full of stumbles and bumbles, poor interviewing skills, questionable follow-up skills, etc., these are all recipes for disaster. One can't take for granted how important each and every step of the job search / interview process is.

From a very early age, we learn how critical it is to "do good work." Teachers used to ask me all the time, "Nicki, is this really good work?" or "Is this truly the best work you can do?" I'm pretty sure this translated into "Is this piece of shit your final draft?"

Hopefully your teachers instilled in you the importance of producing the best work possible. I remember one of my teachers suggesting we ask ourselves if we're extremely proud of whatever it was we were turning in and if we weren't, then "the work" wasn't ready and we needed to spend more time on it. And guess what? This is a question we should still ask ourselves as adults. In a job search or interview setting, it's absolutely critical you make sure every single thing you do is something you're really proud of. Otherwise, you're setting yourself up for failure!

Just OK is not OK (I wrote this before the AT&T commercials were created).

Average is not good enough.

Mediocre is not good enough.

Meh is not good enough.

Doable is not good enough.

If you can say, "This isn't my best work," then it's not where it needs to be. Be honest with yourself. You know what I'm talking about on this front. Don't half-ass stuff. Don't kid yourself. I've had too many candidates readily admit when something wasn't their best work. When this is the case, you're just wasting time because other candidates will outshine you. Hiring managers know the dangers of settling and will wait to find and hire the right person rather than compromise just to find a warm body.

Spelling Is Important

AS KIDS, EARLY IN OUR EDUCATION, we're taught the importance of proper spelling. Many of us can remember bringing home lists of words and studying for spelling tests on a weekly basis. For me, these are vivid memories. My mom was a stickler about quizzing me and my brothers on our spelling lists. And I recall how annoyed I was because all I wanted to do was go outside and play, yet I was stuck in our kitchen going over each word. Good news is, I was pretty gifted at spelling, unlike one of my brothers…he was terrible. It was during those early years in school that the importance of learning to spell words properly was drilled into our heads.

So what does this mean for you in a job search or interview process? Should be pretty obvious, but if you need me to spell it out for you (pun intended), it means pay attention to spelling, because if you have misspelled words, your candidacy may be cut short. Seriously, pay attention to your spelling on every single piece of correspondence because I can't tell you how often I find mistakes in things sent to me. Spelling is vitally important (no matter your age)!

Don't Misspell People's Names

I WOULD VENTURE to guess most people have a personal attachment to their name. It is, after all, their name. I haven't taken a scientific poll on this, but I've taken informal ones, and it's clear: people get a bit perturbed when their names are misspelled. I suppose there are times when this can be overlooked and not given too much thought. However, in a professional setting, especially one like a job search / interview setting, this can be a catastrophic mistake. Knowing that every single communication you send out serves as a representation of the quality of your work and your attention to detail, what do you think misspelling something as simple and as important as someone's name says about you? If you guessed something close to "Yikes! What a dumbass! If you can't even spell my name correctly, what else are you going to misspell?" you're absolutely right! Misspelling a name isn't going to gain you points in "reasons why you should hire _____ [insert your name]." And please don't think you haven't done this before because everyone has (including me)!

If I had a dime for every time I've seen my name, Nicki, misspelled, I might have about $1,000,000. No joke. I realize there are many ways to spell the name Nicki. But honestly, I could not make it any easier for people. My name is in my actual email address, it's also in the signature of my emails, and I always type my name at the bottom of each and every email I send. Hence, it isn't too challenging to take a second and look at how I spell my name and then copy it. For the record, it's Nicki. Not Nikki.

I want you to keep in mind, executive recruiters are often the job seekers' entrée into a company / opportunity. And please recognize, recruiters are tying their professional reputations to the individuals they present / represent. If recruiters present candidates who make sloppy mistakes, those recruiters will lose credibility and be viewed as professionals who don't vet their candidates thoroughly. Thus, when I see my name misspelled, you can surely understand why I can't help but wonder what other things this person might be careless about. I don't mean to sound harsh, but someone who can't take a second to make sure they're spelling something as important as someone's name correctly can create questions in a recruiter's mind, as well as in the minds of any decision-maker. The good news is, whenever someone messes up my name, I'm way more forgiving of this oversight than I probably should be. I try to give people the benefit of the doubt and won't use that as a reason to not engage in a conversation. However, many aren't as forgiving, and misspelling someone's name can quickly be the kiss of death. Some decision-makers automatically reject the candidate when they see this kind of carelessness. If you think I'm exaggerating, I promise you I'm not.

Don't roll your eyes, thinking I'm being melodramatic. This has happened! I've seen it firsthand more times than I can count. People are human and mistakes happen. Knowing someone didn't take a second to confirm the proper spelling of someone's name can quickly lead to all sorts of thoughts about where else carelessness might occur.

People—taking the time to ensure you're spelling someone's name right is common sense! In today's world, we all know there are many names spelled in unique ways. One can no longer assume there is only one way to spell any given name. I wouldn't be surprised to see a silent P in the name John because, today, anything goes. For that reason, take a second to look at how someone spells their name and then use the exact same spelling. And make sure your computer isn't autocorrecting it. Pretty basic…but for some reason, this is such a common mistake and one that spells *careless*!

Don't Misspell a Company's Name

DUHHHHHHHHHH! THIS IS AN OBVIOUS ONE. Goes without saying. Right? One would think…

Unfortunately, this is another one of those mistakes we see all too often. Just like misspelling a person's name, misspelling a company's name can be a devastating and irreparable bungle! Again, I'm quite forgiving and might give the candidate one free pass—*one*. But for many decision-makers, this is a huge problem and, at times, one that is indefensible and unrecoverable. You can only imagine what hiring managers inside a company think when they receive an email, document, presentation, etc., with their company's name misspelled. At a minimum, this infraction raises a few eyebrows, giving cause for concern. After all, during an interview / job search process, one assumes candidates are putting forth their very best work. So like we covered earlier, if someone commits this egregious error during the interview process, one has to wonder what other outrageous mistakes will be made once that person is hired and their guard goes down.

Everyone—please pay attention to what I'm about to say:

It takes a minute (and that's if your computer is super slow) to log on to a company's website and / or to carefully reread prior emails and correspondence. Please, please, please do this!

We all know companies can be creative in how they spell their names, so carefully take note of things, including their use of spacing, capital versus lowercase letters, punctuation, hyphenation, and spacing. I realize misspellings often happen while using smart devices such as iPhones, iPads, etc. Unfortunately, in a job search / interview setting, the disclaimer about possible typos many place at the bottom of emails sent via those devices won't always cover you should there be a mistake.

When you're sending out any communication, regardless of the technology used, take extra caution, because sometimes computers automatically change words and names once they've been typed (autocorrect settings can screw even the best of us!). Double-check your work. Misspelling names of any kind, be it a company's name and / or a person's name, is simply unacceptable and does not bode well for a candidate. Slow down and do good work. Spelling is important. Period.

When I spend time preparing and coaching professionals for interviews, I tend to emphasize this point and find many senior-level execs actually get snitty with me (even though I stroke egos by saying I know it's a basic point but one I've learned never to ignore because I witness this firsthand…yada yada…). Some clearly convey annoyance in their tone and sometimes react by saying things like, "Trust me, I'm a true professional. I would never misspell a name (gasp!). That's soooo basic!" or "Thanks, but you don't need to worry about that with me." In fact, I was recently preparing an executive for his first interview with a client. When I went into my spiel about how important it is to pay attention to spelling, this professional didn't hide how put off he was by what I was saying. In a huffy tone, he emphatically told me that as a senior executive, he never would have reached the high level he had if he had been careless in such a way. (I'm telling you, he may have literally growled. This man's frustration was palpable!) While he finally acknowledged I was "doing my job" and my point was undoubtedly helpful to some (a.k.a. those less fabulous than him), he stressed (in a condescending tone) how it need not be a concern because he would simply never do such a thing. Hmmm…

Really?

Ha!

Guess what?

After his interview with my client, he bcc'd me on the thank-you note he emailed to the executive who interviewed him. I'm sure you can predict the direction this story is headed. The thank-you note was flawlessly written, he got the job, and the salary was twice as high as expected because he was / is that good, and we all lived happily ever after.

Nope!

You undoubtedly guessed it. Throughout the thank-you note, he repeatedly misspelled the company's name. Knowing what a big deal he'd made during our prep call about how he'd never do such a stupid thing, I was all the more embarrassed for him. Of course I had to point this out. I couldn't let it go. I told him the thank-you looked great except for where he misspelled the company's name four times…yes, you heard me, I told him he did it four times! Not once. Not twice. Not even three times. Four. I'm sure he wanted to go hide under a rock. And yes, the silence was deafening. He had to feel like a total tool!

Karma's a bitch.

So, what is the point here? It better be clear by now, or I'm a shitty writer. The point is…no one is exempt! This mistake can happen to anyone. I've done it, and chances are you've done it too. Be careful and take a minute to look at a company's website. Then type their name exactly as you see it on the site and make sure your computer doesn't change it. Don't let a spelling mistake be the reason you're removed from consideration.

Spell-Check Isn't the "End All, Be All"

SPELL-CHECK IS A TRUE GIFT and one I would struggle to live without. Unfortunately, spell-check doesn't catch everything. Lord knows I've certainly learned this lesson the hard way.

Do you know what a homophone is? Homophones are words with the same pronunciation but they're spelled differently based on their context. Words like *to*, *two*, and *too*; *buy*, *bye*, and *by*; *here* and *hear*; *there* and *their*; *your* and *you're*; *do* and *due*; *weather* and *whether*; *then* and *than*; *mail* and *male*; and *role* and *roll*. Spell-check doesn't catch mistakes with homophones, so you need to be mindful—meaning you must *always* proofread your work to ensure you have the proper spelling of each and every word based on the context in which it's used. We can't rely on spell-check—or any other technology, for that matter—to do all the work for us.

When executives receive communications or documents with misspellings, it doesn't leave them feeling warm and fuzzy about a candidate. You may think a company cutting a candidate for misspelling one word is a bit harsh. But it happens, and you *do* not want it to happen to you.

PS: Most people know if spelling isn't their strong suit. If you're in that camp, don't proofread your own work. Ask someone who happens to be good at spelling to review for you. You'll be glad you did.

Use Proper Punctuation and Grammar

I'M PRETTY SURE I'VE BELABORED THIS POINT—I've highlighted how every communication is a representation of you and your professional abilities, the importance of doing good work, blah-blah-blah. Clearly this includes all correspondence: cover letters, emails, handwritten notes, texts, and presentations, along with anything else you've sent to someone.

Aside from typos, I'm sure you've seen emails riddled with punctuation and / or grammatical errors. I sure have. While some executives are a bit more forgiving when emails are sent from smart devices, no one should assume using technology gives you a free pass (regardless of whether you've put the aforementioned disclaimer at the bottom of the message asking people to excuse typos). In a job search / interview setting, all correspondence must always be professional and as close to perfect as possible. There are *no* exceptions! Proper punctuation and grammar are expected. Even if you've developed a strong rapport or friendship with someone, you must keep in mind you're in a business setting and thus cannot let your guard down. How you communicate with a friend is one thing. However, in a professional setting, you must err on the side of caution and make sure your work is flawless at all times. After all, why would you ever want to give someone a reason to think you're anything less than amazing? I know I sound like a broken record, but hiring managers assess everything. And in honor of my very own mother, let me say (in her voice), "If you aren't going to do a good job, you might as well not do it at all!" I'm proud to say my mother is absolutely right! If it isn't good work, it'll be a complete waste of your precious time. So please do everything to the best of your ability or just stop. In addition to spelling, check your work to make sure you're using proper punctuation and grammar.

Similar to the last story, I was working on a senior-level marketing position (base salary was over $200,000 a year) and was quite far down the interview path with my client. There were a number of really strong candidates my client was excited about. The leading candidate had gathered some interesting insight into the competitive landscape and decided to email this information to the hiring manager, who happened to be the president of the company. I was copied on the email, and unfortunately, I quickly noticed six typos in the note (ones I would classify as minor in offense). Subsequently, the president reached out to me and said he was really sorry to do this but he'd decided to remove the candidate from consideration. After receiving two emails from her with typos, he didn't feel she had the attention to detail needed to lead an entire marketing function for his company. You can imagine how devastated this candidate was when I delivered the bad news. But I honestly couldn't blame the president. As much as I adored her and as accomplished as she was, it was difficult to overlook the fact that there were multiple emails containing numerous typos. If she had been interviewing for a position where writing and communicating weren't of the utmost importance, then maybe the president wouldn't have felt compelled to cut her from the process.

The moral of this story: slow down and do good work! Communications have to be typo-free, which means your grammar and punctuation must be spot-on and you can't have misspelled names or words.

Doing good work is key!

Prepare

By failing to prepare, you are preparing to fail.
—Benjamin Franklin

PERHAPS YOU RECALL HEARING when you were growing up, "Eat your breakfast. It's the most important meal. It prepares you for your day."

As children, we're taught the significance of preparation. Whether it's preparing for a test, a presentation, a recital, a game, a play, a concert, etc., we learn preparation is the foundation of success.

Doing good work means you absolutely must dedicate ample time to preparation! Sadly, in a job search or interview setting, many fail to prepare in one or more ways. What do I mean? Well, people often jump right into the mix without spending time focusing on some of (or all of—*gasp*!) the building blocks to successfully launching a job search and / or engaging in an interview process, which often leads to negative results. In working with thousands of people, all too often I've heard professionals admit their lack of proper preparation led to disappointing outcomes. From longer and more difficult job searches to seeing fewer exciting opportunities to surprising rejections—a lack of preparation can lead to negative results.

Whether you find yourself unemployed or unhappily employed and know you need to find a new job—or you're a recent college graduate entering the job market for the very first time—you need to prepare, and I'm going to walk you through what you need to do to be prepared. So buckle up! We're going to cover a ton of ground here. The first thing to know is you need to develop an overarching game plan of how you're going to go about your job search. You will then break it down into finer parts so you can get all your ducks in a row. This means you need to map out your goals by day, week, and month. You want to be thinking about things such as:

- Résumé: Do you even have one? If no, how will you create one? Do you have a template to follow? Or have you found a professional writer? On the other hand, if you do have a résumé, is it updated? If not, when do you want to be done updating it? Set a goal and put this date on the calendar so you can hold yourself accountable to that deadline. By the way, my advice is, if you can afford to have a professional writer help you, I always recommend doing so. But before you hire someone to write or update your résumé, get references and make sure you're comfortable with the quality of the writer's work. I've seen some supposed professional résumé writers whose work wasn't very professional. Buyer beware! If you don't have the money to pay someone, that's fine. You can find resources to help you either by going online or getting a few résumés from others that you can use as a guide. Please, please, please—once you have an updated résumé, have a few people proofread it. Mistakes happen all the time, and nine times out of ten, I find typos or inconsistencies in résumés that need to be fixed. For real! Even some of the most impressive executives have résumés with errors.

    Do you still even need a résumés? Do résumés matter? It's true, some people will tell you with great confidence that résumés no longer matter. They'll say in today's world, résumés are a thing of the past. Here's my two cents—résumés still matter to many, and they are something you must have. If you have a good résumé but find it isn't necessary in a particular situation, no big deal. However, if you need an updated résumé to pursue a certain opportunity and yours is less than fabulous, that could hurt you and your chances badly! Fact: Every client we work with still expects to see a resume when we present a candidate. On the few occasions where I had a candidate who either didn't have a résumé or refused to update theirs, my clients rejected them. Yes, there may be companies out there who no longer care about résumés, but in my experience, that's the exception and not yet the norm. So, in my humble opinion, résumés are still important. Thus, ensuring you have a great résumé when you're getting ready to launch a job search is key. Even if you're not actively job searching, if you're contacted about an exciting opportunity and you want to potentially throw your hat into the ring of consideration, it'll be important to have a strong résumé you can provide to the recruiter(s) and / or to the company's talent acquisition / hiring team. Without one, there's a high probability you'll be passed over.

- Bio and / or Professional Summary: This is typically something more senior-level / executive-level professionals are expected to have. If you fall into that category, do you have a bio or professional summary crafted that outlines who you are, as well as what your strengths and accomplishments are? Can you write this yourself, or do you need to hire an expert? Set a goal for when you want this completed. Reminder: Once it's complete, please have others proofread it to ensure it's ready to go when you launch your job search or engage in an interview process. Again, if you're earlier in your career, this is typically not something anyone will expect you to have and thus one less thing to worry about.

- LinkedIn: Do you have a LinkedIn profile, and is your profile filled out with significant detail? And by significant detail, I do not mean simply having your name along with a running list of companies you've worked at, the titles you've held, and years of employment. If your profile is that barebones, details must be added. This is imperative and needs to be done ASAP! Your LinkedIn profile is your online résumé and something every person who has the ability to rule you into or out of a process will review and assess. Thus, if your profile is not up to snuff, when will you complete this task? This is an absolutely critical step in preparing for a job search. That said, even if you're not actively job searching, having a strong LinkedIn profile is equally as important. By the way, your LinkedIn profile is not a place to simply cut / paste a generic job description about your role / responsibilities underneath each position you've held. You must take it a step further and highlight what you've done, what results you've delivered. This is a place where your stats will truly shine and separate you from others who might have a similar profile. In your profile, if you're merely stating details about roles / responsibilities, this doesn't help differentiate you from other professionals. Highlight what you've achieved. Your accomplishments make a huge difference in how you're viewed. LinkedIn is also a great place to let your personality shine through, albeit to a reasonable extent. For example, I'm a total goof who finds a lot of really dumb stuff funny...others may not fully appreciate how much I love old *SNL* skits from the '70s, '80s, and '90s, as well as how much I love every single John Hughes film, *Wedding Crashers, Best in Show, Tommy Boy,* and more. I might not add all of that to my LinkedIn profile summary. But you don't have to have a totally dull professional summary. You can add some color that lets people in on what makes you unique. This will undoubtedly separate you from others. Be sure to use discretion. If you're just not sure how to improve your profile, read through a lot of summaries and see if there are any ideas you can glean from some of the better ones. If needed, you can find a professional who specializes in writing LinkedIn profiles. These experts will know what you need to do to make your profile more searchable and to help your profile stand out to people like me. As a recruiter, I live on LinkedIn 24/7/365 and can attest to the fact that, to this day, far too many people still have weak LinkedIn profiles. This dramatically affects how many recruiters / companies will proactively reach out to you about their opportunities. Even if you're not in an active job search mode, I'd assume you'd still like to be contacted about exceptional opportunities, and often LinkedIn is where top firms will find you. Thus, it behooves you to have a great profile!

In addition to having a robust profile, do you know how to leverage LinkedIn as a tool? This is an invaluable tool for job searching, and you want to maximize using all it has to offer. If you're not completely in the know about all the different ways to put this technology to use, you need to get some training. What's your plan regarding how you're going to learn? Are there tutorials on the site you can access? (*Hint*: Yes!) Also, doing a quick Google search will undoubtedly net you some great ways to learn. Alternatively, do you have a friend who works there? Or, do you know anyone who's a whiz at using technology? If yes, can you meet with them and have them help you learn? If so, when can they meet? Get something scheduled as quickly as possible, and remember to put all of your goals on the calendar so you can hold yourself accountable and make progress.

Net-net—have a LinkedIn profile that provides the reader with ample depth of detail to help them get a better sense of who you are, why and how you're different from others who might be viewed as your peers. In addition, make it easy for people to contact you for opportunities. Be sure your profile is set up to receive InMails, and be sure to check the box that says you're "open to new opportunities" as this will generate a lot more activity by elevating your profile when recruiters are doing searches. If you're in an active job search, knowing how to best leverage all LinkedIn can do for you as a candidate will pay off in spades. Get yourself prepared on this front.

- Contacts to Target (this includes both people who can possibly help you and companies you want to reach out to): Do you have an initial list of all the people and companies you want to start targeting? (This list will evolve over time, but you need to get one started.) Do you have these broken into subgroups, such as friends, family, current / former colleagues and clients, etc.? You want to have these organized and ready so that when you launch your job search, you're not all over the place and disorganized. Preparing early will help.
- Emails And Templates To Send: Have you crafted emails to send to contacts who might be able to help you? One email you'll send to close friends and family (these are those in your "contacts to target" group[s]) seeking their support and assistance in your job search. Another email, which is likely similar to the friends and family one, for colleagues and professional contacts to let them know you're in the job market. You never know who or what these people know that could help you in your efforts. For example, they may have inside leads on job openings or useful connections. If you have not yet crafted the emails you'll be sending to these groups of contacts, when are you going to craft them, and what's your plan for when you'll send them out? Get dates on your calendar of when you want these emails written and when you'd like to start sending them. Keep in mind, you'll likely tweak the email verbiage as you move into your job search, but having something prepared that you can start with will help you tremendously.

- Job Search Tracking Tool: Do you have an automated tool or spreadsheet created to help you track every single thing you're doing as you go about your job search? Essentially, I'm referring to having something like a CRM. This is absolutely critical to have in place. When you start your job search, you need a way to track everyone whom you've reached out to, when you reached out (date), how you contacted them (via phone, email, InMail, text, social media, etc.), why you reached out (there's a job opening at their company, they're a friend of a friend, you used to work together years ago, etc.), notes about what you did / said along with any information regarding possible next steps, what those follow-ups are and when you're to do them, and then be sure to enter that into your calendar so you're reminded to do those next steps. In addition, this is where you'll note if you applied to specific companies, to certain jobs, how you applied (via the company's career portal or via LinkedIn or via a specific job board or other), if you heard back (who responded, when, how, what they said, any follow up to-dos), etc. This is truly where you'll capture every minute detail, and this will keep you far more organized than if you were trying to put it all on paper. Or, heaven forbid, not even really keeping track of what you've done and just relying on memory! Trust me when I tell you, all of this is impossible to keep straight. A job search quickly becomes overwhelming to manage by memory and / or by hand. It gets super messy really fast, and being organized right out of the gate will help you avoid unnecessary headaches and possible embarrassment. Believe you me, it becomes much more difficult to try to go back and put details in after time has passed. Having it organized right from the start makes your life so much easier. So if you don't have a tool in place, when / how are you going to get one?

    *To recap and to reiterate, you need to be tracking (with detail) who you're contacting, how you contacted them (email, phone, text, etc.), dates, and details of every interaction, whether you had a call or a face-to-face meeting, what happened during the conversation, and if there's any follow-up to be done (and when). You need to know where you applied (name of company, what division, etc.), when (date and perhaps time), and title of position as well as the job number associated to the position if there is one. Get yourself prepared. Be hyper detailed. You'll be so thankful you did!

- Time Management: Have you thought about your calendar and how you'll block out your time so you can best plan and be prepared for each day? I'm not sure people realize how easily the day can get away from you. It's amazing how much time laundry, preparing and cooking meals, doing the dishes, grocery shopping, and cleaning can take. Add on things like getting an oil change, running to the dry cleaner, doctors' appointments, home repairs that have been neglected, and so much more. Five minutes here, thirty minutes there—it all adds up fast. If you don't carve out time for specific tasks (and then actually stay focused on said tasks), you can quickly find yourself being unproductive. Personally, I can get easily distracted if I don't commit to staying 100 percent focused on something. What really helps me is if I block off specific time slots and then label what task(s) I'm going to do in that set window of time. For example, I will block off 7:00 to 8:00 a.m. for exercise. I treat it just like I would a meeting. So I typically allot enough time to go through emails and clean out my inbox before 7:00 a.m. That way, I can get on the treadmill without the anxiety of a full inbox waiting for me and just focus on my workout. Please note: It's really important to think about yourself as you consider how to schedule your days. For example, if you're at your best early in the morning, block off 7:00 a.m. to noon for doing mission-critical tasks that require undivided attention and your best work. Things such as reaching out to companies, reaching out to individuals, and phone interviews. If you know you drag a bit during midday, perhaps you should carve out 1:00 to 4:00 p.m. for researching companies / people and preparation work. Then maybe 6:00 to 7:00 p.m. is for follow-up work, such as thank-you notes and responding to emails. However, if you're not a morning person, the schedule I just referenced is likely not ideal for you. Point is, by knowing your internal clock and what times of day you're at your best, you can plan your calendar. The key is to honor your time commitments and remove distractions. Putting your cell phone away, turning off any email or social media alerts, and minimizing other possible disrupters will help you immensely. Moral is, determine what's best for you. Blocking off your calendar in advance of each day will help you prepare for the day and then on that actual day, be the most productive.

- Precall Plan: If you're going to call someone, prepare for the call by knowing exactly what you want to say so you're articulate. For those of you who saw the movie *Swingers*, remember the voice mail Jon Favreau's character, Mike, leaves for Nikki? (If you haven't seen it, YouTube it. You'll crack up!) The point is, when you're speaking with someone or when you're leaving a message, you don't want to sound like Mike did on Nikki's voice mail. In other words, you don't want to sound like a bumbling idiot! You want to be concise and well-spoken. For many, when the stakes are high and the pressure is on, this is no easy task. Bad things can happen. To avoid this pitfall, I often suggest writing a script. That way, you don't have to think on your feet and can have the words handy if you need them. I think we've all had moments when we've hung up the phone and thought, "I just sounded like a total f*cking moron! I'm a complete buffoon!" What an awful feeling that is! Obviously, we want to do all we can to mitigate that risk. By preparing, we're definitely setting ourselves up for success. PS: I practice what I preach. I'm not just giving you lip service. I'm the queen of writing scripts because I know when stakes are high, if I've prepared a script I can have on hand to help me stay buttoned-up and on point, I'll be way more articulate and smooth. I've gotten tongue-tied before and have had some cringey (as my kids would say) moments and have learned my lesson the hard way. You often have *one shot to* get it right, and you don't want to blow it by failing to prepare.
- Prepare for Every Interview: This is one of the most common mistakes people make and one of the biggest reasons why people are passed over in an interview process. And it is *so* basic! (This doesn't mean it's easy, though!)

    People fail to prepare for interviews. One of the things that quickly tells a hiring manager who hasn't prepared is when they ask, "What do you know about the company?" and the candidate can't provide a good, solid answer. You may be wondering how someone shows up to an interview ill prepared to answer that question. Because let's be honest—it's a basic question, and one everyone should be ready to answer. But I'm not kidding…this happens more often than you can imagine, and it absolutely drives me insane! Every person who has an interview should be able to answer this very basic question. You need to prepare for it!

When candidates are asked what they know about the specific job they're interviewing for, candidates' answers are often weak. It quickly becomes obvious to an interviewer which candidates prepared and which ones didn't. In addition, candidates often have trouble providing thoughtful and articulate answers to one or more (yikes!) of the many questions they're asked throughout an interview. From being long-winded to stumbling over words to going down ten different rabbit holes, many struggle to formulate good, solid, succinct answers. While no one can predict each and every interview question that will be asked, it behooves you to spend time preparing. And as you prepare, I recommend putting possible interview questions into a few different buckets:

- Common Interview Questions: Think about all of the common interview questions you can possibly come up with, and then prepare your responses. Common interview questions are those basic, "vanilla" questions candidates always get asked regardless of the position they're interviewing for. Do a Google search of most commonly asked interview questions. You'll come up with a sizable list. And by the way, you'll find that some of the basic / common interview questions are actually way more challenging to answer than you realize. These are just a few examples of what I'd label as basic interview questions: Tell me about yourself. Tell me your strengths / weaknesses. Why do people like working with you? Why'd you pick the college you went to? Why'd you pick the major you graduated with? How would your friends describe you? What's the one quality you'd like to change about yourself? Who are your biggest role models and why? If you didn't need to make money and could do anything in the world, what would it be? Then, you need to prepare your answers to the basic interview questions. Note: You certainly don't want to sound overly rehearsed during an interview, so I'm not suggesting you memorize a speech. However, by gathering your thoughts and practicing what you're going to say, you'll find it much easier to be eloquent, cogent and succinct when you're in the real interview.
- Questions Specific to the Job: Think about the position you're interviewing for—what questions can you anticipate they'll ask relative to

the role? If there's a job spec, that's a great place to start. Typically, a job description will help you discern what's most important to the company. Ideally there are bullets outlining what they're looking for, and by turning each bullet into a question and formulating your answers, you'll be more prepared for some of the questions you might be asked during the actual interview. In addition, when you're trying to anticipate what questions they might ask you specific to the job, I always recommend you try to put yourself into their shoes and think, if you were the hiring manager interviewing candidates, what would you be asking to best assess their (the candidates') skills and their (the candidates') fit to your (the company's) needs? And then prepare and practice answering those questions. It's virtually impossible to know the exact questions you'll be asked. But by going through this process during your preparation, you'll be improving your abilities to articulately and succinctly answer questions. And what you learn should help you be more comfortable and confident regardless of what questions you may be asked.

- Anticipate Their Concerns: Pretend you're in their shoes hiring someone for this role. Then, look at your candidacy through their eyes. Think about where they might have concerns about your background and where you might have gaps / fall short of their requirements. Are there any concerns you can anticipate they might have? For example, have you stayed at the same company for ten years? Have you been at the same company for eight years without one promotion? Have you switched jobs (and companies) every eighteen months? Do you fall short on the number of years of experience they say they want candidates to have per the job description? Do you lack experience in their field? Have you only worked for big *Fortune* 500–sized companies and this is a very small start-up? Have you been managing direct reports for the past six years and this role isn't managing anyone? Is this role based in an office five days a week and you've been remote for the past couple years? I could go on and on, but hopefully you're getting my point. By looking at your background and résumé through their eyes, ideally you can anticipate some of their concerns so that you can be better prepared to speak to those should they come up. Again, you can't possibly know for certain what questions / concerns might come up during an interview, but the more you prepare, the better you'll do when you're in the actual interview. As previously mentioned, when I go through this exercise of writing out how I'd answer questions / concerns and then practice my answers, I'm able to be more articulate when in the moment. Perhaps such an approach would be helpful to you too?

- Questions to Ask Them: Think about the questions you have for them. Do you have a list of thoughtful questions prepared for every interview you have? Have you put the questions on paper in order of priority and relevance based on whom you're interviewing with, what stage of the interview process you're in, and what's most critical for you to know as you go through your evaluation of them? You never want to run out of questions. When an interviewer asks you what questions you have for them, responding with, "I don't have any. You answered them all" is an almost-certain way to get yourself removed from consideration. The only time you should ever say you don't have any questions is if you actually want to get kicked out of their interview process. If you want to be rejected, go ahead and say you have no questions. Otherwise, you absolutely must have a good list of thoughtful questions prepared so you're never at a loss. And when I say thoughtful, I mean your list of questions can't be only the most basic and obvious questions that every other candidate always asks. This means you need to ask questions with a bit more meat on the bone. Here are just a few examples: Why are you hiring for this role now? What are the most important objectives for this position to accomplish short term and then long term? How are you evaluating success? What metrics is this person tied to, and how did you decide on those metrics? Describe the company's culture and then the team's culture. What's the hiring manager's leadership style like? Why do people like working for this hiring manager? What about their style might be challenging for someone? What's the frequency of one-on-one meetings with the hiring manager? How are you onboarding this hire? Why'd the last person leave? Who internally will this person work most closely with? What / who are the biggest obstacles to success in this role? Before you joined the company, are there any questions you wished you'd asked but didn't? Is there anything that really surprised you when you joined here? What's the career path for this position? How do you like to work with people here? How often does the company have all-hands type meetings? How is the financial health? Have you hit your goals every quarter in this past year? What about in the past three years? What's the long-term vision? What growth goals do you have for the next two years? What concerns you most as you look into the future? What excites you most as you look into the future? If there was anything you could suggest to improve your tech solution, what would it be, and is product working on it right now? Why do you win deals? Why do you lose deals? What are your competitive advantages? Where do you fall short of the competition? What's kept you here? There are many additional questions I could add, but I'll spare you and stop the list here. Being prepared means you won't run out.

When we think about being prepared for interviews, my mantra is "always expect the unexpected." That means even if you're told you're going to meet with certain people (titles and / or specific names) in a certain order and you're likely going to be asked a set of questions, you need to know all of that could be tossed out the window. Thus, during the actual interview, you need to roll with it. Know things can change and sometimes it's for the better and sometimes not. But deal with it. Companies like to see if candidates can be flexible and go with the flow.

Have you ever heard the saying "Luck is when preparation meets opportunity"? I'm a true believer that the more you prepare, the more confident you'll be and the better you'll do when it's "game time." Strong preparation means luck will be on your side.

OK, so we talked about preparing for the interview by thinking about questions that might be asked. We put them into a few buckets (vanilla / basic questions, questions specific to the role, questions around possible objections, and questions you'll ask them). Equally as important to preparing for various interview questions they might ask you is preparing in general. So beyond preparing for questions, I'm talking about doing your homework on the company you're interviewing with, the person(s) you'll be meeting with, and their industry.

To recap:

- Think of interview questions (in all the buckets) and prepare answers
- Prepare by researching the company
- Prepare by researching each interviewer you're meeting with
- Prepare by researching the company's industry

You need to spend a lot of time on each of these. That means don't set aside a mere ten measly minutes for prepping. This is not enough time! Tip: Think about the amount of time you've dedicated to preparing for big meetings or presentations in any job you've held. Or think about the amount of time you spent studying for midterms or final exams. Those who never studied, ignore what I just said. I was a studier, so it's a good point of reference for me. In general, this means carving out a couple hours or more. If that's a bit too much or you're not afforded much notice, carve out as much time as you possibly can.

One very important thing to note: As you're doing your research, do not rely on memory; take copious notes and print off any information you can find. I don't know if it's my age or just me, but my memory has failed me one too many times. So don't put it to chance. Take notes and print off information as you do your research. Prepare!

Company: You need to thoroughly go through the company's website with a fine-tooth comb. This means going well beyond the "About Us" page. I'm talking about taking a deep dive into the details. Go through their website and learn all about them, their products, services, and solutions, their leadership team; see if there are case studies, press releases, and anything else you can glean from their site. If there are financials you can access, you should. For example, public companies have to annually file financial reports such as 10-Ks, which are made available to the public and can provide you with a sense of their financial health. Do a Google search to see what's out there. Are there interviews, articles, or videos about the company? Sometimes, there are videos of interviews with their top exec(s). Maybe an executive sat on a panel and talked about an interesting topic? Use LinkedIn and find / review their Company Page. Print whatever you can so you can easily reference the information as you prepare and so you can save it for future reference. I know this isn't "green" of me to say, but listen closely…you need to be prepared, and having information at your fingertips means you not only present yourself as someone who has and is prepared but also as someone who has lifelines when needed.

Interviewer(s): You need to research the interviewer(s) you'll be "meeting" with. An easy place to start is on LinkedIn. Gather what you can there. Not only is it helpful to see how long they've been at the company and if they've had promotions, but you can also check to see if you have mutual connections. Maybe you have similar backgrounds? Also, check the company's website. See if the interviewer(s) are listed—typically this is found in the "About Us" section or in the "Leadership" section—and if yes, read whatever you can about them. Also, do a Google search. Use social media too. You can find out a lot of interesting (and sometimes fun!) information about some people. By the way, if you do have mutual connections, you may want to reach out to them. They may be able to provide you with valuable insights that will help you determine if the opportunity is right for you. In addition to mutual connections, uncovering any commonalities you share with this person can be quite useful. Perhaps you went to the same college or you were in the same fraternity or played the same sport or share a similar passion, etc. There's a lot you can learn about someone when you do a little due diligence.

Industry: From an industry perspective, doing your research will not only help you be more knowledgeable about the entire space but might also give you a sense of the health of the entire industry / sector. You may realize the industry you're looking to possibly get into is going through a major contraction and, therefore, it might not be the best time to dive into that pool. Conversely if there's rapid growth in that segment, now could be an ideal time.

Spending ample time learning about the company, the person(s) interviewing you, and the industry the opportunity is in is invaluable. Don't cut corners here. I cannot stress enough how essential this step is and how often people underestimate what's required. I have seen so many candidates be rejected when it's obvious to the hiring company that they really didn't prepare. I don't care how polished you are, 99 percent of the time, it won't go well if you wing it.

- Résumé: When preparing for an interview, you need to think about your résumé. How many people think they know the details on their resume by heart? I'll tell you, a lot of people can't answer questions about their resumes with accuracy. It's thus critical for you to always have a printed copy on hand. If your interview is via phone or video, then you only need one copy (for you). If the interview is in person, you need to print off multiple copies. My rule of thumb is to print a résumé for each person you're scheduled to meet with plus one for yourself and bring three additional copies. That way, if there are any surprise interviewers, you should be all set. This might sound crazy, but review your résumé before an interview. Make sure you refresh your memory on the places you've worked, dates you held each position, and what you accomplished. When professionals get later into their careers, many forget or confuse details. While it doesn't happen often, numerous times a year, I'll receive feedback that my candidate couldn't answer questions about something on their résumé. That's never good! This is why it's helpful to always have a copy in hand. Even if your interview isn't in person, having a printed copy you can quickly reference means you won't need to worry about your computer going dark. It always takes eons to boot up in situations like these.
- Location of Interview: When preparing, make sure you know the location of your interview. This sounds so obvious, right? Well, I can't tell you how many times someone either hasn't saved the address into their calendar or brought it with. They're then in major panic mode trying to track me down last minute to figure it out. It's absurd! Save these details on your calendar so you know the location of your interview and where exactly you're going. Again, this is obvious. Yes? One would think. I think it's safe to say most of us have access to a GPS. But still, if you've never been to the location before, it's always a great idea to prepare by taking a test run to make sure your directions are good. Have you ever found yourself in the middle of a construction zone and the exact road you need to turn onto is closed? Or for some reason, the location doesn't show up on GPS? This is no fun when you're headed to an interview and potentially short on time. So driving the route to the destination prior to the big day will provide you with ample time to work out any kinks. It's also prudent to have

a sense of timing and traffic patterns. Be sure to give thought to parking: where you'll find parking, how long it might take not only to find a parking lot and spot but also how long it'll take to walk to the building, and so forth. For example, in a big city, parking can take a substantial amount of time, whereas in a suburban area or small city, parking might not be too difficult. It's extremely stressful to be driving in a city like Chicago, where there's a plethora of one-way streets and parking garages fill up quickly. Perhaps you'd rather take public transportation and avoid the parking dilemma. In that case, you'll want to figure out the best mode of transportation (bus, train, el, etc.) and then determine the route (are there multiple buses or trains you'll need to take to get from point A to point B?) along with their schedules; also figure out what time(s) you need to be at the stations / stops. If possible, do a trial run to make sure you know what you're doing, as it can be quite confusing and somewhat overwhelming. Now, perhaps this all seems way too stressful and you decide to take an Uber or a taxi. Regardless, always factor in some buffer time to give yourself room for unforeseen issues and delays. We all know bad weather can really throw a monkey wrench into our best-laid plans, and thus, you should always have a plan B. After all, it's a plan B world. (Maybe even a plan C world!) Prepare.

Please also be careful when in a metropolitan area to confirm exact addresses, especially if you're meeting at a common spot, such as a Starbucks. It's not unheard of for two locations to be close to each other, and it's easy to see how someone might go to the wrong one (no joke—I've had this happen to a couple candidates of mine).

- Day of the interview: Prepare by giving yourself plenty of time so you can hopefully avoid being late due to transportation issues. Tip: If you arrive at your destination more than five minutes early, kill time somewhere else so you aren't too early to your interview. I'll cover this in a bit, but just know some decision-makers get a bit bent out of shape when candidates arrive too early. By the way, I know this is counter to what many of us learned. I always thought being early was considered being on time. However, having received feedback on hundreds of candidates' interviews, I've found many interviewers are tweaked by candidates arriving early and

interrupting whatever it is they were doing. To be safe, do not arrive more than five minutes early.
- Contact Information: As you prepare for your interview, make sure you have the proper contact information. If the interview is a phone interview, know who is calling whom. Have contact info handy for the interviewer or for whomever scheduled your interview. If you're running late or need to reschedule, reach out asap to notify the appropriate people. Always be on time for your interview. It's incredibly stressful when you realize at the last minute you don't have the right info and you need it. Many of us have learned this lesson the hard way. I may or may not have learned it a few times.
- Make Sure Your Technology Works and You Have the Necessary Links: If you're doing a video interview, make sure you have the right link and you know how to work with the platform being used. It's so stressful when you're expected to get onto, let's say, Zoom and you don't have it downloaded and need to do so. Or, maybe you haven't used the tool in quite some time and when you launch, it starts doing an update that appears as though it might take a while to complete, leaving you unable to log on to the interview. Let me tell you, this can send many into a frenzy. It's not fun to be panicked that you won't be on time for the interview. To save yourself from all of this, it's good practice to prepare by launching the tool the night before your interview and doing a quick practice run with a friend. Keep in mind, this is also why having contact information is very helpful: we've all been in situations where our technology fails for any number of reasons and being able to inform the person(s) is important. With regard to video interviews, you also have to give some forethought to things like making sure your background is decent. No one wants to see an unmade bed, dirty towels, leftover food, etc. These do not leave a good impression. Furthermore, consider how you'll look since you're going to be visible to others. I don't know about you, but I can't just wake up and be ready for prime time. I need to get ready. By preparing what I want to wear in advance, the day of the Interview is less stressful. Net-net—preparing yourself and your space is key. Be presentable and make sure your space is presentable.

- Prepare Your References: OK, so let's say you've been asked for references. Hopefully that's a positive indicator of the direction things are going in the interview process. Hooray—yay for you! Guess what? This means it's time for you to prepare your references! I'm genuinely so confused by the number of people who clearly don't prepare their references. Unfortunately, this can and has led to problems, sometimes big ones! Let's keep in mind that references are typically requested at the end of the interview process. However, there are some recruiters and companies that request them much earlier in an interview process. Thus, it's never too soon to think about them.

    As we start to discuss preparing your references, know that we're going to think about this both for professionals who are newly entering the job market (recent college grads) and for professionals who've been in the workforce for some time. Who your references are and how you want to prepare them might be a tad different, and I'll share thoughts on both.

    If you're newly entering the job market and are getting your first "real" job, your references might not be able to provide the hiring team with the same depth and breadth of insight that references for someone who comes armed with a year or more of experience in the workforce can offer. Either way, the very first thing you want to do is actually contact your references. I know this sounds fairly basic, but when you're asked to provide references, you need to get their permission first. So you'll want to actually contact them. And by the way, if you haven't talked to someone in years, I'd think long and hard about providing them as a reference. If someone doesn't know what you've been doing for the last five years, let alone that you're still alive, that person really shouldn't be provided as a reference. I have been the recipient of calls like this and it's downright weird. So let me repeat as I want to be crystal clear here—the very first thing you're going to do when you're asked to provide your references is contact them to ensure they're available and willing to be your reference. I don't care if someone told you they'd always be glad to be a reference for you. You're still going to contact them to ask if they can be a reference for you at that moment in time.

    Now, if you've been at the same company for the past six years with the same bosses, you might have to provide a reference you haven't connected with in a while. But you really do need to be careful when it comes to thinking through who your references will be. Ideally, you've already discussed your challenge with the hiring team and shared you won't be able to provide references from your current employer. Then, there's no surprise that your references will not include anyone currently working with you.

So you're contacting references, first and foremost, because you want to make sure the reference is still alive. If yes, that they're able to receive a phone call and will take it. We all know people go on vacation. We all know people don't always answer their phones, especially when numbers they don't recognize pop up on their caller ID. We all know people don't always listen to their voice mails. Hence, contacting those you'd like to put down as your references first to ensure they're open to being a reference and that they can have a conversation in the next few days is paramount. If you're not able to get in touch with someone who you want to be a reference for you, odds are the person contacting the reference won't be able to either. And that can be embarrassing.

OK, moving forward—keep in mind, the goal of reference checks is to give the hiring company a chance to find out if you've been honest about your background. Additionally to glean more about what you're like as an employee, colleague, peer, manager, person, etc. People want to find out if you're easy or difficult to work with, if you accomplish your goals consistently, if you actually have the skills you've said you do, and so forth. Thus, as a candidate, it's important to think about this prior to providing your references, because if someone can't speak to these "things," it can raise a whole host of red flags. Honest to G-d, I've called references who've said they haven't talked to the particular professional I'm asking about in years. And due to the time lapse, some references will acknowledge, they can't speak fairly and accurately about the person's current skills because it's been so long since they last worked together. Obviously this is not helpful at all and certainly can become problematic. Why, why, why, why would someone provide this reference? Come on, this is common sense—when asked to provide references, provide ones you've stayed in touch with and ones who can speak to your relevant skills! And by the way, this is a strong reminder to stay in touch with people you've worked with, especially your former bosses. As you move forward in your career, it's easy to lose touch with your prior leadership and this can be a big mistake. Make it a point to at least check in once a year.

In my firm's process, long before I ever put a candidate in front of a client, I ask candidates if they'll be able to provide me with a minimum of three references, and typically I'll note that two of their references will need to be prior bosses. If a candidate doesn't answer that question with confidence, I'll dig deeper. If it becomes clear this could be a challenge, chances are I won't proceed with the candidate. Now, there are some exceptions here. If you're an entry-level candidate looking for your very first job, you won't have deep experience, or possibly any experience, for that matter, in the field you're interviewing in and on top of that, you won't have prior bosses to offer as references. So you may be thinking you won't have two or three professional references to offer. However, I want you to stop for a moment and think again because you actually might have references you can provide. Have you had any internships? Have you had summer jobs or even jobs you've held during the school year? Have you led groups or held positions in extracurricular spaces like athletics, fraternities / sororities, clubs, etc.? If yes, that's where you'll find references. Now, there may be some synergistic skills that a reference can speak to, but more often than not, these types of jobs don't match up perfectly with the job you're pursuing. That's understandable. These references will still be helpful to whoever is contacting them. By the way, if you're remotely concerned about this, bring it up to the recruiter or hiring manager early in the interview process. Share the fact that from a references perspective, you want to ensure they understand your references will be (insert whomever you're thinking you'd use) and find out if there's a potential issue here. Addressing this earlier rather than later is always helpful. They'll be able to provide you with great advice and counsel on how to best prepare such references.

OK, speaking of preparing your references…assuming you're planning on providing references whom you've, at a minimum, kept in contact with, you should speak to each reference before you ever share their name with a potential employer so you can confirm whether or not they're willing to serve as a reference for you. In other words, get their permission first! To recap: You're going to contact your references to be sure they're able to be references at that moment in time. Then, you're going to actually speak with them yourself to prepare them. You want to provide each reference with a detailed overview of the position you're interviewing for to ensure they:

- know the actual position and title along with the key requirements hiring managers are focused on and
- are comfortable speaking about you for this role.

Let's add some color to this:

You need to provide your references with details. This means, beyond asking if they're open to being a reference for you, you're providing them with a detailed summary of the role, you're sharing with them why the hiring manager / company is interested in you, what they believe you will bring to the position / company, and if there are any concerns they (the hiring managers / the company) have about you as a candidate that you've had to overcome in their interview process. Once you've covered all of this with the reference, you need to ask them, "Based on what I just shared with you about this opportunity, do you feel comfortable serving as a reference for me?"

Wait for an answer.

If the person doesn't say yes, you need to dig deeper and determine if it really makes sense to proceed. If the individual says there is no concern, then ask, "OK, just to make sure you're all set and it makes sense to proceed, is there anything I shared that you're not fully comfortable with?"

Again, wait for an answer. Make sure they know roughly when to expect the hiring manager's call. Based on all of this, you need to decide if you feel confident this is a good reference for you.

Look, I'm not trying to rig the system at all. But I kid you not, I've talked to references who, after I've described the position to the reference, have point-blank said they can't endorse the candidate for the specific position because when the candidate worked with them, the candidate didn't hold that type of role and, thus, the reference can't speak to the candidate's abilities in such a position. Now, in my role as the recruiter, I certainly appreciate honesty and am glad someone (the reference) has provided me with such candid feedback. However, if I'm the candidate, I want to try to find people who can speak to my skills / strengths as they relate to the position I'm interviewing for. And if this person can't, I'd like to know this before I embarrass myself and offer this person up as a reference. In this type of situation, whoever is calling the reference will undoubtedly question why you provided this reference. They will wonder why you couldn't come up with a reference who is better suited to speak to your candidacy as it relates to their hiring needs. Or they may consider taking a pass on you and focusing on other candidates who might be better aligned with the position. The exception to this is when you're a candidate who doesn't have the experience they're looking for but you've been completely transparent about this fact and the company / hiring team is OK with this. Despite what you're lacking, the hiring manager(s) still see you as a good, viable candidate for reasons discussed throughout their interview process. In this scenario, your references are going to be asked to speak to the strengths as well as the potential you bring to the company. Thus, the references need to know this upfront so they aren't caught off guard. You'll want to explain to them what everyone knows you're missing and why they're still open to you as a candidate. That way, the potential reference(s) can tell you if they're comfortable serving as a reference for you.

Now, we've covered prepping references for entry-level job searches as well as for established, experienced professionals. Let's add another group to the mix; those who are switching careers (sometimes professionals will refer to this as pivoting careers). When someone changes their career path, they may not have the exact skills or experience a hiring team is looking for, and certainly this should come as no surprise to the hiring team because they've interviewed and assessed the person's candidacy, typically in advance of getting to the reference-checking stage. In this situation, candidates typically won't have references who can fully speak to their capabilities in regard to whatever space it is they're moving into. For example, if a candidate has been in sales for ten years but has decided they really want to move into the marketing function, they likely won't have the exact experience the hiring team is looking for. However, there may be reasons why the hiring team likes the candidate. Perhaps there are aspects of marketing the candidate has done during their tenure in sales. Maybe the candidate has taken a course or has obtained a relevant certification through which they've gained solid experience. There might be synergies and parallels discussed in the interview process providing the hiring team with confidence in the candidate's ability to transition into the position and marketing team. Thus, the candidate will want to find references who can speak to those parallels and synergies as well as the qualities and characteristics the hiring team values. So while the candidate's experience won't be perfect, their references can provide insights the hiring team will value.

A tricky part of reference checking worth noting: There are some people who legally can't and won't give any sort of feedback when contacted for a reference check. Some companies have strict policies prohibiting employees from sharing anything beyond dates of employment. Truth be told, there are some decision-makers who don't want to waste time calling references who will only state whether someone was, in fact, an employee at the company and confirm dates of employment. Those never seem to leave a decision-maker feeling warm and fuzzy about the professional. There's a belief that if there was something good to be said, the reference would say it and not be so strict about the policy. Thus, one can't help but wonder if a reference states the strict policy and only provides dates of employment along with the titles held whether or not the professional has a dark past with some skeletons in the closet no one wants to share for fear of legal repercussions. When it comes to reference checks, I've pretty much seen it all. I've had candidates tell me they don't have any prior bosses. Really? Hmmmm. Weird! I've had candidates provide references who are no longer alive. So sad! Awful! I've had candidates provide references who don't remember them. The reference isn't sure they actually worked with my candidate. I've had candidates provide references who remember working with the person but state due to the lapse in time, they don't feel comfortable speaking to the person's abilities.

I've had references tell me the candidate doesn't have the requisite experience, when in actuality they do but gained the experience after working with the reference so they weren't aware. You get the point…I've had candidates give some lousy references. Moral to the story is, you need to prepare your references because if you don't, things could go sideways.

Oh my goodness—this is a long chapter! We've covered a lot! Let's quickly recap: Preparing is paramount to success. The more you prepare, the better you'll do in your job search and / or interview process. Prepare by developing a plan; know what you want to accomplish and when. Make sure you focus on your résumé and get it in tip-top shape. Have a strong bio on hand if you're a seasoned professional. Build out your LinkedIn profile so you're noticed and contacted for great opportunities and so your experience stands out to all who review it. In addition, learn how to leverage LinkedIn as a tool to help you with your job search. Furthermore, craft an email(s) you want to send out to anyone and everyone who can help you with your job search. Organize your contacts / connections so you can start reaching out to them. Know when you plan to do so. Make sure you have the right technology in place to enable you to keep track of every single aspect of your job search. Then, learn how to best leverage the technology so as to maximize the benefits. Think about time management and how you want to organize your days, weeks, and months. Set goals and hold yourself accountable. Plan for calls as well as interviews by doing your homework and practicing interview questions and answers. When you have interviews, prepare for them by ensuring: you have your résumé(s) ready, you know where you're going if in-person, you have contact information along with proper links if virtual, you have tested your technology to make sure it's ready to go, and you have prepared your references so they are ready for you when you need them.

Do Your Homework

JUST LIKE YOUR teachers checked to make sure you did your homework, hiring managers will do the same. While we touched on this briefly in the prior chapter, I am taking the time to dig in here because this is feedback I receive all too often, and it can't be stressed enough.

"It was clear [candidate's name] did not do their homework prior to our interview!" *or* "[Candidate's name] was not prepared at all!" *or* "[Candidate's name] didn't know anything about us."

Ugh! Are you kidding me? How does this happen? This is basic 101 'stuff'.

During an interview, it never bodes well for candidates when they haven't done their homework and don't know basic information about the company they're interviewing with, the position they're interviewing for, and / or the person they're being interviewed by.

In an interview, you really can't point blame at your dog, saying he ate your homework. In an interview, it's all up to you. Yes, every candidate should know the importance of doing their homework. Unfortunately, though, it seems to be a critical part of interviewing many try to cut corners on, and—*NEWS FLASH*—few do so successfully. Knowing how crucial this step is, let me break it down for you. Here's the homework you absolutely must do before every interview:

1. Use LinkedIn to look up the profiles of the person(s) you're speaking or meeting with. You can also do a Google search and try to check the person out on social media sites. Typically, you'll find useful intel about people fairly quickly. Remember: Take notes about each person and have those notes available during your interview(s). It's virtually impossible to

remember everyone's background. Make it easy on yourself by having some bullets about each person at your fingertips. One of my mantras in interviewing is "Don't rely on memory." Taking notes will help you as you do your homework!

2. Review any and all information shared with you about the position being discussed. Whether it's a formal job spec, an email describing some basics about the role, or notes taken when speaking with a recruiter, please refamiliarize yourself with these points before every interview. It's essential for you to, at a minimum, have a sense of what the position is about as well as what the company is seeking in an ideal candidate. Know the key characteristics and qualities they're looking for. Once you have a good grasp of their "hot buttons," put some thought into how you align with the role. Think about why you're a good fit for the position. (Hint: If you have no clue, then you have a problem and need to figure this out. If after trying to figure it out, you still have no idea how you're a good fit [meaning you're not a fit], then you probably should not pursue it.)

    Assuming you're a good fit, you need to map out how you want to position yourself so that during the interview, you can successfully articulate the value you'll bring to the hiring manager and to the company as a whole. Do you know how many people struggle with articulating these points succinctly? Hint: Significantly more than you'd think. Don't fall into this trap and take for granted how challenging a seemingly simple question might be to answer. Know your value proposition and how you align with the role. Do your homework.

3. If you know the company's name, look it up online and dig in! PS: Reviewing a website does *NOT* mean simply spending a few minutes reading the home or "About Us" page. A few minutes is grossly inadequate! Look through a company's entire website (unless it's Amazon—that's too many pages). Google the company—learn about them, who they are, what they do, what their core competencies are, who their competition is, etc. Check to see if there are any recent press releases. If so, read them! Did they make an acquisition? Did they divest a division? Did they just raise a new round of funding? In addition, learn all about the company's industry. You must know your stuff! When you demonstrate knowledge about the company

and their industry, you'll stand out as a professional who did their homework. I realize some recruiters may keep their client's name confidential. In that scenario, it can be a bit of a challenge to figure out the exact company. However, if you know enough about their industry, doing a bit of research often helps to narrow down which company it might be. And if you've been given a job spec, this can sometimes help you determine the company.

4. If you're interviewing with a company that makes a reasonably priced, easy-to-purchase product, guess what you should do? Yup—buy it! Use it. Get to know it. Experience the product from the consumers' perspective and have thoughts about it. Read reviews. See if the company responds to reviews and what they tend to say.

   If the company you're working with has an app, it would be wise to purchase / download the app and actually spend time with it so you understand and can articulate the users' experience firsthand. Net-net:

   o If you're interviewing with a company like LinkedIn, you might want to make sure you have a profile set up on LinkedIn.
   o If you're interviewing with Facebook, make sure you have an account. X—the company formerly known Twitter? You better be X-ing or what we used to call, tweeting. Uber? Better take a ride! Tinder? Grinder? Get ready to go on a date (kidding!)!
   o If you are interviewing with a brick-and-mortar retailer and you've never been to their store, go! Walk the aisles, talk to some employees, and buy something. And use a credit card so you're "in their system."
   o If you're interviewing with an online retailer, spend time on their site and buy something (assuming it's affordable). Feel the consumer experience firsthand so you can speak to it.
   o If you're interviewing with a CPG company (consumer packaged goods company), use their product(s). If they make beverages, drink some. If they've just launched a new laundry detergent brand, try it. If they're an energy bar manufacturer, eat some. If they make potato chips, get on your couch and start crunching them!

Hopefully you're getting my point. These are all commonsense, simple things you can do to do your homework and help get ready for an interview while also putting your candidacy in a better light. Failing to take these steps can have consequences.

Quick story: I was working with an iconic Chicago-based retailer, and in a first interview, it was quite common for candidates to be asked if they'd ever shopped at their store. If a candidate hadn't been to or shopped at the store, that wasn't helpful to their status in the process.

Another: I have clients who've developed apps, and it's typical for them to inquire whether or not someone has the app downloaded. Furthermore, if they use the app and what the experience has been like and / or what suggestions they may have, etc. Obviously, it helps when candidates can answer these questions with a solid yes and have insights to support that answer. This is pretty basic stuff we can't take for granted.

Doing your homework is a must! In the vast majority of cases, it's very easy to determine if a candidate hasn't done their homework before an interview, and sadly, the grade received is typically below a passing one.

Don't Be a Know-It-All

YES, I SAID doing your homework when looking for a job and when preparing for an interview is super important. That said, equally as dangerous as not doing your homework is doing way too much homework. Here's what I mean—there are candidates who go to the extreme. These folks will spend days upon days doing research. They will go to such great lengths, often utilizing CIA tactics, to uncover any and every morsel of information possible about the company, the competition, and the interviewer. These professionals, whom I affectionately refer to as the "Cliff Clavins" of interviewing, do so much prep work they're literally oozing out information. Proud of the insights gathered, Cliff Clavins often have trouble tempering both their enthusiasm and the amount of detail they spew forth. In an effort to impress their audience, they'll regurgitate obscene amounts of information (be it in writing or verbally). Unfortunately, this can have the reverse effect and completely backfire. Rather than impressing decision-makers, Cliff Clavins sound more like "know-it-alls," which can (and often does) irritate their audience. Yes, Cliff Clavins can be amusing. But they also run the risk of being incredibly annoying. There's a fine line here, and one needs to be careful not to go overboard. Being knowledgeable is important, but being a know-it-all can be a turnoff, and some decision-makers will reject candidates for this very reason. I've received feedback such as, "Adam spent ten minutes telling me everything about our product, all of which I knew. He then went on to explain to me the dynamics facing the market, which again, I already knew. It was annoying. And a waste of precious time."

By the way, in the bucket of know-it-alls are name-droppers. Many hiring managers have little tolerance for candidates who name-drop excessively. Being a know-it-all and / or a name-dropper can do more harm than good.

Another way candidates can come across as "know-it-alls": some candidates like to tell the interviewer what they should be doing and / or what the company should be doing, as if they know what's best. For example, telling an interviewer how their company should be going to market, who they should be targeting, how they should innovate, not to pursue going down a certain path, etc., can really rub a decision-maker the wrong way. For example, saying to a hiring manager, "You need to go after XYZ retailer and stop wasting time with ABC retailer because… [insert reason]"… may not be a smart move on the candidate's part. In fact, it might be downright dumb! Perhaps the company's had tremendous success with ABC. Maybe they pursued XYZ a while ago and decided for a myriad of reasons, they didn't want to do business with XYZ. Look—as a candidate, you don't have all the inside scoop. So, unless specifically asked your thoughts on something, be cautious. Candidates aren't inside the company and privy to information, thus it's extremely ballsy to tell a company / hiring manager what they need to be doing, thinking about, focusing on, innovating toward, etc. It's like telling someone how to raise their child or how they should run their own life. Tread lightly. Rather than making bold statements, formulate questions. For example, a candidate could ask, "Have you ever thought about going after XYZ retailer? If you did, what happened?"

For the record, being a know-it-all isn't only a negative in a professional setting. This can turn people off in your personal life too. We all have that friend who will voluntarily tell you something about every single thing! Even if you didn't ask, they'll share their wealth of knowledge. Sometimes it's exhausting because you just don't care one bit and just want to move the conversation along or end it. Other times it's annoying because they're telling you stuff you already know or worse, stuff you just said. Other times you don't think the know-it-all is right. You may have different thoughts on the topic, but with this individual, you're always going to be wrong. Why? Because they know everything. They know it all! They're an expert on every subject! I could keep going on this topic, but I'll spare you.

You get the point…there's a fine line between being able to share information that demonstrates you did your homework versus going overboard. I realize it's hard to know exactly where that line is. This is where being able to "read the room" is really important. You need to pay attention to the body language of those you're speaking with, along with their tone of voice. If people appear annoyed or disengaged, if they sound a bit different than they did earlier in the conversation, you should make a change in your approach. That might mean shortening your answers and refraining from regurgitating details they already know about their own company. I'm a big fan of putting yourself in the other person's shoes and hearing what you're saying through their ears. Ask yourself if this would annoy you in anyway. Consider whether what you're saying includes too much detail. If you think you might be coming across too much like a know-it-all, you probably are, and that means you need to hold back a bit. You might want to let them do more of the talking and possibly ask some questions to shift the conversation. Let the interviewer take the lead to guide the conversation along.

Look Over Your Work Before You Turn It In

WHEN YOU WERE IN GRADE SCHOOL, did your teachers tell you to be sure to look your work over before turning it in? Mine always did! Teachers stressed how careless errors could largely be avoided simply by taking the time to review your work so you could find and fix mistakes before turning said work in. This, of course, resulted in better grades.

For those who aren't sure what I'm driving at here, this means proofread your freaking work! Proofread. Why? Because proofreading helps ensure you're doing good work. Remember? We talked about this before. All of us need to proofread! Every single person must proofread.

We can't assume we're consistently putting forth work that's 100 percent perfect—we need to check it. In fact, 99% of the time I proofread my own work, I find at least one error, and the same goes for when I review someone else's work. We talked about the dangers of technology and how many falsely assume computers can be relied upon to uncover any and every error. When none are highlighted, people feel they're in the clear. Not so! We can't count on computers—or any other technology, for that matter—to find every mistake. The only thing we can count on is the fact we're human and thus prone to making errors. So take time to look over your work! And by all means, fix your mistakes!

When in job search or interview mode, you absolutely must proofread every single piece of "work" put out into the market. This includes your résumé, cover letters, emails, projects, thank-you notes, texts, etc. Can we please commit to proofreading everything so we can catch our errors before it's too late? It's insane how many typos I see on a daily basis coming from professionals at every level. And please don't roll your eyes at me, and don't you dare think to yourself, "Puh-leeeze—I would not be at the level I am if I had typos in things I write!" Because guess what? The doorbell just rang, and do you know who's there? Why, it's Murphy's Law. By thinking you're above this, you just invited Mr. Law over for a visit, and believe you me, you'll regret it!

Heed my warning.

I'm 100% serious—typos happen all the time, and typos can spell disaster. I've seen it too many times to count—candidates cut from consideration because of one measly typo. When there are other candidates (I don't care if it's one or hundreds of other candidates) vying for the same role, one single solitary typo can knock you out. Right or wrong—fair or unfair—it's a fact.

Résumés: Why are there so many typos in résumés? One document you must, without fail, proofread a gazillion times is your résumé! This is common sense, yet the number of typos I find in résumés literally boggles my mind; it happens at epidemic proportions and is absolutely asinine! As we talked about earlier, this isn't a mistake only the rookies make; typos are prevalent in the résumés of some of the most impressive professionals out there. Across the board, there are people at every level with mistakes in their résumés. No joke, I've worked on senior-level communications / PR positions with applicants who hold very high positions within our nation's most impressive companies, and you'd be astounded by the number of typos I've seen in résumés and cover letters, emails, InMails via LinkedIn, and texts received during those searches. I'm pretty sure professionals in communications, of all the functional areas within a business, should be the ones with perfectly crafted, typo-free résumés, cover letters, and emails. Surprisingly, this isn't the case!

I think we can all agree, your résumé is an extremely important document. Like it or not, résumés are not yet obsolete. Yes, your résumé may still be the document used to determine whether or not you will be asked to interview for an opportunity. It's supposed to separate you from all other applicants…in a good way…not a bad one! Thus, why would you risk being passed over due to having careless mistakes in your résumé? Even though spell-check doesn't catch everything (as mentioned earlier), please use it. Some typos might be identified. In addition, most of us have someone we can ask to proofread our résumés (a friend, spouse, neighbor, etc.). Alternatively, you can always hire someone. There are many experts out there who will gladly take a few bucks to proofread your résumé. While money may be tight, you have to know this is some of the best money you'll ever spend. If it means getting a job faster, which means you'll start making money sooner, can we agree it's a wise investment?

Keep in mind, this goes beyond résumés. This extends to all work because we're human and humans are infallible. Mistakes are bound to happen. So catch typos to ensure others never see them. I know it sounds counterintuitive to some, yet by slowing down and looking your work over (proofreading) on the front end, the timeline to achieve desired outcomes will be accelerated on the back end!

Make Your Work Look Nice

I DON'T KNOW ABOUT YOU, but I have G-d-awful handwriting. When I was growing up, my teachers consistently noted this and were always on my case, encouraging me to improve my penmanship. I recall conversations about how my work looked sloppy and because of that, it looked like I didn't care and / or take pride in what I was doing, yada yada yada. Time and again, I remember being lectured on how I needed to make my work look nicer. And funny enough, my kids' teachers had the same conversations with them. Apparently bad handwriting can be passed down through DNA. You may be wondering what this has to do with job searching and / or interviewing. Why am I bringing this up? While I'm fairly confident this might be rather self-explanatory, I won't put the onus on you to unravel every mystery. Here's what I mean…in a job search process and / or interview setting, every single thing you do, along with every single thing you put forth, is being evaluated. Thus, every single thing needs to be done as close to perfectly as humanly possible. What you produce and put forth should look like it came from a true professional and not some random fourth grader. (Not that there's anything wrong with random fourth graders. I've had two of my own, and they were pretty darn cute!)

Résumé

MAKING YOUR WORK LOOK NICE sounds pretty obvious, right? I assure you, it's not! Let's start with our current favorite topic, the résumé. Can we please make résumés look nice?

We're going to simplify this into two areas: the aesthetics and the content.

<u>Aesthetics</u>: I'm literally talking about how the ink looks on the page. Suggesting you make your résumé look nice should be a slam dunk, a "nonissue." Unfortunately, it isn't. This drives me absolutely bonkers! Nothing screams "schlump" more than a poorly crafted, lame-looking résumé. I constantly receive résumés reminiscent of the work my boys brought home from their fourth-grade tech class. Of course, at the time, I was incredibly proud of what they brought home because it was great work…for a fourth grader! When you're well beyond fourth grade and in the working world, I'm hoping we're aiming a bit higher. A professional-looking résumé provides the reader with a positive impression right off the bat; picture someone driving up to your home in a gorgeous Porsche versus the 1976 AMC Pacer used in the movie *Wayne's World*. What would your first impression be? With a nice-looking résumé, it's easy for the reader to quickly assume the professional must be impressive, which obviously sets things off on the right foot. A pitiful-looking résumé…well…not so much!

Some of the things I see on résumés that aren't nice aesthetically include the following:

- Headers: If you use headers, make sure they're where you want them. I see many résumés in which the headers are clearly not where the author intended them to be. For example, a header might not be centered on

the page. Or it says Page 2, but it's at the bottom of the first page when it should be at the top of – guess where – the second page.
- Page Breaks: Make sure page breaks are where they're supposed to be. (This often goes hand in hand with the point about headers made above.)
- Consistency: Make sure the bullets, dates, margins, and borders are lined up in a consistent fashion. Have consistency in all areas, including things such as: font (style, size, color), where and what you bold / don't bold, what is or isn't underlined, what's abbreviated, how and where you place dates of employment, spacing between paragraphs, periods / no periods at the end of bullets, margins on each page, etc. I find the easiest way to check all of this is to print a résumé onto paper and view how it looks on the page(s). Yes, this isn't "green," and I'm sure there are some who will tell me how many trees we're killing when résumés are printed. But it can be really hard to know with certainty if things aren't lining up when viewing documents on a computer screen. Just be sure to recycle the paper, and you won't feel so guilty.
- Easy to Read: With regards to the ink on the pages and the words being used, a résumé needs to be easy to read. Unless you're in a highly creative position or field, a résumé should not be written in some sort of crazy font style, in an insanely small size, or in funky color(s) and / or wacky format. These things can make a résumé extremely difficult to read.

    Easy to read also means you cannot load each page up with so much text that there's no white to be seen. If you cannot see white on the page because it's completely covered with words, you need to trim it down ASAP. If you've opted to have your résumé written in paragraphs versus utilizing bullets, it can be harder to read. It may be difficult for the reader to quickly identify who you are, what you've accomplished, and what makes you unique. If you have a résumé in which the layout has differing borders with text going in multiple directions, you're creating a challenge—the eyes of the reader don't know where to focus. Some résumé-writing experts have said such formats create confusion and note that whatever message you're trying to convey might be very hard to discern.

Tip: If you aren't sure how your résumé matches up to others aesthetically, ask some friends to share their résumés with you. In addition, if you've ever hired people, go through old résumés and look at the ones you were impressed by. Research to find résumé-writing experts. Read what they've written as many will tout what the most current trends and styles are for having the best, most professional résumés. Another good litmus test is the feedback you're receiving. If you're hearing people say, "Your résumé is extremely impressive" or "Wow-your résumé rocks!" then you're probably in good shape. Conversely, if you're not hearing such compliments, your résumé may very well need a shot of Botox or a full-blown face-lift. If that's the case, do yourself a favor and seek the advice of a professional. There are many professional résumé writers, so find a few. Take some time to research them; ask for some references and samples. Then pick the one you feel is best. If spending the money to have a professional write your résumé is simply not in the cards, then jump online and search for résumé-writing tools / formats. There is absolutely no excuse for having a lame résumé. I know money might be tight and many people are counting their pennies. While I'm definitely not a money manager or investment adviser, I can assure you that a sorry-looking résumé is going to make your job search a lengthier and more challenging endeavor. If spending a few hundred bucks to have a professionally written résumé results in a shorter job search, guess what? This means you'll be getting a paycheck sooner. Do the math! Make the investment! Also, do keep in mind once you have an amazing résumé, you'll have an exceptional foundation to build upon for years to come. All you'll need to do is update it from time to time. It'll be a cinch! And trust me, you'll be beyond thankful you had this professionally done.

Content: Let's move beyond the aesthetics of the résumé and talk about the actual content – this is what is IN the résumé. First of all, you absolutely need content. I don't see it very often, but once in a while, I'll receive a résumé with a list of companies, titles held, dates of employment, and education credentials. This is too bare-bones. What you need when it comes to content:

- Provide Ample Detail: The reader wants to see more than a simple list of the names of the companies you worked for, what your titles were, and dates showing when you were there. Readers want to know what you did in the positions held during your tenure. So it's important to provide detail around roles, responsibilities, and, ideally, the results you achieved.

Having a bare-bones résumé isn't going to help hiring managers get to know you and see how you compare to others who might be applying for the same position.

- Confusing / Unclear Verbiage: While most professionals I've worked with do have (some) content in their résumés, sometimes the content is unclear, and this can present challenges. People use verbiage that's confusing or vague—for example, "go-to person in charge of everything," "jack-of-alltrades," "chief problem solver," and more. Uhhh—can you help me understand what those all mean? When your content isn't clear, the reader won't be able to determine how you compare to others they might be considering.

  Some companies use specific acronyms or abbreviations others might not know. Be sure to explain those if you use them. For example, a professional I was working with had this on their résumé: "Go-to SME for annual PA and KPIs." Not everyone knows SME means 'subject matter expert' and that PA means, 'performance appraisal' and KPI means, 'key performance indicator'. It's best to explain what the acronyms and abbreviations mean to your audience because you don't know who will take the time to look it up and try to figure it out.

- Concise: Yes, we want detail in the content, but it's important to be concise. There are many résumés with a lot of verbiage considered fluff. If you can take words out, especially if your résumé is long, do so. Edit to remove personal pronouns, redundant bullets, and unnecessary use of words (i.e.— 'the' or 'that' or 'and so forth') to make the document more concise.

  Many people ask me questions about how long a résumé should be. Does it have to be one page? Or can it go beyond? Are three pages too much? What about four? The right length for a résumé is definitely a controversial topic as there are many differing opinions. If you've been working for a while, many agree it's OK to have a résumé that's more than one page. That said, I don't care who you are or how long you've been working; six pages is a bit excessive, and much of it likely won't be read. In fact, statistics say decision-makers spend on average about six seconds reviewing your résumé, which means you're pushing your luck with six pages. Hence, when it comes to the length of your résumé, you need to exercise some discretion. If you've worked twenty years and only have a one-page résumé, it might look a bit short to executives reviewing it. On the other hand, if you've only worked five years and your résumé is three pages, you might be working with a document a tad too long. Remember, most people don't have the interest or patience to read through a lengthy document. This is where a professional résumé writer can be tremendously helpful, as they will know how to pare it down. They can help you weed out the fluff, condense any redundancies, and articulate your professional background with impactful verbiage that'll help you stand out. Short of working with an expert, seek the advice and counsel of other professionals you respect. Show them your résumé and get multiple opinions. If the consensus is that it's too long, trim it down.

- Strong Verbiage: Many underestimate the importance of the verbiage used in a résumé. The words used throughout a résumé need to be strong. This will help you stand out. For example, what do you think is more impactful: "Responsible for $24 million territory" or "Successfully identified and closed $24 million of new business revenue in 2023, achieving 120 percent of annual plan"?

    As discussed, if decision-makers spend approx six seconds reviewing your résumé before making their decision as to whether or not to continue evaluating you as a candidate, you better believe the verbiage you use makes a tremendous difference. The more your words can convey authority and expertise in a particular area, the better.

    From a verbiage perspective, also take into consideration what's casual and conversational language versus what's professional. For example, "Got President's Club award" is better stated as "Achieved President's Club award."

- Results: Throughout résumés, many professionals do a fabulous job outlining the roles / responsibilities of positions held but fail to denote the results delivered in each role. Many résumés read like job descriptions. They offer a running list of day-to-day duties. However, they don't highlight the professional's achievements and impacts. Think about it—let's simplify this by using sports as our example. If you're a pitcher in the MLB, there are lots of pitchers whose roles and responsibilities are the same as yours. However, what differentiates you from all the other professional pitchers are your results and achievement—they're what count. Not every pitcher has thrown two consecutive no hitters. Not all pitchers throw twenty-four complete games in their rookie years. As teams evaluate who to recruit, they look at these stats to determine who has the best results.

Let's go back into the corporate world. There are a lot of operations executives. Some have had mediocre success, while others have had phenomenal success. One operations leader might have helped their company successfully expand into three new markets, add hundreds of millions in revenue, all while leading a team of over thirty. While another might have helped his company add two million in revenue (which is nothing to laugh at) while leading a team of three. Clearly, these two execs are different!

I recently had to research heart surgeons. There are a lot of them out there, but they aren't all the same. There are some I would never want operating on my mom. There are tons of restaurants in the city of Chicago. All serve food. However, all are not equal, and there are many I would never go to. This is why review sites are so popular. Results matter! Hopefully you get the point—hiring managers reviewing your résumé want to know the details of your results. How can you tell if you have results highlighted? When looking at your résumé, at the end of each bullet, ask yourself, "So what happened? What was accomplished?" If you can't see the answer in the bullet, then you probably haven't fully highlighted the results delivered.

When bringing forth results, think about things like: Did you help make money, save money, increase growth, reduce time wasted, create efficiencies, streamline processes, mitigate risk, reduce turnover, reduce time to hire, find savings, uncover discrepancies, identify and minimize redundancies, etc.? Everyone wants to know your accomplishments, your achievements, and the results you delivered. Do the best you can to make them stand out.

- Tailored: Where appropriate and if possible, résumés should be tailored to the position you're applying for. Your résumé should use keywords and phrases mirroring verbiage used in the job spec and / or echoing what you've been told by the talent acquisition executive(s) or hiring manager(s). Don't panic—tailoring your résumé doesn't mean reinventing the wheel every single time. What it does mean, however, is that as a candidate for a particular position, you need to help the reader easily see how you align with the position you're pursuing. When you tailor ("tweak") your résumé to a job spec, you'll do yourself an enormous favor by "connecting the dots" for the reader. Ultimately, doing so puts you in a better position to be considered for a particular role. Yes, this will take you a few minutes to do, but I can assure you it will pay off in spades. You're potentially wasting a bunch of time if you are not doing it. By the way—you really need to pay close attention, especially if you have a few versions of your résumés as it's easy to mess things up. For example, if a job spec highlights the position as an individual contributor sales position in the telecom space, you should NOT send a résumé with the headline "Top Medical Device Sales Executive—Successful track record of building and leading large sales teams…" Hopefully you can see what's wrong here. This person not only positioned themselves as a sales manager, which clearly differs from an individual contributor position, but also highlighted that they're in the medical device arena. By their saying this, the hiring manager may assume this person is in the medical field and is a sales leader and may not read further. Even though the résumé may outline experience in individual contributor roles and experience in other fields, this candidate potentially cornered themselves and significantly increased the odds of their résumé ending up in the delete folder. Not good! Now, if this professional has held individual contributor positions in the past and has worked in industries outside of the medical device field, my advice is to create a more broad-based summary to cover their bases, such as "Top Sales Executive—Successful track record of consistently meeting and exceeding aggressive revenue targets in both individual contributor as well as sales leadership positions across a variety of industries, including _____." Such a headline has a better chance of getting the reader to take a bit more time before making the decision to pursue or reject this candidate.

Another example, I was working on a digital marketing position and the job spec clearly laid out how critical certain aspects of digital marketing experience were. I was introduced to someone who had a wealth of digital experience and after a first phone conversation, I asked her to send over her résumé. When I reviewed, I noticed much of what she'd shared with me wasn't on the résumé. It was obvious the résumé was much more geared towards a generalist marketing type role. I reached out to her and gave her that feedback. She acknowledged the version shared was in fact written from more of a generalist perspective and that for the role we discussed, she should probably tailor it to better fit the digital aspects. Now, if she wasn't working with me and just blindly submitted her resume straight to the company, they probably would have taken a pass because they would view her as a generalist. They would not know she truly checked the boxes on many of the digital marketing 'must haves' because she didn't have any of that incredibly important detail listed.

Before you submit a résumé for any position, use some common sense and put yourself into the shoes of the hiring managers. Read your résumé through their eyes. This will aid you in evaluating how to best position yourself as a viable candidate. Doing good work means you have to take time to tailor your résumé to help others quickly see why they should spend more time evaluating you and your candidacy for a specific role.

A good résumé must be impressive both aesthetically and in its content. This will absolutely help you get noticed faster. And, getting noticed faster typically results in someone having more opportunities.

Beyond the Résumé

MAKING WORK LOOK NICE extends beyond just the résumé and permeates into every aspect of a process because, as discussed, every single thing is being evaluated and examined. From emails to thank-you notes, to texts, to presentations, to projects, and so on. It all must look as close to perfect as one can get.

In many of the searches I work on, candidates are asked to work on a project of some kind, which may include creating a presentation. I'm amazed by some of the work people put together and ultimately present. During an interview process, the assumption is candidates are putting forth their very best work. Needless to say, if the work provided is subpar, well…it's highly unlikely the person will advance beyond that round. If you don't know how to put together a sharp-looking presentation, you better get help quickly. Take a class, buy a book, or have a friend help you (but learn so you can actually do it yourself). I have had innumerable candidates lose out on being the one to get a job offer due to their presentation / project being average or even weak. I realize if you're currently employed and in the midst of an interview process where you're asked to work on a presentation, it can be time-consuming and a lot to ask. However, if you're seriously interested in the opportunity, you need to carve out the time needed to do your very best. You've made it this far; why ruin it for yourself at the last stage? If the time frame given to you just doesn't work with your busy schedule, ask for more time. Let someone know you won't be able to do your best work unless you're allotted more time. See what they say. If they can't give you extra time, then you just do the best you possibly can in the time you have or bow out. Often people are willing to offer some concessions if they know in advance the issues you are having.

If you're in an interview process for a PR role, you may be asked to do a writing test. You may have to do it on the spot, or you may be given a fake assignment and asked to work on it overnight. If you're interviewing for a role in finance, you may be asked to take a math test or work on something in Excel. If you know these things are coming, get yourself ready. If it's been a while since you used Excel, brush up!

If you're sending correspondence via email or text, make sure it's good! This means you need to reread it before sending to ensure it's professionally written. This means you can't write like you do to your friends. No shorthand; no abbreviations; no emojis. Be clear, concise, succinct, and professional. Do good work!

Doing good work is a concept that touches every aspect of a job search and interview process. As I've stressed repeatedly, every single thing you do is a representation of you as a professional, and thus every single thing needs to be done to the best of your ability. This will help you stand out and have better results!

Cut and Paste Carefully

WHILE THE CUTTING AND PASTING I'm referring to is a bit different from the safety scissors and Elmer's glue we all recall from our youth, the principle is still the same. Our teachers taught us how important it is to be careful when cutting and pasting. If you use too much glue, it'll seep out of all the edges and be a big old mess. If you don't cut carefully, your edges might not be straight and your work won't look great. Now, I'm pretty sure most people who are job searching aren't using scissors and glue in their applications. However, cutting and pasting is still a thing professionals need to pay attention to, and here's what I'm talking about:

In an effort to be more time efficient when job searching, many professionals craft templates they use for things like: cover letters, email and InMail outreaches, follow-up notes as well as thank-you notes, and so forth. Often these templates are used as a framework and are then tweaked to each unique situation. This saves the individual from having to retype a lot of the same verbiage from one note to the next. For example, someone may create a basic thank-you note template that says something such as:

> Hi, _____,
> Thank you so much for your time today. It was wonderful to speak / meet with you and learn more about your company, [insert company name], as well as about the position. I truly enjoyed our conversation and appreciate all the invaluable information you shared. As discussed, I am absolutely confident I will be an asset to your team.
>
> I look forward to hearing back from you about possible next steps. Thank you again.

For every interview someone has, they may cut and paste this into an email and then fill in specifics relevant to the interview and opportunity. For example, this note might be tailored to read:

Hi, Sue,
Thank you so much for your time today. It was wonderful to meet with you and learn more about your company, ABC LLC, as well as about the HR director position on your team. I truly enjoyed our conversation and appreciate all the invaluable information you shared. As discussed, I am absolutely confident my ten-plus years of experience as an HR generalist, during which I've built and led top-performing HR teams, will be an asset to you and to the company as a whole. Having revamped an entire HR function for a company of similar scope and size, I will be able to bring a depth and breadth of relevant experience enabling me to make a significant impact quickly. The ATS system we implemented at XYZ company will work perfectly at ABC. I can leverage our experiences to help you avoid many of the unnecessary hiccups that ultimately delayed our go-live date.

I look forward to hearing back from you about possible next steps. Thank you again.

Unfortunately, what people don't always realize is when a template is cut / pasted and tailored and then it's emailed, things can get a bit wonky. What the recipient sees may appear goofy. Sometimes the texts are mismatched; the font, style, size, and color of the template verbiage can be visibly different from whatever has been added, and the end result can look as though some of the text was pulled from somewhere else. Essentially, it can appear like someone was trying to cut corners.

Why this happens, I don't know. I'm not remotely techy. But I've seen it enough times to know it can and does happen. Therefore, when cutting / pasting, it's absolutely critical to take extra care to ensure whatever you're sending does not look cut and pasted. One way to try to cover your bases is to send the note (or document) to yourself first and see how it appears in your inbox. When you open the email, look closely. Make sure it's all consistent. Alternatively, you may need to retype into a fresh email. While that may seem to defeat the purpose of having a template, having the verbiage prepared in advance will still save you time. Also, by typing a fresh email, you can be certain what you send won't be mismatched. Unfortunately, if a decision-maker receives something that appears cut and pasted together, they might assume a candidate was trying to cut corners, which in turn might give the hiring manager the impression that the candidate is lazy. And I think it's safe to say lazy is not what a candidate wants an executive thinking as their candidacy is being evaluated.

The moral of this story is, if you're going to cut and paste text or forward something, please take a few minutes to make sure everything stays consistent with regards to the font used (style, size, color) and nothing reformats or changes after being sent by sending to yourself first and seeing how it appears. When in doubt, retype into a fresh document or email. I promise you, I see this mistake all too often, and it's not a good look. Over the years, I've received numerous emails from hiring managers in which they've forwarded to me whatever it is they received, highlighting parts of the text and pointing out the inconsistencies. Many are astute enough to state that it looks as though the candidate cut and pasted together various sentences and note it was obviously a mistake on their part. Unfortunately, I've witnessed executives decide to eliminate candidates for this offense. Some may think that's a bit too harsh. However, when there are great candidates to choose from, the littlest of infractions can get you cut from the process (pun intended).

Don't Be Lazy

THIS ONE IS TOUGH because I love—love—love—love being lazy!

Deep down, if I could, I'd truly love to be a lazy-couch-potato-y, never-get-out-of-my-comfy-cozy-clothes type of person. Lazy often sounds so appealing... kind of like the softest pair of warm pajamas on a cold winter night worn in front of a roaring fire with a great movie playing and a nice glass of wine in hand. (OK, so maybe we trade the movie for an episode of *Dateline NBC*, *48 Hours*, or *20/20*. Perhaps a season 4 of *Ted Lasso*? Any of those will do!) I absolutely love those rare days or nights with nothing on the calendar. But that kind of lazy is different than the kind of lazy I'm talking about.

For the purposes of this book, "Don't be lazy" carries enormous weight and needs close examination, so pay attention! What I'm referring to here is professional laziness. Whether you're actively in a job search or find yourself in the midst of an interview process, you cannot afford to be lazy. Typically, there isn't an easy button when it comes to getting a new job. I'm sorry to tell all the job searchers out there, you cannot cut corners! You just can't! As discussed, job searching requires attention to detail and a lot of hard work. Sure, once in a blue moon, someone might get lucky where things come together without a ton of time and effort. However, the vast majority of the time nothing is easy and laziness won't net you the results you're after. In fact, laziness tends to bite people in the ass!

Heads up—if you're job searching, it *ain't* easy! This is no stroll in the park! And no—job searching is not a hobby; you don't pick it up and put it down like a crossword puzzle. If you are unemployed and searching for full-time work, job searching isn't something you do for a part of the day. This requires a lot of very thoughtful and extremely hard work all day, every day.

Did I just say "hard work"?

Yep—I most certainly did! And let's be honest with each other: everyone has a different definition of "hard work." So I'll break it down. Hard work means if you are currently unemployed and you're serious about finding a new full-time job and you want real results, you can't put in a three-hour day and then "punch out" at some virtual time clock, consider your job search work done for the day, and head to the gym for a two-and-a-half-hour workout (unless you're a trainer earning some cash on the side). "Don't be lazy" means if you are putting permanent dents into the cushions on your couch, it's highly likely you're watching too much TV (or you have a shitty couch). Hard work means that job searching is a full-time job. And please note—to be very clear, "full time" is no longer the stereotypical forty-hour workweek. Today, "full time" tends to be more like fifty hours (or more) per week. So unemployed professionals seeking full-time jobs who are dedicating forty hours a week to job searching—this is really the minimum amount of time you should be dedicating to your efforts. (I'm not kidding around when I say job searching is a full-time job in and of itself!)

"Don't be lazy" means you need to be ready to put in the work! Now, if you're currently employed and proactively in job search mode because you want to leave your current role, you won't be able to dedicate the same amount of time an unemployed person can. In this situation, you're undoubtedly juggling your day job, along with any other priorities you may have (e.g., spouse / kids), while also trying to conduct a job search. Here you need to be very strategic about finding chunks of time to do your search, and this may include time later at night and on weekends. Certainly, there may be times during your workday that you'll need to carve out for your job search, perhaps to do an interview, and this is something to be very careful about because you do not want to abuse your current employer by collecting a paycheck from them while using your "time on the clock" for other things. You really need to protect the integrity of your day job and continue to produce great work for your employer. In this situation, because you won't be able to job search full-time like someone who is unemployed, you need to recognize your search may take a bit longer and plan accordingly. And to maximize efforts, you'll want to make the best use of any resources and connections you have to try to advance your search. If there are people whom you can trust to keep your search confidential who may be great to network with, reach out to them. They may have some viable leads for you at that moment in time or in the future. If you're gainfully employed but know it's time to seek a new job, it takes work on your part to manage it all.

"Don't be lazy" also means that when in job search mode, if you're trying to get someone to help you in any way or if you're trying to get someone to consider your candidacy (e.g., a recruiter), make things as easy as possible for that person so they will want to work with you.

I repeat—* Make things as easy as possible for others.

Remember the famous line from the movie *Jerry Maguire* "Help me help you"? Well, those four words are akin to gospel, and I advise you to take this advice to heart!

Here are some examples of the laziness I see:

- Frequently, I receive emails with no subject line. This seems awfully lazy of the sender. I mean, c'mon…who hasn't heard of an internet virus? Or who hasn't received a bajillion spam emails? How many people do you think want to open an email from someone they don't know, especially when there is no text in the subject line? Most people I know aren't likely to open such an email, and who can blame them? If you've ever had a virus on your computer, I'm sure you don't want another one. It can wreak tremendous havoc and create a lot of unwelcome pain. People are übersensitive to this. They'd rather risk missing something important than open up a random email, because it could potentially be tied to a nightmare virus. And we've all heard stories of viruses taking over someone's computer, ultimately wiping out their hard drive while holding their documents hostage until an enormous ransom gets paid. Super scary stuff! Hence, please think twice, and take a moment to put something in the subject line. This helps the recipient gain comfort that their computer won't blow up if they open your email. And PS, another good reason to fill in the subject line is that some computers will automatically filter emails without a subject to a junk folder / spam account. This happens to me all the time. While I try to remember to check my junk folder daily, I often forget, which means precious time can be lost. Even if the recipient knows your name and you assume they will open any email you send their way, just take the extra twenty seconds of time needed to type a proper subject into every email you send. That way no recipient will hesitate before opening, miss your email, or delete the email without reading it. Fill in the subject line.

- I receive emails with an attachment but no text in the body of the email.

    No text…

    Really?

    Why wouldn't you type something that helps me know why you sent me the attachment?

    If you're the sender of such an email, you're basically expecting the recipient to be a mind reader. You're forcing the recipient to guess what you're thinking. Would you want someone guessing what you're thinking? Seriously, if you receive a blank email with an unknown document attached, what's your first thought? By the way, the sender's name might not be familiar to the recipient. Thus, the recipient might not have any idea why they're getting this email, what the sender's point / goal is, and they might fear clicking on the attachment will be detrimental. Even if the attachment is named something that possibly makes sense to the recipient, the sender is still taking quite a risk. Many recipients will opt to skip opening the attachment and just delete the email, which means the sender completely wasted their time.

    Now, you might think this doesn't happen often. But I can tell you firsthand, this happens to me with frequency. And going back to the water well of "We all have too much going on, not enough hours in the day, blah-blah-blah," a lot of people don't have time for, or much interest in, solving the *Scooby-Doo* mystery the sender has set into motion. Recipients are wondering, "Who are you? Why'd you send this email? Is the attachment legit? Do I dare respond to this email? I'm not sure what I should do…moving on to the next email in my inbox…"

    Similar to many in my field, I'm typically juggling numerous searches at any given time, and often, some of those searches are in the same functional areas. For example, let's say I'm working on three senior-level marketing positions, and I receive an email with an attached résumé and no text. First off, this professional put me in a position where I first have to ascertain if I even know them. If I don't, I have to do the leg work to figure out who they are. Once that's done, I then need to decide if I'm even comfortable opening the attachment because I'm in fear of unleashing a virus. If I end up opening it, I have to try to figure out why this person reached out. It is now my job to determine their intent and put the pieces of the puzzle together without any help from them. Did they reach out to me about one of the three marketing roles my search firm is currently working on? Or are they simply a marketing professional reaching out to me, not about any particular search I'm working on but just to be on my radar so that should I have a suitable position, I can reach out? Whatever the reason is...I have no idea because the sender didn't give me a clue! With so much on my plate, I need to decide if I want to take the time to reply to the sender and ask them these questions or simply move on to the next to-do on my list. The sender has put their outreach in peril by not taking a minute to provide the recipient necessary context.

Recently, I received an email from someone whose name I didn't recognize with the subject "HR Generalist" and then an attached document entitled "HR July 20__" (the date). Quick recap: I didn't know the sender. There was a subject and an attachment.

When I saw the email, I actually did have a couple free minutes to look up the sender on LinkedIn, which isn't always the case. (What if I didn't have time?) On LinkedIn, I saw the person and I were first-degree connections and that he was, in fact, an HR generalist. So I felt more comfortable opening the attachment, and with slight trepidation, I did so. Thankfully my laptop didn't explode! The document was his résumé (phew!). That said, there wasn't a note to me or an introduction of any kind to let me know why he was sent his résumé. Now, I did have a few minutes to review his résumé before a call and did just that. I was moving quickly to get on my next call and closed the document and email and went about my day. About a week later, I received another email from this person. Once again, the name rang a bell, but I didn't instantly recognize who this person was. This time, there was a subject header ("Follow Up"), and there was text in the body of the email. He said something to the effect of "Did you get my prior email? Why didn't you respond? Can we discuss your CHRO search? Or do you have anything else that might be a fit for me?" Honestly, I was pretty bugged by his note because it forced me to have to go back through my received emails to determine whether or not I did get an email from him. Once I found the email he was referencing and realized he was the HR guy who had sent only a résumé (and no text), I responded and said I had received the email he sent but because there was no text in the body of his note, my assumption was he'd simply reached out to share his résumé so we could have it on file. I also pointed out that I almost didn't open the attached résumé for fear it wasn't a legit email. Well, let me tell you, this guy was not very nice in his response to me. He told me I was rude for not responding to the prior email. Furthermore, he had sent his résumé because he'd heard my firm was working on a CHRO search and wanted to know if he could interview for the position. As you can likely predict, I could not respond saying what I actually wanted to say. Instead, I took what I thought was the high road and said, essentially, "First, apologies for not responding. As I mentioned before, your email had no text written in it. All I received was an attachment of your résumé. There was nothing to indicate your interest in a CHRO search we were working on. However, we'd already completed that search and didn't have any other HR searches in motion." I said, "I'm sure you can relate—I receive hundreds of emails daily and simply can't respond to all, especially when people's intentions aren't explicitly stated. I did update our database with this latest information though and will reach out when we have a search that could align." Now, if he had been smart, he would have responded either saying "sorry" or "good point(s)" or that I had offered wise advice and he'd make sure to include text in future outreaches. Let's just say…he wasn't smart. His response didn't include any such sentiments. After my blood pressure returned to normal, I made a note on his LinkedIn profile saying, "Do not contact about HR searches. Was very rude."

Here's the deal: If someone doesn't provide any insight as to why they're reaching out by typing some sort of message stating what role (if any) they're expressing interest in and why they might be a fit, guess what people like me are inclined to do? Yep—part of me might be tempted to hit delete!! (Settle down; I said "tempted." I don't always do that…but I have hit delete many times.) Not to be a coldhearted asshole, but I, along with millions of others, stink at guessing what senders of emails are thinking and possibly wanting us recipients to do.

Hint: If you want people to help you, then you need to help them!!!

Here's the moral of this story—in the body of any email sent, be sure to craft an overview clearly articulating to the recipient *who you are*, *what your purpose is*, and *why you're reaching out*. Spell things out so there's no guesswork involved. Talent acquisition professionals and hiring managers alike feel incredibly frustrated by people who don't take the time to provide some degree of information. (Can you tell this is something that irks me?) Sending emails without detail in the subject and / or in the body of the email isn't helping your job search. It's just wasting your time. When emailing an attachment, be sure to put information into the body of the email so the recipient doesn't have to guess your objective for contacting them. Don't be lazy by skipping this important step.

- I receive emails with *"generic"* notes or attachments. On a fairly regular basis, I'll receive an email with a quick note saying something like, "Attached is a copy of a *generic* cover letter I use and my *basic* résumé…"

"Generic"?

"Basic"?

OK, so why is this so bad? What's the big deal? You may be thinking, "Gosh, this lady is a piece of work! Why does she get irked by the words *generic* and *basic*?" Allow me to answer. First, I'm old (ish), and the word *generic* conjures up visions of "off-label" groceries people who were trying to save money would buy in the '70s. Google this and you'll laugh at the images. The boxes *generic* groceries were packaged in looked like prison garb. A box of *generic* corn flakes cereal, for example, was a big white box with only "Corn Flakes" written across the front in big black thick letters. The way it was packaged made you think it was cheap and probably didn't taste good. You might have assumed it was nothing special and definitely not as good as the real, more expensive version. Whether or not you're my age and remember these groceries, if you receive an email with an attached document that has the word *generic* somewhere in its title, you're probably not flattered. You probably don't feel special. You're possibly assuming you're getting something more "lower end." The recipient might think the sender doesn't value them. Or, possibly the recipient thinks the sender is moving quickly and might be trying to cut corners to save some time. Now, let's add to this: Let's say the sender didn't put anything (no verbiage) into the body of the email—if all the recipient is getting is an email with a document attached that has the word *generic* in its title, they may assume the sender's thought process went something like this:

Recipient: I'm *not* going to take time to craft a thoughtful note to you to explain why I'm reaching out and why you should want to open the attached document. There's no time for pleasantries. I would like for you to take *your* time to open the document(s). After all, that's your job! I'm not going to take any time to customize this email and / or attachment to you or to anything you might be working on. You can figure out who I am *and* how I might be a fit for one of your job searches. You should want to take the time to do that! I make you money.

Now, even if the sender isn't remotely thinking these thoughts, the recipient might assume this IS in fact what sender is thinking. Even if this wasn't the sender's intent, perception is reality. And if your recipient thinks you don't value them enough to put a little more time into your outreach, that won't help you win any points. It truly takes a minute or two to put something in the subject header such as, "HR professional reaching out re your CHRO search" and then in the body of the email, put something like, "Hi, Nicki—I heard about your CHRO search and wanted to send you my résumé as a potential candidate. I bring over ten years of HR leadership experience in rapidly scaling health tech companies. I see in the job spec that your client is prioritizing finding someone who has implemented strong talent management solutions, and this is something I've done. As you'll see on my attached résumé, I've accomplished [say a few things that align you with the role]. I welcome the opportunity to schedule a conversation to explore this further. Please feel free to respond to this email or you can call me at_____. Thank you!"

See how easy that is? It makes a world of difference and will net you way more positive results than not having anything in the subject and / or in the body of the email!

Recently, I received an email that read, "Hi Recruiter. I'm back in the market. I encourage you to take a look at my *basic* cover letter (attached). I use this along with my *standard* résumé (attached). Please follow up with me to schedule our next steps." I'm sure you've already conjured up visions of where I'm going with this one…but for clarity's sake, let me walk you through the many issues with this scenario. First, why didn't the candidate take a second to tailor the cover letter to the recipient (me)? In this situation, the candidate knew he was emailing me because he used my email address (which has my name in it—sooooooo…you know my name, use it!). Second, back to what was just mentioned, why didn't you give me more detail in the body of the email so I could feel more comfortable opening attachments from you? Also, please don't make the recipient (me) do any more work than necessary. By asking me to open the attached documents, he's asking me to take a risk, especially if I don't know who he is right off the bat. Additionally, he's putting more work on my shoulders. The contents of a cover letter can be cut and pasted into the body of an email. Why do I need to be the one taking the extra step of opening the document? By the way, I know there are naysayers out there who will hammer me for this point and accuse me of being the one who is lazy. To those, I respond by saying you don't have to like it, but this is reality, and if you're the one job searching, the recruiter / hiring manager has the power. They can get you into opportunities. Thus, you should want to do whatever makes things easiest for them. Perhaps your work life isn't as hectic as others' and you may not fully appreciate where I'm coming from. Take it or leave it. I'm just trying to help.

Here's the deal—if I'm the professional looking for a job and actively seeking the assistance of others, I'd certainly want to boost my odds of success. So I'd be sure to do everything possible to make the lives of those I'm trying to get help from as easy as possible. It goes a long way to address the recipient by name and tailor the communications to that person. Refrain from using labels such as *generic / basic / standard*, as they can take a level of professionalism away from the message. If you want to increase the likelihood of someone actually reading what you're trying to communicate, take the time to either type customized text or cut / paste text from another relevant place into the body of an email. Be thoughtful and take a few extra minutes to do things right so you set yourself up for success. Cutting corners to save time means you end up wasting time. Do: Take a minute to customize your outreach to the recipient.

- I receive vague texts and / or emails forcing me to guess who you are and what you want. While I'll get into this in another section (yay for you!), one of the most frustrating things is when candidates send vague email messages like:
    - "Hi. I'm back in the market. If you have suitable positions, please let me know."
    - "Hi. Just checking in to see if you have anything for me."
    - "Hi. Let me know what you're working on."

Vague notes like these present numerous challenges to the recipient. First, as stated before, I don't always know who the sender is. I know other recipients find themselves in this same predicament. Often, an email address may not provide someone's full name, and if I don't have them in my address book, I can't easily figure out who they are. If the message is sent via text and they're not in my contacts list, I might not have a clue who the sender is. Yes, I can try to do a search of my database, but this takes precious time out of my day and if I have a lot going on, I might not take the time.

Alternatively, let's say you do provide your full name (thank you!); there's still a chance your name may not ring a bell with the recipient. (Who the heck is Tim Morris? Do I know a Tim Morris?) Perhaps your name does ring a bell but it's such an obscure recollection that the recipient isn't *really* sure who you are. (Is Tim Morris that guy who I spoke with around the Fourth of July who got laid off from that digital start-up? Or wait, maybe Tim is the one who had a really bad cough when I talked with him? Huh, I'm not sure that's right...could he be the guy who...)

In any of these scenarios, the recipient is once again responsible for putting a detective hat on and piecing together the puzzle. Needless to say, the sender is rolling the dice because there's no guarantee the recipient will do the legwork required to figure it all out. I'm sorry to bark up this same tree yet again, but the truth here is, most people's days are jam-packed without time to spare. Given that recruiters (and many decision-makers) have hundreds of emails coming into their inboxes daily and knowing they're often racing from one interview to the next (conducting five to ten interviews daily), it becomes easy to understand how counterproductive it is for people to send emails and / or texts like the ones just detailed. Keeping every professional who we've "met" straight is simply not possible (unless you're Marilu Henner...her photographic memory is *uh-maze-ing*!!!). And as stretched as we all are, in a situation like this, when vague messages come in, a recruiter or hiring manager may not do the necessary research to refresh their memory, and thus candidates can easily get lost in the fray and miss good opportunities. And by the way, for those of you rolling your eyes and thinking it's the recipient's laziness that's the problem, not yours...well, I have news for you...roll your eyes all you want...but the reality is, you may lose out on something great because you chose not to take a minute to give the necessary background.

To summarize, candidates are doing themselves a huge disservice by not providing an adequate amount of detail in the emails / texts they send. Not only can it appear completely lazy, but candidates are potentially missing out on opportunities while wasting their own precious time and energy.

Listen up! It takes a couple minutes to provide a quick synopsis of who you are, how you know the person you're reaching out to (if you actually do know the person), why you're reaching out, and what you're looking for / in need of.

While this will take candidates a bit more time on the front end, enormous time will be saved on the back end. And in the end, more people will help you, which makes job searching easier and more fruitful. Do: Provide detail around who you are, how you know the recipient, and why you're reaching out so no one needs to guess or make assumptions.

- I receive "applications" from people who clearly didn't pay attention to the details. I know job searching can be an exhausting task. Yes, reading through every job spec is time-consuming. But I gotta tell you, it can be really obvious and extremely frustrating when someone clearly doesn't read what's written on the page. If you are provided instructions detailing how to apply and it is stated you need to provide a résumé along with an overview of why you feel you're an ideal candidate for the position, guess what? You need to do just that! If you don't—if you only submit your résumé and opt to refrain from providing said overview—there's a strong possibility your candidacy will not move forward. Keep in mind, stating in your email something like, "Please see attached résumé" as your overview of why you feel you're an ideal candidate is flat-out unacceptable. Of course whoever you sent it to knows they should review your résumé... duhhhhhhh...that's why they requested it. If you decide not to give more detail, you're basically telling the hiring manager you're too lazy to read what they wrote and / or you're too good to have follow their instructions. Either way, you're being viewed as lazy (and possibly as a jackass). Either way, you're not going to like the end result.

Now, if you submit your résumé and it's clear you don't align with the job description, you obviously didn't pay attention to the details. And that's f*cking annoying to hiring managers because there are typically a lot of applicants and résumés they need to go through. If a job spec says you need eight years of HR experience and you have zero years, yet you decide to apply, you're an idiot! You're wasting everyone's time.

If the spec clearly states that applicants are to use email only and specifies "no calls please," guess what? Don't call. Do. Not. Call. If you call, it's obvious you either didn't read through the spec or you simply don't care. It doesn't matter if you think it's bad business for the hiring manager and / or company to ask applicants not to call. You're certainly entitled to your opinion. But that's the request. That's the decision-makers' prerogative, and they have the power. If you opt to ignore this, you're not helping yourself become a candidate who will be invited to interview. Do: Pay attention to the details / instructions / preferences noted on a job spec.

- I frequently receive unsolicited emails from professionals asking me to review their résumés and / or bios and give them feedback. I don't always know the senders of these requests. As a courtesy, whenever I can, I'll gladly provide professionals with my thoughts on "things" they send me. Whether it's a résumé, a bio, an email, a cover letter, a thank-you note, an outreach, or anything else. If I have time to help, I will. (I don't always have time.) What's infuriating, though, is when I review a document and find typos. I'm not overly tweaked if I find one or two. But, if there are more than two, I'll circle back with the sender and, in a nice way, I'll ask if they took the time to proofread prior to sending to me. I'll note the reason for my asking is due to finding a number of typos. Often, the person will respond saying no, they didn't proofread before sending it to me. Ummmm, thanks for your honesty, but I'm sorry...what? When you're asking someone for their help and not paying them for it, why in the world would you send them something you didn't proofread?

Why? Why? Why?

Why is it my job or someone else's job to find all your errors? I'm taking time out of my day to help you, and time is my commodity. Yet, you're too lazy to proofread it before getting it to me? I'm sorry, but I've become a little less nice about this and am now much more direct in my responses than I was when I first started out a bajillion years ago. Now I simply don't have time or patience for this nonsense. People, you must think! Put yourself in your reader's shoes. Let's say one of your direct reports sent you something with numerous typos and when you voiced your findings, he admitted he didn't proof it before sending it to you; how would you feel? Unless people want to pay me for editing, I will stop when I realize the document has too many errors to count. It's just unacceptable and totally lazy! Proofread your work before you ever send it.

Advancing your career is hard. Just like anything in life, you get out what you put in and if you're not putting in your full effort (if you're being lazy), you're going to find yourself in lengthier and more frustrating job searches and / or missing out on amazing, career advancing, opportunities.

Read with Comprehension

IN GRADE SCHOOL, I remember taking a lot of those standardized tests, and they all had a "reading" section. I remember reading these long and boring paragraphs and then having to answer a lot of questions, all designed to assess one's "reading comprehension skills."

Because reading with comprehension is so vitally important, most children are taught early in their education the importance of carefully reading through directions as well as the importance of following instructions, written and verbal. I recall learning this important life lesson while in science class. I hate to admit it, but I had a few experiments go sideways because I didn't read with comprehension. Unfortunately, I broke a few beakers.

Reading with comprehension is absolutely key. While we touched on this a little bit in a prior chapter, here's how it relates to job searching:

- Carefully read each and every email, job spec, job posting, etc. so you comprehend what is stated.
- Carefully read through instructions of any kind. Please read every single word closely so that you comprehend what is written.

    Doing so will enable you to respond properly and more successfully. You want to be successful, right? I can't even begin to tell you how many times I find myself gritting my teeth or pulling my hair out thinking, "This person didn't read my email / job spec / job posting." Please know, this is a huge mistake! You are truly doing yourself an enormous disservice by failing to read carefully so you comprehend fully. Reading with comprehension pretty much goes back to "slow down...careful is better than quick."

First of all, the best way to ensure a position is even worth your while to consider, and possibly spend time applying for, is to actually look at what the role is about and what the requirements are. If you don't align with the role (meaning you don't meet a majority of the requirements), please do not apply. It's an enormous waste of your valuable and limited time.

I repeat—If you do not meet or align with a majority of the points on a job spec, please do not apply!

Example: Sally is an HR professional with three years of HR experience as an HR generalist. Sally does not have any experience overseeing compensation and benefits. There is a Director of Compensation & Benefits where she currently works. In addition, Sally doesn't have any experience leading a team of direct reports (she hasn't managed people). She's ready to move on from her company and is looking at an exciting position with a company she has always liked. On the job description, it is noted in the requirements section that candidates need eight or more years of HR experience and must have two or more years of experience overseeing compensation and benefits. In addition, candidates must have leadership experience. Question: Should Sally apply to this job? Answer: No. She is missing three key requirements. Now, let's say Sally sees a job opportunity at this same company. For that position, they're seeking candidates with four (or more) years of generalist experience, but she has only three. She aligns with everything else. Should she apply? Answer: Yes. If a job description says the position will be working from an office four days a week and you are not willing to go into an office at all, do not apply. If you know the job requires someone to travel over 50 percent of the time and you only want to travel 10 percent (or less), don't apply. If a job description says you must have your CPA but you don't have it, don't apply. If a job description wants you to have or be willing to get your CPA and you're open to sitting for the CPA exam, then you absolutely can apply. If a job spec for a marketing role wants someone with three-plus years of marketing experience and you've spent the last ten years working as a third-grade teacher, don't apply. Now, if your best friend works at a company with a job you don't align with on paper and they're willing to hand deliver your résumé to the hiring manager and vouch for why they should consider your candidacy, go for it. Sometimes crazy things happen. But if you do not have an inside track, don't waste your precious time applying for jobs you don't align with.

Why shouldn't you throw caution to the wind and take a chance by applying? We've belabored the point—job searching takes a lot of time, and there aren't enough hours in the day. Using your precious time wisely, where it can pay off, is a critical factor in proficiently and successfully conducting any job search.

I see people—lots and lots of people—wasting ridiculous amounts of time applying for and pursuing positions not even remotely aligned with their backgrounds and skill sets. This is absurd! Not only is this a total waste of everyone's time, but it can also be viewed as a poor reflection of you and your professionalism. This world is indeed a small one, and it's remarkable how often I see the same résumés being sent to me for various positions that don't fit. Guess what happens when you're the professional who's doing this? It's like the boy who cried wolf—you end up not being taken seriously. And every time your name pops up, people won't give you the time of day.

Do yourself a favor and take a second to carefully read through communications fully. This attention to detail will serve you well.

In job searching, there are some professionals who opt to use what many refer to as a "shotgun" approach, where one blankets the marketplace with their résumé, applying to as many positions as possible each and every day, hoping they'll get lucky and something will be a match. Simply said: This. Is. A. Horrible. Strategy.

Sure, you'll feel productive as you press "send." Sure, you might get a hit at some point. However, I promise you, your time is far better spent being strategic, targeted, and thoughtful. Find positions your background and skill set align closely with and apply only to those roles. Before you apply, make sure you craft targeted and tailored résumés along with overviews / cover letters. This might seem and feel less productive in that it will take you significantly more time to apply to far fewer positions. However, you will see your odds of getting positive results increase dramatically.

Do not mistake activity for productivity!

The number of résumés sent out in a day is not equal to how productive the day was!

- Read with comprehension also means you need to look for key words, points, phrases, and numbers.

This is so important, so pay attention! Another reason reading with comprehension is critical is because within the text of things like job descriptions as well as communications from hiring managers, you'll find the key words and / or phrases highlighting the most important criteria being assessed.

This is like getting the answers to a test before you take it!

And, who doesn't love finding out what questions will be on an exam? I know I loved when teachers told my class exactly what would be on the test. It made life so much easier! (Not sure how much the student learns when a teacher does this, but that's another book…)

Here's the deal: Take note of what you read on the job description, and then use this prized information to align yourself with the position you're applying for (this assumes you do in fact align). Echo the company's thoughts by using their same verbiage and you will be way more successful in your endeavors. Think of a job spec as a pirate's map leading you to the Holy Grail. You wouldn't ignore a map full of fabulous clues, would you? No! Of course not! Because you know full well you'd end up wandering aimlessly and probably walking some stupid plank! You know the map would save you significant time and energy by providing you with valuable insights needed to find the hidden treasure.

Breaking news- The information imparted via the job posting, email, etc., provides you with clues, so use this knowledge to help you tailor your résumé and outreaches. You'll do better work, ultimately netting more positive results! While a commonsense pointer, it's one many professionals fail to follow.

If you take a moment to think about how you personally make many decisions, I guarantee you'll quickly realize the importance of key words and phrases. For example, let's say something is wrong with your knee and you want to find an orthopedic doctor to evaluate what's going on. Like many, you may jump online to do some research. As you find physicians, you'll be far more likely to consider those who highlight knees as an area of specialty versus those touting expertise in shoulders and hips. If you don't see anything about that doctor helping with knees, you wouldn't schedule an appointment, would you? Drawing the parallel, find out what a company is looking for in an ideal employee by reading closely, and then align your background appropriately by using their same verbiage in your communications.

Note: If, after reading, you can't align yourself, then do not apply. It's not worth your time and energy. The only way you should apply is if they say no experience is needed.

Play Nice; Treat Others the Way You Want to Be Treated

WHEN MY KIDS WERE LITTLE, my husband and I were constantly telling them to play nice. We warned them that if they didn't play nice, no one would want to play with them and they'd end up as miserable failures, living in our basement forever and ever. Just kidding. We didn't say that second part. Further, we always stressed (and still do) the importance of treating others the way they want to be treated. While I've long since forgotten all the stuff I learned in the child psych course I took in college, I'm pretty sure this is partially how children learn empathy (or how to *not* get their asses kicked on the playground).

Depending on your age, you've probably heard about and / or experienced a down economy. If yes, it's probably not too hard to recall how stressed everyone quickly became when the economy faltered. The anxiety around the unknown during 2008 and during COVID was palpable. As I type, this economy is very unstable and many are rightfully anxious. In down economies there are layoffs left and right. Startups go out of business. Money worries get worse. It's truly no fun. Now, rationally, we all know when things get bad, they eventually improve. But, for many, the 'during' part totally sucks.

OK. So, you're likely wondering, "What does this have to do with 'playing nice'?"

Good question! Let's look at it like this…when things are bad, people get mad. And when mad, some people can be short, testy, mean, aggressive, etc. When someone is rude, that = not playing nice. Not playing nice does not help someone have more success when job searching and / or when interviewing. I recommend professionals refrain from taking their anger, aggression, hostility, and stress out on others. No matter how difficult times are for you personally or for society as a whole. In the professional world, regardless of whether you are job searching, interviewing, or gainfully employed…

Don't be a jerk!
Don't be an ass!
Don't be a schmuck!
Don't be a punk!
Don't be a dick!
Don't be a bitch!
Don't be an asshole!

Whatever you call it, I'm telling you, don't be f*cking rude—play nice!

Now, I'm hopeful you have a few ideas around why being any of the above is awful and completely counterproductive. I'm hopeful I don't really need to break this down for you. But, for shits and giggles, I will.

First and foremost (this is basic), if job searching / interviewing, not playing nice is not going to help you, your career, or any possible candidacy you're aspiring toward. This will not propel you forward professionally in any sort of positive direction—period! How many people like helping assholes? Personally, I don't like helping jerks. I know I'm not alone. People trying to help you don't want or need your abuse.

Second, simply said, being rude is not only not helpful, it's totally unnecessary. I think we've all experienced and / or witnessed people who just aren't nice, and for what? Does it give them a thrill to be mean? Do they think it's advancing their cause? Because the answer is, NO! No one—I mean absolutely NO ONE—enjoys being treated poorly!

In addition to being completely unpleasant, it's really quite ugly and can be truly hurtful. Over the years, I've had numerous encounters with extremely rude (I'm talkin' downright nasty!) professionals, and here's the deal…if you are the candidate, unless someone has been a complete asshole to you, being a jerkwad is entirely uncalled for. Being rude, condescending, or insulting to those trying to help you is flat-out dumb! Let me be clear, it's really f*cking stupid! I've worked with many professionals who are actively job hunting and are clearly frustrated with their personal situation. I'm empathetic to that. But that still doesn't give the person the right to be mean. If you want help, treat people with respect!

Here's a good example: I interviewed someone who stated his three most recent job moves were due to being laid off from each company. We all know reductions in force (a.k.a. RIFs) happen, but let's be honest, most people aren't that unlucky to be laid off three times in a row. Can it happen? Sure! But I also expect candidates to know and understand interviewers will likely ask questions. After all, this situation can raise a few red flags in the hiring manager's eyes, and it is the recruiter's job to anticipate the hiring manager's concerns and get answers to their questions, ideally, before they have to ask them. Some hiring managers / interviewers might wonder if the company was going to fire this professional but gave them the option to resign instead. They (hiring managers) might wonder if the candidate just isn't that good (skilled) a worker and / or is possibly difficult to work with. Because the hiring manager(s) will want to understand the professional's career progression story and will undoubtedly start asking questions, I always dig in and try to get my arms around what happened. When taking candidates through my interview process, I ask questions, lots of questions (this is a recruiter's job):

- Why were you hired at the company?
- What was your role (provide details)?
- What goals / objectives did you have, both short- and long-term?
- Did you achieve the objectives? If yes, how? If not, why not?
- Why did the layoff happen?
- How many people were laid off in addition to you?
- What reason(s) were you given as to why you were included in the layoff?
- If I talked to your leadership team, would they be able to answer that question for me?

Going back to my example, when I asked these questions of Mr. I-Got-Laid-Off-From-The-Last-Three-Companies-I-Worked-At, he got extremely frustrated with me and, in an overly huffy tone, wanted to know why I needed all this detail. I explained hiring managers always like to understand the reasons a RIF happened and why the candidate was part of the layoff. Before I could finish my response, he cut me off and aggressively snapped, "Do you think I want my résumé to look like this? Do you? DO? YOU?" And then there was silence.

I'd like to say I was stunned by his extremely caustic tone. (His anger was palpable.) But I wasn't. Having done this as long as I have, I can say he wasn't the first to be so worked up in response to my line of questioning. And for those of you who might assume the way I asked the question likely warranted such a response, I'll have you know that one of my biggest strengths is my EQ. My ability to empathize and my ability to be extremely sensitive to the other person's situation are exceptional. So no, I don't position my questions in a way that necessitates such defensive responses. And for those of you who might be thinking you'd be frustrated having to answer those questions, too, after probably having already answered those questions before with other interviewers and thus was founded in letting some frustration show through, nope! It is not OK. It is never OK. As a candidate, you need to suck it up and recognize the person asking the questions has a right to know and this will help them help you.

Going back to my example, after my candidate snapped at me, asking if I thought he wanted his résumé to have three RIFs in a row and I sat in silence for what was a very long pause, I calmly explained to him how clients always want to know the story of someone's career progression. I said based on my years of experience working with this particular client, during which I had previously presented candidates who'd been laid off, I knew the questions they'd want me to have answers to and thus the reason I had asked him those very questions. I stated quite directly that if he didn't want to answer my questions, I understood but doing so would mean we couldn't continue to explore the opportunity. Somewhat to my surprise, he decided to answer the questions, albeit in a tone of total annoyance and what I sensed was utter disgust. So, truth be told, at that juncture it didn't matter what he said as he was not going to move beyond our conversation. There was absolutely zero chance of me presenting his candidacy to my client. Instead of recognizing that as the recruiter, I was in a position of trying to help him by understanding the story so I could do my best to get him an interview with my client, he lashed out at me. Keep in mind, I was not the one seeking a job! I have a job—a very good job, at that.

If you're a professional looking for a job, you might want to think twice about the way you treat all the people who are trying to help you find a job. Be smart and play nice! Put yourself in the other person's shoes, and think about how you'd feel if someone was treating you the way you're treating them. Take a moment to consider this: If you're being mean, is that person really going to want to go out of their way to help you? Is that person going to put their reputation on the line to assist you?

Hint: The answer is...no!

Now, I learned a long time ago, you never know what's going on in someone's life. Therefore, I try to be forgiving of those who are rude and disrespectful. However, I'll always opt to work with those who are kind, polite, and respectful, and I know I'm not alone on this. If you're frustrated with anything in particular, like the fact something you posted only got two likes or job searching or interviewing or the color of your walls or the fact you haven't had a date in six months or you're simply frustrated with life in general, do yourself a favor and refrain from taking it out on those who are trying to help you. Find a way to deal with your frustrations: exercise; watch a great movie; read a book; scream into your pillow; take a class; pick up a hobby; volunteer to help others. But...

Do not act rudely toward those who are trying to help you!

Better yet, just don't act rude—period! Call me old-fashioned, but I'm a believer in the concept of good things happen to good people. Be nice because the universe will notice, and at some point, good things will come your way.

It's no secret many have a negative view of the overall field of recruiting, which obviously includes all actual recruiters themselves. Over the years, I've had interesting encounters with professionals who seem to be angry with the entire talent acquisition process and / or industry as a whole. Candidates love to share their war stories with me, and I've heard innumerable unflattering accounts about executive search professionals, both internal and external.

Now, you must know that every single industry will always have a broad spectrum of talent, ranging from professionals who are at the top and stand out as "best in class" down to some really G-d-awful professionals who would definitely be awarded "worst of the worst." Hence, we all know in the world of executive search, there are undoubtedly some less-than-stellar professionals. Regardless, don't generalize and assume every recruiter is terrible. Most people don't want to totally suck at their jobs, and most people don't have bad intentions. Please keep this in mind and just be nice. Treat people with respect.

Remember, executive recruiters are tasked with finding the best talent for the particular positions they've been hired by their clients (companies) to work on. When working with those in the talent acquisition field, reflect on what was just said—most people want to do a good job. Most don't want to waste anyone's time (including their own). Most are doing what they're paid to do. So when recruiters ask you questions (or when any interviewer asks you questions, for that matter), they're doing it for a reason, and I promise you, 99 percent of the time, their goal is not to tick you off, play games, or trick you.

Recently, I was interviewing a candidate whose résumé appeared to have seven jobs in the last fourteen years. I had to ask him about this not only for my own knowledge but also because I knew this would be my client's first question and having a clear answer would be absolutely critical to whether or not he'd be invited into their interview process. So I needed to know why he'd had so many changes.

In a very casual, matter-of-fact, nonjudgmental sort of way, I asked him, "It looks like you've made a number of moves over the past fourteen years. Can you tell me about that? If we proceed, my client will want me to walk through why you've made these changes. I'd love to hear why you joined and then left each company detailed on your résumé. Let's go through this together, starting back when you were with _____."

Between the incredibly deep breath he took and then the aggressive / caustic tone he used when responding to my inquiry, it was obvious he wasn't pleased with my question. He tersely barked, "Do you think I want my résumé to look this way? I mean, really. Do. You. Think. I. Am. Happy. About. It? Do you think it's fun for me to have to answer this question during each and every interview I have? Do you think that I might want to be in a different situation?!" And then he made a strange growl-like noise.

My initial thought was: "Do you think I want to punch you?"

Next thought was: "Yikes! Wow! Weird…I think he just growled. OK…so I've seen enough *Dateline NBC*s to know people are crazy and his response was really uncalled for."

Then my next thought was this: "Do you think I want to represent you after that outburst / temper tantrum? Do you think I might get a wee bit nervous you'll behave just like that in front of my client? Do you think I want to risk my reputation by presenting you to any of my clients?"

Answer: Big fat n + o = NO!

Now, in the candidate's defense, I'm sure it is really frustrating to be asked this question over and over. Clearly it struck a nerve. But his tone, his aggressive nature, and his overall response all quickly ruined any chance (remote chance) he had. How in the world could I have moved him forward?

Answer: I couldn't.

By the way, in certain industries, it's accepted as normal for professionals to move around with a degree of frequency. For example, in the world of advertising, professionals switch companies with a bit more regularity, and as long as the reasons make sense and don't discredit someone's professionalism and skills, many decision-makers won't be concerned. Thus, movement doesn't have to be the kiss of death. Most interviewers realize asking some basic questions to uncover the story can help ease concerns around the many job changes. But the job of a recruiter is to ask questions in order to obtain the long and short of it so they can clearly present a candidate's story. However, when someone immediately gets defensive and aggressive like the professional I just referenced did, it really doesn't matter what the story is because the vast majority of people in my shoes won't feel comfortable moving the candidate forward in a process. And please note—nothing I'm saying is unique to me. I hear this from other decision-makers / gatekeepers all the time.

Listen up—you won't do yourself any favors by mistreating the person(s) holding the keys to getting your information into the hiring manager's hands. Beyond that, consider the big picture—as a candidate, even if you aren't selected for a particular position, recruiters are bound to have more opportunities in the future. As a recruiter, time and again, I'll reach out to professionals I previously worked with whom I really liked and ranked high. These are candidates who, for one reason or another, weren't right for the position I was working on at that time. However, knowing they might be a fit for a current search, they're the ones I typically contact first. I don't know about you, but as a professional, I think it's prudent to be on the radar of reputable recruiters so they're motivated to share future opportunities with you, right? Don't you want to be the first person who comes to mind whenever (good) recruiters have a position you might align with?

This leads me to my next point, which is…don't shoot the messenger! I will repeat this: Do not shoot the messenger!

I am pretty confident I speak for 99 percent of recruiters out there when I tell you one of the worst parts of our job is telling a candidate they aren't moving forward in an interview process. No matter what stage of the search we're in, it always stinks to have to deliver bad news. As often as we do this, it never gets easier. Many professionals, dare I say most, do truly care. We hate to see people disappointed. Sometimes, we know the bad news is crushing someone's hopes and dreams. Therefore, when recruiters (or anyone, for that matter) provide this feedback, please play nice and don't lash out. We're just doing our jobs...I can assure you we're not trying to ruin lives. If you want information as to why this decision was made, I promise you, being nice and politely asking for feedback will get you a lot further than verbally attacking the person delivering the bad news. Play nice, and it's highly likely you'll be on someone's radar for future positions. Be a jerkwad, and congrats—you've just increased your odds of being put on the shit list (a.k.a. the do-not-contact list).

I recently contacted a candidate to share the dreaded bad news. Unfortunately, Jan wasn't selected to move forward in a client's interview process. I explained to Jan their reasoning and shared they felt other candidates were more closely aligned with what they were seeking. Jan could not have been more gracious in her response. Very professionally, she thanked me for following up to let her know she was no longer being considered and respectfully inquired as to whether any feedback was provided. Jan thoughtfully stated she respects their decision but was always looking to improve and thus, if I was given any helpful feedback, she'd love to learn from it. In this situation, it truly was all about being one of many incredibly impressive candidates. So I highlighted how tough the competition was and stressed how impressive all of the professionals Jan was competing against were. Because my client said it was OK to do so, I noted a piece of valuable information shared with me. I explained the hiring manager felt she (Jan) didn't do a great job of directly answering some questions asked during their interview. My client said Jan had trouble getting to the point and staying on any given topic without veering onto tangents. While negative feedback can be difficult to receive, Jan was amazing! She was extremely appreciative of this feedback, and rather than getting defensive, rather than ripping the client and saying they were totally wrong, rather than attacking me, she thanked me profusely for sharing such valuable feedback and promised me she was going to work on this and be better in upcoming interviews.

Moral of the story—this candidate was an absolute doll and made it incredibly easy for me to speak candidly with her. It's always refreshing to work with people like her! On the other hand, recruiters and hiring managers alike have had people receive feedback in the exact opposite fashion, and ouch, it's never pleasant! I've had professionals respond with palpable aggression, to the point it's truly uncomfortable. I've been yelled at, sworn at, and had people scream that the feedback was complete BS (or insert other colorful language). People have accused hiring managers of all sorts of things. They've ripped decision-makers, said they're total assholes who have no clue. They've verbally torn people apart. I'm talking, completely shredded my client(s) to pieces. Candidates have found everyone to blame while never taking a moment to look inward and accept any level of responsibility. And yes, in their defense, it's absolutely possible some feedback might not have been fair. However, not being present for the interview, it's impossible for the recruiter (me) to know exactly how things played out and comment. Recruiters are simply delivering the information we've been given. Clearly, when the candidate reacts aggressively, it becomes virtually impossible to feel comfortable disclosing any amount of frank information. In addition, it makes it impossible for us to want to do business with the candidate again in the future. All this said, if the person delivering the feedback is doing so in a less than professional way, I understand this can affect a candidate's response. However, many approach this conversation the same way I do, which is gingerly, empathetically, with grace and compassion. So, please don't beat them up!

As discussed, no one is perfect; we all have flaws, and we've all had bad days on which we've said, done, or acted inappropriately. No matter what side of the desk one sits on, people should always be treated with respect and dignity. In a job search setting (or any professional setting), emotions may be high, but that's no excuse for mistreating others. Be it fellow job searchers, hiring managers, or executive recruiters, it's vital we all play nice and stay professional. Even if the other person is being rude, bite your lip, stay composed, and be nice. It's easier said than done, I know! But you'll walk away with pride. Your reputation will stay intact. And good things will happen.

Tell the Truth

TELLING THE TRUTH should be a part of most people's moral code (notice I said "should be"). After all, it is one of the Ten Commandments. Whether you were taught this very important lesson at home, in religious school, or during your early education, at some point you hopefully learn failing to tell the truth can (as my dad always said) "get you into deep doo-doo." My parents used to tell my brothers and me that failing to tell the truth would cause our noses to grow just like Pinocchio's, which totally scared the bejesus out of me. Who wanted that huge nose?!

Unfortunately, when job searching, people are tempted to do whatever they can to make themselves the "perfect" candidate. Sadly, many are inclined to exaggerate their skills and accomplishments, while others will just flat-out lie. In fact, statistics state about 85 percent of candidates lie on their résumés and / or in interviews. Here's the deal…don't do it…it will come back to haunt you! I'm not lying, it will.

Tell the truth!

Today, more than ever before, it's so easy for potential and / or current employers to research anything and everything about a candidate, and trust me, they will do just that! If a lie is uncovered during the interview process, most companies will not hesitate to automatically reject the candidate. If a lie is discovered after a person has been hired, many companies will terminate employment immediately. It doesn't matter if the person is doing well at the company; a lie could be automatic grounds for dismissal. Regardless of these consequences, there are innumerable professionals out there who know lying is a slippery slope but opt to roll the dice, hoping no one will catch their indiscretion(s). Big or small, a lie is a lie, and if you misrepresent yourself in any way, you run the risk of getting caught. Lying, fibbing, misrepresenting, altering, misstating, exaggerating, strategically omitting—whatever you want to call it, it's an awful idea and can really damage a person's reputation. Whether it's a lie about yourself on a professional level or a personal one, don't do it! Tell the truth.

On a professional level, tell the truth about your skills, the jobs you've held, your titles, dates of employment, etc. With regards to telling the truth about your skills, an important point to note is that companies hire professionals for the skills and accomplishments the candidate claims to possess in the interview process. Think about it—it's awfully hard for a candidate to live up to expectations and do what they say they can do if they've exaggerated or flat-out lied about their skills. Aside from potentially landing in hot water, at a minimum, or getting fired (even possibly sued!), misrepresenting your skills, strengths, and achievements is a surefire way to set yourself up for failure. Don't lie to yourself (ha!)—this will come back to bite you!

No company is perfect and neither is any one candidate. Thus, it's rare for candidates to align 100 percent with any job spec. When someone seems to be a perfect match for a job description, I often joke that there must be a personality flaw. Now, because it's rare to find a candidate who's a perfect match on every single front, as long as a candidate meets most of the requirements, they typically have a shot at being considered for the position. Therefore, it's absolutely critical for a candidate to highlight where they do align with the requirements of the job and underscore the strengths they bring to the table. Equally important, though, is for the candidate to properly position any gaps they have (areas where they don't align with the job spec) so companies know where they may need a bit more time to get up to speed. Believe it or not, many hiring managers subscribe to the school of thought "Hire for DNA and train for skills." This means companies may prioritize how a person is hardwired over the background experience(s) they bring. Thus, if someone can demonstrate that they are hardwired with a strong work ethic, that they're resilient, they like to learn and grow, they show passion and perseverance, they're resourceful and bring positive energy, etc., those qualities and characteristics can be, and often are, more important than some of the gaps the professional may have skills-wise. Hiring managers know those skills gaps can be lessened with training. However, what can't be easily taught or trained are those DNA characteristics.

I'm sure you don't need me to fully spell out why misstating or misrepresenting your skills can be incredibly stupid, so I'll keep this brief. If you're applying for a job wanting someone who has experience using, for example, a certain SaaS-based product and you say you have that experience when you really don't, guess what happens when you start in that job and have no clue how to use the solution? Do you think they'll be upset to learn you're not proficient with the tool? Will you be freaking out when you actually have to use it and don't know how? Let's say you're an HR professional and the job you've been interviewing for wants someone who has experience overseeing benefits. They want someone who has led open enrollment. You say you've done that when you really haven't. Do you really think you'll be able to simply wing it if you're hired? Do you really think they won't quickly realize you're not experienced on this front? As you can see, if you don't tell the truth about your skills, you're bound to be exposed, and this often leads to very short tenures in positions. Tell the truth, because you don't want to be set up for failure in a job.

Aside from misrepresenting one's skills, strengths, and accomplishments, another area where telling the truth tends to present a challenge is noting employment "end dates" on a résumé. Here's the deal—every single date placed on your résumé must be accurate! If you're no longer employed by a company, you absolutely cannot misrepresent this on your résumé. There are many professionals who purposely choose to keep their last position listed as "current" or "present" even though their employment has ended. This is a very dangerous game of Russian roulette! Of course the psychology behind this is, many professionals feel they're more attractive to potential employers when they're currently employed. Unfortunately, this can and often will backfire. The reality is, when your résumé is not accurate, many will question whether you're knowingly being deceptive and might automatically reject you for this infraction.

Pay attention- The dates stated for every single position held, past and current, need to be correctly represented on your résumé.

Tell the truth. Don't misrepresent. Don't fudge. At some point, you will get caught.

As I've shared with you before, when interviewing candidates, I ask questions probing into their past and current employment situations. In scenarios where the candidate has either directly claimed to no longer be in their most recent position ("I left there a few weeks ago…") or has insinuated in some way that the position is no longer "current" ("When I was there…"), I'm going to dig deeper to understand what happened to them. And you better believe, if a candidate's résumé states they're still currently there by noting the date as "MM/DD/YY–Current" red flags start swayin' in the wind! If it comes to light the candidate is no longer employed there, and if it's been more than a couple days (OK—maybe two weeks), questions are going to be asked. A typical question might be "Your résumé says you started your position in March 2021, and it says 'to present.' Are you still there, or have you left?" In response, here are some examples of the excuses people have come up with:

- "Oh, gosh, I'm so sorry…I accidentally sent you the wrong version of my résumé." (Really? This was an accident? Not sure I buy that! You just said you've been gone for over three months. Hmmmm…)
- "I know. I need to update my résumé and put the actual end date in. I just haven't done it yet." (Why haven't you? What are you waiting for? You just admitted you left six weeks ago. I assume I'm not your first call.)
- "Oh, I didn't realize it wasn't updated." (Whaaat? Really? C'mon- You've been gone for two months now. I call BS! However, if true, I'm even more worried!)

Whatever the excuse, it doesn't sit well with most decision-makers. Their spidey-senses will go up. When you are no longer employed with a company, you absolutely must update your résumé immediately. Feigning ignorance or surprise doesn't typically sit well with hiring managers. Rather, it can lead to questions about a candidate's honesty and integrity, ultimately disqualifying them from consideration. I'm not overstating it when I tell you, this is something hiring managers are extremely sensitive about.

By the way, I realize there's a bit of a gray area when it comes to those receiving severance packages. If you receive a lump sum payout right after your employment is terminated (or severed), that's technically your employment end date. However, if you receive a payout spread over numerous months, many believe you can technically be considered employed until you receive the very last installment. I'd encourage a great deal of discretion here. If you're being paid a year of severance on a monthly basis but haven't stepped foot into the building and / or done one thing for that employer since the day you left eleven months ago, you might want to discuss with them what end date they're using and stick with that.

OK, with this talk of layoffs and severance packages, one of the questions I frequently hear from those who've been impacted by a RIF is one we should explore further. People often ask me, "Is it true that employers have a bias against unemployed candidates?" In other words, do companies prefer job applicants who are employed over those who are unemployed? Unfortunately, like it or not, fair or unfair, in most job markets, there is a preference for considering candidates who are employed. However, during economic downturns, like we saw in '08 and during COVID, we all witnessed many great professionals lose their jobs through no fault of their own. The myth that good employees never get "let go" was turned on its head. During those daunting economic times, many hiring managers realized this and were able to capitalize by snatching up top talent. As the job market recovered, though, the pendulum swung back, and decision-makers seemed to fall right back into the pattern of placing a premium on candidates who were employed. So let's take a sec to explore what an unemployed professional can do to help their cause. The great news is there are many options!

One option is to form your own company (set up an LLC) and do some consulting work. Incorporating isn't too arduous, and in most states, it isn't too costly. Once you've created your LLC, get out there and find a consulting assignment. This will enable you to have current work you can detail on your résumé. How do you find a consulting assignment(s)? Well, you start by asking current or former colleagues, clients, friends, neighbors, and others if there's anything they need help with. Even if they can't pay you, strongly consider accepting the work. You'll be able to detail it on your résumé, and it'll go a long way. Whether you're being paid or doing the work pro bono, no one needs to know. And hiring managers will see you're actively engaged in the workforce, which is always a good thing. Another option is to volunteer and put those activities on your résumé. Some professionals take the opportunity to further their education. Investing in your own personal and professional growth is always a great idea! Whether it's full-time schooling or online courses, it will be money and time well spent. Maybe you want to get certified in project management, brush up on Excel skills, take a few leadership workshops, etc. All can help you strengthen your resume, your confidence and widen your list of contacts. Whatever path you choose, though, please be honest about your current status. If you're no longer with an employer, you need to accurately state your end date.

I'm sure you've heard the saying "Too much of a good thing is bad," and in the spirit of telling the truth, it's important to note, sometimes people tell too much of the truth and, in so doing, can actually damage their candidacy. Once in a while, I come across a professional who is so brutally honest, I need to help them understand the difference between telling the truth and telling too much of the truth. Clearly, I'm promoting honesty and always stress the importance of accurately representing oneself. However, professionals need to be mindful of presenting themselves in the best light possible and refrain from sharing (or over-sharing) information that isn't helpful to their plight. For example, a while back (pre-COVID), I was working with a New York City–based company on a search where they wanted to find local talent only. They were not willing to relocate someone for the role because they felt the talent pool should have been plenty deep in NYC. Early in the search, someone referred a candidate to me who was absolutely perfect for the role! She was spot-on in practically every single way, except for the fact she wasn't local to NYC. This candidate knew the client was interested in local candidates only and, from the start, assured me she'd be more than happy to cover all relocation costs herself and stressed we shouldn't let geography stand in our way of moving forward. Because of how perfectly her background aligned with the position, I decided to take things to the next step. My client agreed she was an outstanding candidate and requested an interview with her. Sure enough, this candidate did extremely well and quickly progressed forward in my client's interview process. Every step of the way, she was crushing it! The entire team absolutely loved her. Her final interview started with regrouping with the hiring manager, whom she'd previously met with a number of times. Assuming that went well, they then planned to present her with an offer. Yay! Exciting stuff! So the first half of this final interview with the hiring manager went great! From there, though, things didn't go as swimmingly. The relocation topic was brought up one last time, and the conversation went something like this:

Hiring manager: I know I asked you this before. But seriously, are you absolutely positive you're really willing and able to cover the costs of relocating yourself to NYC? It's a big move and as I've said, we have no budget to relo someone. I need to make sure you're absolutely positive you won't have any issues with this.

Candidate: Yes! This is no problem! I'm so excited to come here. And as I said, I will absolutely cover all the costs. You have to realize I just lost seventy-five pounds; I just finalized what was an awful divorce and a very dark time in my life. I am soooooo ready to move on to the next chapter! I can't wait to leave Boston and my old life behind and start over fresh and new in New York! I'm in a great mental place now and know it's the right time to move.

While some of us may not be able to relate to her situation fully, we can all appreciate it, right? I'm sure you'd join me in applauding her for getting healthy and losing weight! That's not easy! And hooray for finalizing an awful divorce! Having that done had to be a major relief for her. Most can understand why she was excited to move into that next phase of her life. Unfortunately, though, sharing those details raised a number of red flags in the hiring manager's mind. She couldn't help but wonder whether this candidate was truly interested in the particular position and company OR if she was really just looking for a ticket, any ticket, out of Boston. Was she still emotionally unstable from the rough divorce? She said she was in a dark place. Hiring manager worried, could she slip back into that place again? How could hiring manager trust that she'd be able to fully focus on this new position and do great work? We all know new jobs are very stressful and quite overwhelming. Could she handle it, or would it be too much? Were her priorities going to be here or elsewhere?

The hiring manager suddenly had a lot more to worry about. Rather than answering the hiring manager's direct question with a direct and concise answer, the candidate provided so much detail. The candidate could have said, "Yes, I am absolutely sure! I can and will relocate myself. This is not a problem!" (She should have stopped there.)

Now, in this candidate's defense, she definitely told the truth. And, I'm glad she said all this because I always want my clients hiring the best professional. I don't want things going wrong. That said, this is an example of telling too much of the truth. The question was simple and could have been answered with, "Yes." Instead, she gave a lengthy response and the details she imparted were not necessary; they weren't relevant to how she'd add value to the position / company. She could have been the perfect person for the job, and it could have been a great match. She didn't need to share those details, and they turned what should have been an offer into a rejection. Now, maybe that was a good thing in the end. However, when everything went sideways, it was devastating to the candidate. Once the toothpaste was out of the tube, there was no turning back. She couldn't change the course of events. After she said what she did, my client had new concerns they couldn't get past and thus opted to pursue some other highly qualified candidates, ultimately hiring someone who turned out to be a great fit. Perhaps my other candidate would have been as good or better. We'll never know, though. She shared too much and it ruined her chances. Was my client being too judgmental? Did they make too much out of nothing? You're entitled to your opinion. But when hiring for a role as important as this one was to the company, where so much was on the line and the impact on the business was large, details had to be scrutinized, and I couldn't blame my client for opting to take a pass. Like it or not, they made what they felt was a prudent business decision.

Another quick example on this topic—in our hiring process, we create a customized questionnaire for each and every search we work on. (This is something repeatedly touched on throughout this book.) One of the many reasons we use this tool is to help ensure we're consistent in our approach to evaluating multiple candidates for a specific search. While conversations will vary slightly from one candidate to the next, by asking every professional to complete this questionnaire, we can more easily compare and contrast them with one another. We'll ask candidates to email their responses / answers back as quickly as possible. This "homework assignment" helps us assess candidates on many levels.

- We like to see how candidates respond to our request. (Trust me, you quickly learn who's truly interested by gauging their initial reaction to this assignment!)
- We're able to get a sense of a candidate's written communication skills.
- We're able to get a sense of the quality of work the candidate puts forth.
- As stated above, by asking candidates the same list of questions, we're then able to compare them apples to apples.

Recently, I was scheduled to have a follow-up conversation with a woman I'd had a first interview with and subsequently sent my questionnaire to. I'd asked her to submit her completed document to me in advance of our call so I could review and be prepared with my follow-up questions, which would make the best use of our time. It's important to note that she had six whole days to get this homework assignment done. Yes, you heard me. From the time of our first interview to the time of our second conversation, there were six days! That's basically a whole week. Yet she didn't email it to me until approximately twenty-five minutes before our call. Right away, she began the conversation apologizing for not sending me the questionnaire sooner, which was nice of her. I certainly appreciated it. From there, though, she really got herself into a pickle. She continued by saying, "Ugh, I don't know what's wrong with me. This just felt so much like the homework I never wanted to deal with in high school, so I just kept putting it off. I'm sure it isn't very well done and that my answers could have been way better. But I wanted to get something into your hands prior to our call, so I threw it together at the very last minute. If it's awful, I'm really sorry!"

Ummmmm...wtf? Did she really just say that to me? Oh lordy! By now, you have a sense of how I think, and I'm sure you can imagine what my thoughts were. We'll just leave it with that...

Now, she should have stopped after apologizing for not getting her answers to me earlier. She didn't need to provide me with the additional detail. She told the truth, and I do give her credit for that. But she told way too much of the truth, and this did not help her candidacy in the slightest! It actually hurt her. Think about it: Maybe her answers didn't totally suck; maybe what she put together *was* in fact decent. Unfortunately, though, by telling me she procrastinated until the last minute, that she half-assed it, and that her answers likely stunk, well...I then assumed her answers were lame and was not able to look at the document with an open mind. In addition to tainting my view of her responses, she provided me with insight into her maturity level, and this didn't help her win any points with me. Being a procrastinator isn't necessarily a sought-after character trait, and thus her admission helped her dig her own grave. As highlighted umpteen trillion times, hiring managers (and recruiters) are going to assume candidates put their best foot forward in an interview process. Thus, if half-assed is your best effort...well...it ain't good enough and usually leads to a "Thanks for your time. Buh-bye!"

At every step of a process, hiring managers are thinking you're providing them with insights as to what kind of employee you'll be for the company, and most managers don't want to hire the person who blows stuff off and then produces subpar work at the buzzer. Now, from my vantage point, I appreciated the honesty because, as a recruiter, I actually do want to know who the real person / real candidate is. Not the fake "this is their interview self." So I'm always happy not to waste any additional time working with candidates who could really bait and switch me or my client. Anyone who has managed people long enough has had the experience of hiring someone who ends up being totally different from the person they met in the interview process. And by the way, it's normally not "totally different" in a positive way. As much as it stinks to have a candidate disappoint me in an interview process with *true confessions of a procrastinator*, I'll take it over having a client calling me a month into that person joining their team with complaints about the person they've hired.

Another place where telling the truth is really helpful is if you're considering other opportunities and / or are in other interview processes and are asked about it. Many candidates feel they can't be honest about this. You can and you should be. Most people know top talent is highly sought after and thus expect those A+ professionals to have more than one opportunity, especially if the person is in an active job search. Recruiters like me will always ask a professional if they're currently exploring other opportunities and if yes, to please let us know so we can try to help manage the timing for them and help them as they think it through. Quite often professionals feel nervous to disclose this information, often fearing it'll come across as them trying to pressure or strong arm the other company. Most of the time, such information isn't perceived in that light. Rather, it's greatly appreciated as it helps everyone to feel there's a level of openness and transparency. And let's be honest—people want people who are wanted. If another company is interested in the same candidate, that seems to help validate that person's candidacy.

On a personal level, telling the truth is important too. Now, if someone asks you a question they legally can't ask you, you don't have to answer. For example, if someone asks you if you're married, what religion you are, whether or not you're currently pregnant, or if you plan to start a family, you can refrain from answering. However, if you know a company is going to do a background check and you know your record isn't squeaky clean, you might want to fess up sooner rather than later. I am not a lawyer, and thus I am by no means giving you legal advice here. But, I can tell you from firsthand experience that if you provide a potential employer (or recruiter) with information about your past…things such as a DUI, a bankruptcy claim, an arrest record, etc., they might be more open to continuing down the interview path with you than if you hope they won't uncover the truth and they eventually do. I know this is a tricky topic and a very sensitive one. In my experience, being forthright has been the better path, leading to better outcomes. For example, I was interviewing candidates for a CFO position and a candidate I really liked shared he had to declare bankruptcy ten years prior to us speaking. He explained his late wife had a terminal illness and their insurance didn't cover enough of the medical costs. He shared the details, they made a lot of sense and I was able to share with the hiring team when I presented his candidacy. They greatly appreciated the information and understood the decision he had to make. Now, had he not shared and had my client found that out on a background check, knowing a CFO deals with revenue / money, that could have been a deal ending situation. By the way, I dive a bit deeper into this topic in a later chapter, called "If You Did It, Admit It."

My point in this chapter is that telling the truth in an interview process is very important. Hiring managers want to know the *real* you. Remember, though, telling too much of the truth can be dangerous. Think about what you're saying in an interview, and assess whether or not the information you are about to impart is critical. If it's not relevant to how you will positively impact the job and / or how you'll add value to the company, it's probably not important to share.

People Lie

FOR SOME REASON, it's human nature to lie. I don't know at what age people start lying, but I'm pretty sure it's quite early in life. I'd love to understand the psychology behind why we humans do this. (Add this to my "to research someday" list.) In the meantime, let's just agree we all know people sometimes lie. In fact, a quick Google search of this says people lie, on average, twice a day (which seems low). While we discussed the importance of telling the truth and presenting oneself in an accurate light, professionals also need to recognize that during a job search and / or interview process, people do not always tell the truth. In other words, people lie.

For example, I remember Chad, a senior-level sales professional who, when we spoke, explained he was laid off a few months prior to our call and had been in job search mode ever since. Chad provided details around why he was laid off and assured me it wasn't due to his "on-the-job" performance. During our chat, Chad confided he was growing increasingly frustrated with the whole job search process. He shared how he'd been very close to the offer stage with a number of companies but in the eleventh hour, those companies decided not to move forward with him. Chad claimed each company chose to hire the other finalist candidate and he was told the decision ultimately came down to the other finalist having a more robust list of contacts and companies in the industry they wanted this hire to sell into right out of the gate. In other words, each company felt the other finalist could get more meetings faster, which hopefully meant more sales faster ($$$). Now, from my many years of experience in recruiting, I know the reason provided to a candidate isn't always the real reason (or whole reason) why they didn't get an offer. I've had numerous experiences where "the better contact list" reason was only part of why someone didn't get an offer. It wasn't the only reason, though. Now, knowing this, I didn't want to make Chad feel worse when I gently probed for more information. I asked Chad a number of questions to better understand the situation, and ultimately, he was absolutely convinced the only reason he lost out on those positions was his list of connections and contacts. Chad was 100 percent certain he was absolutely perfect during the interviews (his words, not mine). And he had an unwavering conviction that there was absolutely nothing (not one thing?) he could have done better. Even though he didn't know his competition, and even though he wasn't privy to all the behind-the-scenes detail, Chad was 100 percent confident he was the ideal candidate for each position he interviewed for and lost only due to his contacts / connections not being as robust as those of the other candidate(s).

OK, so let me be the bearer of bad news. I'm going to give it to you straight!

While Chad's list of contacts may have in fact been an issue in some or all of the aforementioned opportunities, my guess is there was probably more to the story of why one or more of those companies chose to present offers to the other candidate(s) and not him.

My point in sharing this example of Chad—unfortunately, there are times when candidates aren't going to hear the (whole) truth from the hiring manager and / or recruiter. Thus, as a candidate, you can't assume the feedback you receive is 100 percent complete; some details may not be shared with you. In this situation, perhaps a hiring manager did some checking behind the scenes and heard some less-than-flattering scoop about Chad. If that was the case, the hiring manager couldn't tell Chad what he'd heard or reveal the sources. The hiring manager may have fully trusted whoever shared this less-than-flattering review of Chad, ultimately causing them to lose their enthusiasm for Chad and make the offer to the other person. Another possible scenario is that Chad showed up for interviews looking completely disheveled and made a poor impression. The hiring manager might not have felt comfortable telling Chad, "Hey, you looked like a total schlump at the interview. Your clothes were all wrinkled, and your sport coat had a big stain on it." Or maybe for the final interview, the candidates were given a case study and asked to put together a presentation that they'd deliver in a mock meeting, and Chad bombed on the assignment. Maybe he didn't do nearly as well as the other candidate. Perhaps Chad's presentation completely missed the mark, and he didn't command the room the way the other candidate did in the mock meeting. Maybe Chad struggled to articulate succinct answers to questions he was asked. Another possible scenario is that in the final interview, Chad bad-mouthed a former employer. Or it's possible Chad came across in such a way that the hiring managers didn't view him as a fit for their corporate culture. Maybe he seemed really high-maintenance, bossy, or rude. Or perhaps it wasn't actually about Chad and how he interviewed. Maybe the company insisted on there being two finalists in their interview process, but everyone at the company pretty much knew they were going to hire the other candidate, Jenna, because she worked for the hiring manager at another company years ago. While they couldn't tell Chad this, unless a bus hit Jenna, the job was going to be hers. Another possible scenario is that a member of the company's board of directors personally recommended a candidate, Mark, who was touted as "the ideal candidate." The hiring manager didn't want to be viewed as going against that board member's recommendation and thus made the offer to Mark. This list could go on and on, as there are so many different possible reasons why Chad didn't get the offer. Whatever the case was, though, candidates such as Chad need to know they won't always hear the whole truth; they may only be provided with parts and pieces. Or they may not get any of the truth. Sometimes there's a reason, but the candidate is told something basic like "The competition was really strong, and it was a tough decision" because the true reason can't be revealed. Sometimes the reason provided is the easiest and safest one for a company to use. What this means is, unfortunately, sometimes candidates are lied to. For that reason, being self-aware is absolutely critical for candidates. Professionals need to have honest conversations with themselves every step of the way. I don't know about you, but after every call / meeting I have, I always take some time to reflect. I ask myself what went well, what I would change, where I could have improved, etc. And I can't think of a single time when I didn't come up with something—anything—I could have improved (and typically I have way more than one thing). I'm not trying to make people hypersensitive and completely paranoid. Rather, I want to encourage professionals to realize the feedback provided might not be all the information. It might not be fully honest. Thus, professionals need to consistently critique themselves while also seeking out candid feedback from others as a means to elevate their interview game and job search process.

Additionally, it's really important for professionals to understand those delivering feedback, such as executive recruiters, don't always know all of the reasons why a company won't move a candidate forward and / or have been asked to not share some / all of the reasons behind a decision. Remember, recruiters are being paid by companies and thus their loyalty is, and has to be, to the company first. So please don't beat up executive recruiters for the news (or lack thereof) they deliver. People in my field have had many candidates lash out at them when they're unable to provide details around why they were rejected. Personally, I've had people insult me and my ability to work effectively with my clients. Here's the deal—at the end of the day, you weren't picked. If the person delivering the news knows why you were removed from consideration and wants to share, and can share, any level of detail with you, they will. If not, berating someone isn't going to win you any friends and likely won't net you additional information. And repeatedly asking someone over and over again will probably prove fruitless too. Furthermore, asking in an angry and abrasive tone will definitely damage your chances of working with the recruiter again on any future opportunities. If someone can't provide you with the detail you're looking for, kindly and respectfully leave it alone. Remember the idiom "You can catch more flies with honey than vinegar"? This means, if you want to persuade someone, you will have an easier time by being polite versus confrontational. Therefore, if you're trying to get information out of someone, being nice and thoughtful in your approach might net you the desired results.

When job searching and / or interviewing, it's also important to keep in mind people may knowingly or unknowingly "lie"; they may purposely or accidentally fail to share important information. And unfortunately, this impacts a candidate's ability to accurately evaluate an opportunity.. Over the last fifteen years, I've seen and heard quite a lot. When I have questioned professionals about their backgrounds and have dug into companies they worked for and the positions they held, along with why they left, I've heard things like the following:

- "They weren't honest with me about the roles and responsibilities of the job."
- "They weren't honest with me when describing the company's culture."
- "They totally misrepresented the company's finances. They didn't have enough runway for more than ten months and I had no clue."

- "They failed to share with me that they were in the midst of losing their largest client account."

This underscores the importance of making sure, as a candidate, you are thoroughly researching every opportunity you consider. You need to be asking as many thoughtful questions as you can when exploring the role. Do detailed background checks on the company and the people. If you aren't being given complete answers, or if the answers you're being given don't sit well with you, you need to pay attention to that and dig deeper. That said, as a candidate, you can do a masterful job of asking all the right questions and looking under every rock possible and still end up feeling duped. It doesn't happen often, but it happens. So it's not always the candidate's fault. However, the better you do at inspecting an opportunity, the more likely you are to unearth the truths you want to know.

Because hiring managers and interviewers may leave out important details (knowingly or unknowingly), it's imperative for candidates to be thorough in their assessment(s) of opportunities.

As we've discussed, job searching and interviewing can be very difficult. Recognizing you won't always hear the whole truth is an important step in being honest with yourself as a candidate so you can learn from your experiences and so that you can best assess opportunities. If you've had a negative experience, or more than one, dissect it. Learn from it. Determine what you could have done better so that you don't find yourself in that same boat ever again. Know that you're not always given the full picture. Sometimes candidates are a bit misled, or more than a bit. This is one of the many reasons why asking really good questions matters!

Hide-and-Seek Is for Kids

I WAS FORTUNATE to have a great childhood. Growing up, I lived on a beautiful tree-lined street with lots of kids, which meant there were always others to play with, especially when the weather was nice. One of our favorite go-to games was hide-and-seek. I have such fond childhood memories of playing this fun game outside for endless hours during the summer months. It was an absolute blast and it seemed we never tired of this game. As I reflect on my teen years, I also have many vivid memories of fun times with friends. But for the life of me, I can't recall one game of hide-and-seek. I'm not sure when we stopped playing, but I know it was before high school, and here's the key point: hide-and-seek is a game for children. Not adults. It is a kids' game!

You know my job as an executive recruiter is to find the right professionals for specific positions. As I navigate my way through the process, it never ceases to amaze me how many candidates who were once very responsive and engaged simply disappear, only to reappear days or even weeks later. If you're in job search mode or if you're engaged in an interview process for an opportunity you're excited about, I highly recommend…no, let's take this a step beyond simply recommending…I seriously and emphatically implore you to consistently check your email as well as your phone for voice mails and / or texts! For those who need me to be more specific, "consistently" means, at a minimum, you need to check a couple times a day. Those who don't will inevitably lose out. Candidly, it's difficult to feel good about any candidate who doesn't respond to an email, voice mail, or text in a timely fashion. This means you need to respond within twenty-four hours (preferably before a full day has passed). I certainly don't have time to track professionals down, and I know the vast majority of recruiters and hiring managers feel the same way. Would you want to hire someone you couldn't count on to answer your emails / voice mails / texts? Worse yet, what if the position you're considering the candidate for involves working with customers? Yikes! People are inevitably going to be thinking, "If this person can't respond to me, will they be lax about responding to our clients?"

If you're the hiring manager, wouldn't you view that person as unreliable and pretty unprofessional? If you want people to take your candidacy seriously, then you better demonstrate that you, too, are taking the process seriously. You better not hide! If you do, odds are they'll seek other candidates! (By the way, make sure your phone doesn't block callers with numbers not yet in your contact list. That could create unnecessary issues for you.)

I've had numerous situations where a client was interested in a candidate whom I could not seem to get in touch with. In fact, I recall a time when I was working with someone my client was really impressed with. I was asked to schedule a third interview and tried calling, emailing, texting this candidate for days to no avail. Unfortunately, I simply could not track this candidate down. While I was extremely frustrated by her lack of response, the mother in me was rather concerned something bad had happened to her. Naturally, my mind raced. What if she was kidnapped by wild wolves? What if she decided to hike and got lost? What if she was driving in the mountains and her car fell off the side of a cliff? What if she went skydiving and her parachute didn't open? My list went on and on! Needless to say, I was quite thankful when she finally contacted me many days later (five, to be exact). However, when she did reemerge and called, she did not provide me with any sort of apology or even one good reason for her disappearance. While I try to give people the benefit of the doubt, she didn't acknowledge the precarious position she put me in, herself in, and / or my client in. Unfortunately, I could only tap-dance with my client for so long and ultimately had to tell them I wasn't sure why she wasn't responding to me. Once they learned she'd gone dark, it didn't surprise me that they decided to move on and pursue other candidates. When I told this woman the company was no longer interested in her candidacy, she wasn't happy. In fact, she was shockingly surprised the client questioned her level of interest, professionalism, and maturity. And by the way, claiming "I've been really busy" doesn't help. She tried to play that card. Uh, nope! Sorry! Doesn't work! Everyone's busy. If someone is truly interested in an opportunity, there's always a minute to be found in the day to respond. People don't typically fall for the "I'm busy" excuse. So don't use it.

Yes, life can get really complicated and some days will be full of fire drills where you lose all track of time. It happens. But, that's rare. And when it does happen, people tend to be forgiving. That said, most of us know in advance if our lives are going to be so insanely busy that, for a certain period of time, we're going to struggle to find open windows of time to respond to those outside of our day jobs. And, if that's the case, it's a very strong indication that it's a bad time to interview for a new job. In my experience, when people can't seem to respond to me in a reasonable time frame, they're going to struggle with finding time to interview. In addition, finding time to adequately prepare for interviews is going to be a huge issue too. Do not put yourself into a position where you look terrible because your responsiveness is awful. You're wasting time and potentially damaging your reputation and future opportunities. Companies, hiring managers, and recruiters will all move forward with those who show respect for the process by being responsive and flexible.

This is pretty simple—if you're going to be traveling or plan to be offline for any reason, be sure to let people know in advance. It's also wise to have an extended absence greeting on your voice mail and email so people know not to expect a quick response. Other than an emergency, there are no excuses. If you want others to take you seriously, demonstrate you take them seriously. If you make it difficult for people to find you, you'll make it easy for them to seek others. Hide-and-seek is not a game to be played when job searching or interviewing.

People Don't Like Braggers

KIDS LOVE TO BRAG. Hearing them, with their lack of inhibition, describe how great they are at just about everything is hilarious. My husband and I were at the community pool one day with our boys, and I heard a little boy announce with tremendous excitement (and for all to hear), "I'm the bestestest, most greatest swimmer! *Everrrr!*" As he said it, he threw his arms up as if he'd won a race and concurrently melted the hearts of pretty much everyone who saw him. He was super cute! But then, on the other side of the spectrum, when at a soccer game where older boys were playing, we saw a player (I'm not naming names) score two goals a few minutes apart. He ran along the sidelines right in front of the fans holding his finger up (gesturing they're #1) while repeatedly shouting, "I'm the best! I rule!" over and over again. His coach was ticked off big time. He pulled that kid right off the field and benched him the rest of the game. His coach didn't think that was so cute and neither did the fans.

As a parent, you want to raise your kids to have confidence. At the same time, though, you want them to be humble, kind and self-aware. We tried to instill in our boys that no one likes a bragger. We said it's great to be proud of yourself but not great to be full of yourself. There's a difference!

Throughout my career, I've been extremely fortunate to not only work with, but also become friends with, some incredibly impressive executives, many of whom are humble, genuine, kind, brilliant, and confident. I've also been lucky enough (or shall I say unlucky enough?) to work with professionals who have grotesquely inflated egos. During conversations with those people, I'm often reminded of a precious nugget of advice one of my first bosses ever gave. He said, "Always have quiet confidence." How right he was! There are definitely many professionals who know the difference between confidence and cockiness. But I've worked with plenty who either don't know the difference or simply don't care. I can wholeheartedly tell you that confidence is great, especially when you're a candidate interviewing for a job! Cockiness and overt bragging, on the other hand, typically don't sit well with hiring managers. Professionals who gloat about every single thing tend to quickly turn off those making hiring decisions. Earlier, I stressed how crucial it is to highlight results in terms of what sets professionals apart from one another. While we need to focus on results, there is a positive way to articulate them with confidence. And conversely, there's a negative / braggadocious-ey way, which can be perceived as obnoxious. Be careful and keep this in check! Those who believe they're capable of and have accomplished *ALL* things, including parting the sea, won't win too many fans.

Be confident, not cocky. Note, when you brag too much, it becomes sus (as the kids say). There's a fine line you mustn't cross. Position your successes appropriately, but keep in mind that no one operates independently. We're not in vacuums. There are always contributing people and / or factors helping one achieve along the way. So, take notice—do you say "I" and "me" about every accomplishment, while never saying "we," "our," or "us"? You can't possibly achieve everything by yourself. Thus, it's important to recognize the roles others play in your successes. Remember, we're all human and we all put our pants on one leg at a time. People like to hire professionals who don't have to receive all the credit all the time. Braggers are annoying!

Mind Your Manners

MANNERS AREN'T SOMETHING learned in early childhood only to be forgotten (or disregarded) over time. Manners are extremely important; after all, they tell us a lot about someone. Just as good manners make a wonderful impression, bad manners, or even a lack of manners, can quickly lead to a negative impression. And, believe it or not, in the world of job searching / interviewing, manners really do make a difference. Manners are definitely one area where "nice guys" don't finish last! You may not realize this, but in a job search setting, people truly do pay close attention to the manners of others, and I frequently receive feedback from clients in this area. Way more often than you'd guess!

For example, I've had clients highlight if a certain professional was extremely polite to their administrative assistant, the doorman, and / or other people within the company or building. In fact, a while back, there were two executives who were neck and neck in a search we were conducting. One of the deciding factors as to who got the offer came down to the manners of a candidate. One professional was extremely thoughtful toward others whom he came into contact with during his day of face-to-face interviews at the client's office. Throughout the day, he was polite, said please and thank you, smiled, and said hello to people who passed by him. He was a true gentleman. He held doors open, helped a woman carry heavy boxes to her car, and let others get on and off elevators first. These gestures were noticed, and the impression they made on the hiring manager helped to separate him from the other candidate. Ultimately, his manners were what tipped the scales in his favor, and he was the candidate they extended the offer to! It goes without saying: you should always be polite and have good manners because it's the right thing to do. Aside from that, the bonus of being polite is that others notice. All things being equal, good manners can be the game changer working in your favor.

Remember to Say Please and Thank You

SAYING PLEASE AND THANK YOU... it's pretty basic, fairly simple, yet widely underutilized. When people feel appreciated, they tend to be more inclined to help others. This is a well-known fact. It's rather astounding how often people seem to expect others to do things for them yet really don't seem too appreciative of the person's efforts. If you want people to help you, say those three little magic words, "please" and "thank you," so people know you recognize all they're doing for you.

In life, we often talk about how the little things make the biggest difference. In a job search as well as in an interview process, little things can become big. Above and beyond simply speaking those three words aloud, taking a minute to send a quick thank-you note via email is a must! This is nonnegotiable. If someone helps you, without question and without hesitation, thank them. Period! Even if someone is a friend, requesting something with a "please" and acknowledging them with a "thank you" is important. When you're in a job search and / or interview process, these are basics you cannot skip. I'll tell you what you need to know.

A nice touch beyond merely sending an email is to craft a handwritten thank-you note and send it via "snail mail." People don't do this often enough, and believe me, a handwritten note is a simple way to make someone feel recognized and appreciated. In addition, you'll definitely stand out from the crowd. I realize due to remote work becoming so popular, this may be impossible to do. So, don't worry if you can't. Regardless, here's a bit more on thank-you notes...

Be forewarned, I'm going to tell you thank you notes are a must for basically every interaction. But, pay attention. Whether you're asking someone for their help or you've just had an interview, send a thank-you note. Every time you have a conversation with someone who is involved in an interview process (even if the conversation was impromptu and unexpected), you must always send an email to thank the person. I know, I know…you're rolling your eyes. But, a quick thank you is important. By the way, if you want to really stand out, send a thank-you to any admins who assist you. Often their jobs can be thankless and it means more than you could know when you take a second to recognize them for their efforts.

From a timing perspective, the jury is (somewhat) out as to when a thank-you note must be in the other person's inbox. I'm a firm believer that thank-you notes need to be sent within twenty-four hours. This means, after an interview, conversation, or meeting, the thank-you note must exit your outbox and hit the other person's inbox within a twenty-four-hour period. And as mentioned above, if at all possible, a handwritten note is a nice compliment to the email sent. Obviously the handwritten note will take longer to be received, and this is reason the email is nonnegotiable. And yes, in our COVID / post-COVID world, fewer people are working from a company's office, which means sending thank-yous via snail mail is a lot more challenging than pre-COVID. Handwritten might not be an option.

Whatever you do, do not underestimate the importance of this step in the interview process. Thank-you notes serve as a representation of your follow-up skills, speak to both your level of interest in the position and your level of professionalism, and provide decision-makers with insight as to the quality of your work. It's safe to say if you take longer than twenty-four hours to email a thank-you, many hiring managers will frown upon this. I have heard every excuse in the book as to why a thank-you note wasn't sent in a timely fashion, and quite frankly, unless there was a medical or family emergency, there is no acceptable reason. (By the way, I have too many examples to count of times when thank-you notes were sent well past the twenty-four-hour mark and negatively impacted a candidate's ranking. It happens!)

Thank-you notes should not be painstakingly difficult to write. Now, I'm not suggesting you rush through the process and send out meaningless babble. You definitely need to create a note that is not only professional but that stands out and is memorable.

Note: A poorly crafted thank-you can certainly do more harm than good, so it is critical these are created with care. Typos, poor grammar, punctuation errors—these can and often will damage your candidacy! On the flip side, an articulate thank-you note can help to advance your candidacy. I look at the thank-you note like a bow on a beautifully wrapped present or the cherry on top of an ice cream sundae—it brings everything together.

My parents always said I had to have the last word. Well, guess what? This is your opportunity to get in the "last word"! (No wonder I'm such a huge fan of them!) As many job search experts will state, thank-yous are where you can do any OR all of the following:

- Underscore your candidacy by restating how you will add immediate and long-term value to the company and team.
- State something you didn't get a chance to say during the interview but wished you'd said.
- Clarify any points you feel you may not have articulated clearly during your interview.

While you don't want to go overboard with lengthy thank-you notes, a nice, crisp, succinct, and impressive thank-you note that's a few paragraphs long (my preference is no more than a third of a page) will help you differentiate yourself from the competition. While this was already mentioned, I can't help but stress the importance of being hypervigilant about spelling, typos, grammar, and punctuation. It's really sad and rather alarming how many thank-you notes are sent with errors. We've already covered how such errors can make-or-break your candidacy. So take time to double and triple-check your work.

Here are the properties of a great thank-you note:

- It's personalized to each individual interviewer and is specific to the particular opportunity. It should not be some canned, generic, standard thank-you that appears to be one you've sent to every interviewer you've ever met. That's tacky.
- It highlights what *you* can do for the company / hiring manager and why they should hire *you*. It should not address all of the reasons why the opportunity is good for you. Keep in mind hiring managers are less likely to

be concerned about what they can do for you and are much more interested to know what *you* can and will do for *them*.
- It's not a novel. People have short attention spans.
- It's typo-free. Spelling, grammar, and punctuation all matter.

Candidates often ask me what the proper protocol is for sending thank-you notes after participating in a group interview, where there are multiple people in attendance interviewing the candidate at the same time. My recommendation is to send each person an individualized thank-you note stating something specific to that person. This is much more personal than sending one thank-you addressed to the whole group. While sending to the group is certainly better than nothing, taking the time to personalize each thank-you note / email is more professional and a nicer touch. Now, you don't need to make every thank-you note completely different. Simply adding a couple sentences specific to each interviewer will accomplish the goal of personalizing while saving you from reinventing the wheel with each note.

To summarize, use your manners! Please and thank you are three words you should both say and write with frequency!

Don't Eat Like a Pig

CHEWING WITH YOUR MOUTH CLOSED and not talking with your mouth full are manners my mother was overly strict about. In our house, these were rules you simply didn't break (or you got a death stare like none you'd ever seen before). My kids will tell you I'm critical of this faux pas too! I can imagine not every mother is as vigilant, but many children are taught proper dinner table etiquette. Things like, put the napkin in your lap, chew your food with your mouth closed, do not talk with food in your mouth, use your napkin to wipe your mouth (not your sleeve), no elbows on the table, etc., are all accepted as pretty common rules of the dinner table road.

In business, people tend to "break bread" together. During an interview process, many companies will take a candidate to lunch or dinner as it's a wonderful way to really get to know someone in a less formal setting. Unfortunately, once outside the four walls of a company's office space, many professionals forget the fact that they are still interviewing. I'm sure you've already assumed I've got a list a mile long of all sorts of crazy things that have happened during interviews, and some of the funnier stories stem from lunches and dinners clients have held with candidates. To put it bluntly, it's fair to say on more than one occasion, I've wondered whether or not a candidate was raised in a barn. Sadly, there are many people with horrible table manners, and many candidacies have been negatively impacted because of this.

In some cultures, eating everything with your hands is acceptable. In our culture, we use silverware. In some cultures, it is common practice to pick up a soup bowl and drink from it. In our culture, we eat soup with a spoon. In some cultures, slurping loudly is commonplace. In our culture, not so much. In some cultures, it might be deemed acceptable behavior to reach your arm across someone's plate to grab the salt or the butter. In our culture, it's frowned upon. I'm not sure if there are any cultures that tie professional status to how loudly someone chews (or *chomps*!) their food. But I'm confident our culture does not embrace chewing, smacking, gnawing, or chomping one's food at sound levels remotely audible to those sitting at another table. Nor am I aware of any culture that embraces having food all over one's face. I don't know…maybe there's a culture somewhere on this earth where people who get food all over their faces while eating are revered. Maybe it's a means to elevate one's place in society? However, I'm 99.9 percent certain that, in civilized nations, food all over your face is considered totally gross / borderline repulsive. Clearly, these things aren't acceptable in our culture, so don't do them! Stop eating like a pig! Use proper table manners!

Eat slowly, carefully, and respectfully. It's not a contest of who can eat the fastest.

No one wants to see the food in your mouth as you chew it, and certainly no one wants any of that food flying their way because you're talking with your mouth full.

No one wants to look at salad dressing all over your lips and face.

No one wants to hear you chomping every bite of your food.

And no one wants to hear you slurp soups or beverages from a mile away.

While I'm on a roll, let me also home in on those of you who love to chew the ice from the beverage you're drinking. While your mouth may be cool, you likely won't be if you chomp on ice! Don't do it!

Make wise food choice selections in these situations. Now is not the time to order a slab of ribs. Maybe skip the spaghetti and meatballs and order pasta that's a bit less tricky to eat so a rogue noodle isn't smacking you in the face or hitting your shirt. While you may love a juicy bone-in pork chop, you can order it, but don't you dare pick up the bone and gnaw on it like you always do when in the privacy of your own home.

In interview settings (and, quite frankly, regardless of the setting), one should always remember proper table manners, and one should always be polite. This includes how you act toward the host / hostess, the wait staff, and all others working within a restaurant (or other patrons). When on an interview, every little thing matters and will potentially affect an outcome. I've had candidates cut from a process because they were rude toward the waitstaff. Not good!

Speaking of manners, let's switch gears a bit and talk about interviews that are not in person. Let's start with phone interviews. Did you know there's proper phone etiquette?

I'm not sure why anyone thinks it's OK to eat food or chew gum while on a phone interview, because it isn't! Even if you ask the person you're speaking with if it's OK for you to eat during the call and they give you their blessing, it's still not OK! Trust me, they're just being polite. No one wants to hear it. I have yet to meet someone who isn't perturbed by the noise of someone biting into food and chewing it on the other end of the phone. I assure you this is incredibly annoying and completely distracting! Not to mention that sometimes it sounds absolutely disgusting in the listener's ear. For some people, it's literally like listening to nails on a chalkboard (misophonia is a real condition!). You should want the interviewer focused on what you're saying, not what you're chewing. In addition, sucking on candy is only OK if you have an awful cough and need a cough drop. Otherwise, have some self-restraint and refrain from eating, sucking, or chewing during a phone interview! If you absolutely must eat, do yourself and your audience a favor and mute your phone because I can promise you, as quiet as you think you're being, everyone can hear you. And it's gross!

In addition, when on a phone interview, it's rather rude and, again, completely annoying and distracting when someone is clearly doing housework during a call. I've interviewed people while they've washed dishes, started loads of laundry, run up and down flights of stairs, cleaned windows, rearranged closets, started springcleaning, prepped veggies for dinner, etc. I can absolutely appreciate a good multitasker (if there even is such a thing!), but this is inappropriate. Period. End of story. This is not the right time. It comes across as unprofessional and tells the interviewer you don't take their process seriously. You wouldn't do all this during a meeting. During an interview, professionals should be focused, engaged in the conversation, and hopefully taking notes. Keep in mind that those who are so busy getting stuff done while interviewing via phone are setting themselves up for a lot more free time to get even more stuff done, because their odds of advancing in a process have greatly declined.

Oh, and by the way, please refrain from exercising while on a phone interview too. I'm glad you're trying to stay in shape, but listening to someone pant heavily into the phone is not only bizarre and creepy; it's also unprofessional. I shouldn't have to say this, but walking your dog during an interview is bad timing too.

Bottom line is that all manners matter. That includes table manners!

Use Common Courtesy

IT'S EASY TO get self-absorbed when in a job search. Afterall, it's typically a very stressful time. Plus, we all know how hectic life is, and often our minds are focused on twenty-five things at any given time. However, part of "minding your manners" is remembering to use common courtesy by showing others you care about them. If you're reaching out to someone and / or responding to an email, it goes a long way to have some common courtesy and ask the person how they are. If you know they have a family, asking about them is courteous. If you know they were recently ill, asking or commenting to show you care is kind. It's courteous.

Showing you care, even just a tiny bit, goes a very long way. A quick example—I worked on a search. We were filling a senior-level marketing position. I really liked a particular candidate who made it far down the path but ultimately wasn't selected. I felt terrible about it, but fortunately the candidate truly understood and appreciated all I did throughout the process with him. We agreed to stay in touch. Because we spent so much time together, we learned a lot about each other's families, etc. It seemed we really connected and I truly liked him. Subsequent to the process, I checked in with him numerous times just to say hi and find out how things were going. Every single response he sent was a couple sentences long. He provided me with a brief update on his search, his life and then would close by saying, "Please keep me in mind for any future searches." Not once did he ask about me, my family or my business. I know it's hard because we're all moving two million miles per hour, but it takes one second to type such a sentence every now and then. After a while, people do take notice of little things like this. And many ultimately prefer to work with those who show they care. Remember that and use common courtesy.

Many candidates have reached out and expressed frustration that we don't have roles / searches for them. We gently remind them that we're hired by and paid by companies to help them with specific hiring needs and when we have a search that might align, we'll be sure to reach out. Essentially, we remind them that we don't job search on behalf of individuals. No matter how nicely we position this, there are some who still express frustration or who get downright angry that we don't have any opportunities to discuss. Ironically, they never seem to ask how they can help us in return. They never even offer to help. They love to take, but never to give. Some professionals get frustrated when calls and / or emails aren't returned immediately. Frequently people fail to recognize they're not the only person we work with and that they will sometimes have to wait just a little bit when trying to get our attention. Again, we all have a lot going on, but be courteous of others. Especially when you want their help.

Watch Your Mouth— Don't Use Bad Words

DON'T CUSS IN AN INTERVIEW.

    Never.
    Ever.
    F*cking.
    Cuss.
    In.
    An.
    Interview.

Seriously, I don't care how comfortable you are with the interviewer, don't swear. Even if the interviewer does, you don't! Or you could f*ck it up. Got it? (This is one of those "do as I say, not as I do" situations.) It hasn't happened often, but we have had clients take candidates out of consideration because they used a swear word (or two) in an interview. It's a total shame when a four-letter word undermines your candidacy. Mind your manners and save the colorful language for later.

No One Likes a Crybaby

GROWING UP, were you a crybaby? Did you know any crybabies? As a mom, I've come to realize just how annoying crybabies are. No one likes a crybaby!

Many of those colloquialisms we've heard since birth, such as "Life is hard" and "Life isn't fair," are very true. From a young age, we quickly learn life is truly hard—there are going to be good times and bad times. The tough times are…well, they're tough. Not fun. When bad economic times recover and go into the "good times," there are still people getting laid off and companies going out of business, downsizing, rightsizing, etc. Good people can lose their jobs. A lot of crappy and unfair things happen in the work world. It's life. And it can be hard.

As empathetic as people can be, I assure you in a job search and / or interview situation, no one likes a crybaby! No one wants to hear yet another sob story. My mother used to say, "Sweetheart, whining is simply not becoming," and, boy, was she right! Not only is it not becoming, but it can also be flat-out annoying! Most people reading this can attest to the fact that bad things can and do happen to really great people. During the economic crisis of 2008 and during the pandemic, there were millions of extremely talented people who were laid off through no fault of their own. They found themselves in a brutal job market seeking employment. Those were very difficult times! You had to be coldhearted to not sympathize with those people. Bad times eventually get better. But, better times will eventually get badder (not a word, I know!) again.

Regardless of whether times are good or bad, our 24-7 news cycles will always play up the negatives, and people are barraged with endless stories that are depressing, unsettling, and, at times, downright scary. Everyone is surrounded by doom and gloom constantly because that's what sells. So, what's my point? Well, I can promise you, interviewers and hiring managers are not excited to hear lots of doom / gloom / negativity from those they meet.

In the laws of human nature, we know people are more attracted to happier, upbeat individuals. When given the choice, most people would rather not hang out with negative, mopey, whining individuals who play the victim card any chance they get. Everyone's life has ups and downs, and none of us knows the trials and tribulations others have faced. In the work world, it's important to keep things professional. Hearing a candidate bitch and moan about how crappy things are or how unfair this or that was is exhausting and a quick way to cause an interviewer to want to cut the conversation short.

Life isn't fair!

There will always be someone who has more money, has more connections, has a higher IQ, has better looks, is funnier, is taller, is shorter, is better at sports, is better at the arts, has access to better schools, has a less dysfunctional family, has cuter feet, has a better voice, has a faster metabolism, has a better sense of style, has more confidence, is more popular, is more worldly, is more well-read, is better at debating, is better at math or science, went to a better college, had more access to technology, got to play more video games, had cooler gym shoes growing up, or...I could go on and on for days.

Do yourself a favor.

Let it go! Sing it, think it, say it out loud. You gotta let it go.

Back when I was twenty-one and just starting out, I was told by a mentor of mine that luck doesn't just happen. He said luck comes to those who work hard and work smart. He said people create their own luck.

So rather than thinking about all the things you don't have, start embracing what you do have! Adjust your attitude and put the energy you're wasting on whining toward working hard. Also, keep in mind, in today's world, we have access to so much information. So if there's a skill or a degree or something you're missing experience-wise, see if you can figure out a way to learn it. Is there an online class? A video? A book? I know it's not always as easy as just reading an article, watching a YouTube video, or taking a class. But the lesson here is a simple one—when interviewing, don't drone on and on about all the terrible and unjust things that have happened to you. Don't blame the world and give a sob story. Save it for a therapist or friend. Think of interviewing like you would dating. When you first start dating someone, you typically put your best foot forward. Early in a relationship, most people know not to dump out all their baggage because doing so can scare someone off. Am I right? Well, it's the same thing when interviewing. Whining about your life and the situation(s) you've found / find yourself in is not going to help you advance your candidacy. Yes, you need to be yourself in an interview, but I highly recommend being the most positive version of yourself. This will help you move an interview process forward versus derail it. Plus, if you think yourself happy, you'll become happier, and happier people are healthier, so it's good all around! Sometimes you need to convince yourself to be happy and that's OK!

I recall a conversation with someone I was interviewing for a senior-level position. This person had been laid off a few months prior to our call and shared how he'd been actively searching for a new job ever since. When I asked him how his job search was going, he replied with something like: "It is so f*cking frustrating. I'm getting sick of it. No, actually, I'm not 'getting,' I am sick of it! I am so sick of it!! I am so sick and tired of every flippin' company having some jerk who decides they don't like me for some dumb reason and that one person ruins the whole thing for me. It is ridiculous! It's SO unfair! And it's completely maddening that it keeps happening to ME!"

He bitched for another minute or two, and as he was ranting on and on, his tone grew angrier. He was worked up! Can you guess what I was thinking? In case you need my help, let me break it down for you. My first thought was "Wow! Do not give him anything with caffeine."

Then my next thought was "Ugh! I do feel bad for you, but there's no way I could ever present you to a client of mine. If you said this or something similar to this during an interview, my client would question my ability to evaluate talent."

My next thought(s) revolved around figuring out how to get off the call without pissing him off any further, because…well, because his anger was palpable, and I could feel him seething through the phone. He started to scare me a bit. I mean, this man's voice was totally shaking, and I didn't want to cause him to completely erupt.

Now, if he'd gotten himself together and said something like, "Oh, man. I'm sorry! I just went off, and I don't know why I said all of that, especially in such an aggressive tone. I'm really sorry!" then maybe, just maybe, I could have worked with him. But he didn't. Clearly, he felt justified in his anger and was standing by what he said.

Yes, the old saying "Misery loves company" might hold true in some settings, but definitely not in an interview setting. Letting others in on your challenges, misfortunes, disappointments, heartaches, and woes will likely send them running in the opposite direction. I realize this is easier said than done, and sometimes we can all get carried away. But if you catch yourself in a "woe-is-me" moment, try to pivot quickly and change your tune. However, if you're so upset you can't control it, then you're not ready to have conversations and need to wait until you can get your emotions in check.

Don't be a crybaby! Get yourself together and keep your thoughts positive! Don't be a victim. Take control of what you can. Keep the laws of attraction in the back of your mind, and remember, people are always more attracted to individuals who are positive and upbeat. When you drone on and on about things such as how unfair this world is, how you've been unjustly victimized, and / or how no one will hire you, I can pretty much bet the farm that you're giving people cause for concern. Seriously—after hearing you moan about how no one will hire you, do you really think a hiring manager will walk away from the conversation feeling convinced that, even though no other company is willing to hire you, they should be the one to roll the dice and take the risk by offering you employment within their organization?

Clearly, an interview is not the appropriate time for a bitch session or pity party. Don't be a crybaby! Pull it together, think good thoughts, and exude positive energy into the universe so positive things can and will come back to you!

Sometimes You Win, Sometimes You Lose, Sometimes It Rains

BULL DURHAM, ANYONE? That's where this quote comes from.

"Sometimes you win, and sometimes you lose." That's the quote I remember from when I was a kid. The "sometimes it rains" quote came along later, when the movie *Bull Durham* coined that phrase.

When growing up, if you played sports or participated in contests or games of any kind, you learned how fun it is to win and how crappy it is to lose. As a mom, I learned how hard it is to teach a child how to lose and how to lose gracefully. And truth be told, as a parent it's also important to teach your children how to win because there is an art to that as well. We've all met sore winners and sore losers, right?

In job searching and interviewing, sometimes you win and sometimes you lose. At times it can feel like you lose a lot more than you win. As discussed, job searching and interviewing are really hard! In my fifteen-plus years of being in this field, I honestly can't think of one person who has told me their job search was easy. And what that means is you need to be prepared to sometimes win, to sometimes lose, *and* to know it sometimes rains. (I will discuss each part of the quote… keep reading!)

Rejection in any form is not pleasant, but job searching is typically full of rejection—*a lot* of rejection! Therefore, you need to prepare yourself to deal with this unfortunate reality. Are you someone who takes literally everything to heart? Do you take everything personally? Or are you someone with a tougher exterior? Have you had a lot of experience handling rejection in a professional setting? If you're a seasoned salesperson, you should be equipped to deal with ups and downs. Even so, you may find yourself being tested on this front. So what can you do to arm yourself with the right skills to aid you in getting through the tougher patches, the losses? If you know you're not great at handling rejection, do some homework. Undoubtedly there are books, TED Talks, videos, podcasts, and more all addressing this very topic. If you have any friends, family, or (ex-) colleagues who either are currently in or recently went through a job search, seek them out. Or form a group where you can support one another. Ask for advice on how people dealt with the losses, the rejection.

For me, one of the things I always lean on to help, especially when times are hard, is humor. I encourage people to try to find the humor in anything they can. I have a million stories I could share (but won't!) about people's job searches / interviews. Please note—finding humor does not mean you're completely minimizing or disregarding how challenging job searching / interviewing can be and how difficult the rejection(s) / losses can be. Mental health is a real issue in society, and a tough job search can really take a toll on every aspect of your life. Hence, you must figure out how to best handle the tough times because they're inevitable. Just to be sure we're all on the same page, a "loss" can be in reference to things like:

- not finding any good opportunities during a window of time you sat down to job search;
- finding an opportunity and applying only to be told the job was already filled;
- applying and never hearing back;
- having a great exchange / conversation and then being ghosted;
- a hiring manager telling you you're doing great and being advanced in an interview process, but that doesn't actually happen;
- having an unproductive meeting / interview / networking event; or
- being told you're not the finalist getting the job offer, the other candidate is.

On the other side, there are times when you'll "win." And by winning, I'm not only referring to getting job offers. Winning can mean things such as:

- getting a response to an outreach (typically positive responses are the better kind here);
- scheduling an interview / meeting / event;
- having a great interview / meeting / event;
- finding out there's an opportunity you didn't know about that could be good for you;
- being told you're advancing in a process;
- being a finalist advancing to the offer stage; or
- receiving an offer / accepting an offer.

You're possibly wondering why I'm going to spend a minute on "winning" as this is undoubtedly good, right? Well, yes, but there are some challenges in winning you need to be cognizant of. When something good happens, you can feel like you're "winning." And as such, it's natural for people to consciously and unconsciously "take their foot off the gas," which can serve as a special invitation for Murphy's Law to rear its ugly head. Let me expand with a few examples.

Let's say you had a great interview with Company A that ended at 2:00 p.m. on Tuesday. You leave the interview, and you feel great. Because of how well that interview went, you may decide to blow off the remainder of the day. Perhaps you had planned to log a few more hours of job searching, but now you decide to go to the gym and then meet a few friends for a drink. OK, that's terrific! I'm a big fan of making sure you celebrate the little milestones (in addition to the big ones). However, in a situation like this one, it can be really easy to lose focus and get out of the good habits you developed. I counsel people about the importance of doing the right things every day because that's what's going to net you good results. Continuing with this example, let's say you go to the gym, have a great workout, meet friends for drinks, and go to bed a little late. The next morning, maybe you wake up and decide you're not going to do the couple hours of job searching before lunch you normally do because you're feeling very optimistic. You may know firsthand that it's awfully easy to get out of good habits quickly. As you can see, this can become a slippery slope quickly derailing your productivity. Now, what if this company that you're feeling so great about calls you in a day or two to let you know they aren't actually moving you forward (for whatever reason)? You've lost a lot of time job searching. You once were winning. Now you're losing. UGH!

Let's add another example: In the aforementioned situation, where you had a great interview at Company A on Tuesday...let's say this job with Company A is one you're *really* excited about. You can totally see yourself there. Knowing this, you may decide to back out of other opportunities you're exploring because they aren't as exciting. Advice I give every job searcher is "Don't put all your eggs in one basket" (in this case Company A's basket). Thus, you never want to explore and solely rely on only one opportunity. Now, if you know deep down that an opportunity with, let's say, Company B is definitely one you would *never* take, then yes, cut it out of the mix. *But* if you don't yet know enough about Company B to make such an assessment or if you desperately need a job, then keep pursuing Company B. Things go sideways all the time, and you don't want to get caught flat-footed if the Company A opportunity suddenly disappears for any of a variety of reasons. I've seen this happen so many times, and it's never fun.

Sticking with this example. Let's say there's no Company B yet. The only opportunity you're focused on is with Company A. Without one iota of doubt, you need to be working your tail off to find more opportunities. If you're a salesperson, you're familiar with this concept; this is referred to as filling your pipeline. This means, you need to find as many viable opportunities as you can because some will be interesting, some won't, and some won't move forward, etc. So despite Company A, you need to be working really hard to find other opportunities. And you need to work as if you don't yet have a Company A. This means you can't half-ass how hard you work on your job search. Some people will think, "I have Company A in the works; I don't need to put the pedal to the metal to find other opportunities. I'll look, but I won't look as hard as I would if I had nothing going." *Ummmm*—in the words of Julia Roberts's character Vivian, "*Big mistake! Big! Huge!*" Again, we never want to put all our eggs in one basket, or even just two baskets. Keep your head down and focus on filling your pipeline. By the way, success breeds success. When things are good, normally more good things happen. The universe knows it, and it's amazing how things start to come together. Use the good to find more good and ride the wave.

In addition to making sure you're working hard on your job search, when good things are happening and you're feeling like you're "winning," you need to pay attention to your attitude. Don't get cocky. You can have confidence. Confidence is great. But cockiness will turn people off. If you're not sure whether or not you come across cocky or with too much arrogance, ask some friends and colleagues. We all know someone who will tell you the truth. Ask them!

OK, so we've covered the importance of knowing how to deal with your wins and losses, so let's address the "sometimes it rains" part. What does "sometimes it rains" mean? In baseball, we know some games get called off before they even start due to rain.

Other games might get called off midgame due to rain. Putting this into the context of job searching and interviewing, I'm viewing "sometimes it rains" as sometimes things get cancelled, stalled out or put on hold. You haven't necessarily won or lost yet. But things get delayed. I've been through enough economic downturns to know that many companies will either cancel searches or put them on hold for an indefinite period of time. When this has happened and candidates were in the interview process having success, some of them wanted to sit tight and wait for the opportunity to "come back to life". Certainly, some people can do this. Those who can are typically employed and aren't actively looking because they're not miserable in their job but see something compelling about my client's opportunity. For that reason, they're fine sticking with their current day job and waiting for this to come to fruition. I'll tell them we can stay in touch but to remain open to learning about other opportunities because you never know when another amazing one might appear. On the other hand, I've had candidates who were either miserable in their current job or unemployed. When my search was put on hold, some would want to wait for the search to relaunch because they were really excited about the opportunity. My advice is: *Do not do that!* You never know when a search will relaunch, and in my experience, it's never as early as the company predicts. So you could be waiting a long time. Sometimes it never relaunches. For that reason, you must continue to look and write off this opportunity. You can stay in touch, but do not count on that one. Move on! Sometimes it rains!

In job searching and interviewing, it's always a mixed bag. You're going to have good days and bad, steps forward and steps backward, successes and failures, *and* you'll have things that fall into the middle. You need to learn how to deal with all of it because it's an emotional roller coaster, and you need to be ready. Unfortunately, many professionals admit they didn't anticipate how difficult this time can be on their emotions. If you've been diagnosed with anxiety and / or depression, please make sure you're taking good care of yourself. Pay close attention…you may need extra help and support. For others, this time in your life can bring on never-experienced-before bouts of anxiety / depression, especially if your search takes a while. Please know that this is normal and seek some help. I know this is easier said than done, but anxiety and depression aren't always easy to handle by yourself, and you might need to find professional support. There's no shame in that. I always say those who admit they need help are actually the bravest and strongest. I can't tell you how many times people have confidentially admitted they'd always been super happy but their job search sent them into a dark place. By the way, I've been medicated for depression for over twenty years. So I come at this as someone who is supersensitive to mental health and the toll stressful times can take on one's well-being. While many think they should be able to simply shake it off, it's not so easy to do. Keep in mind, mental health issues can impact your ability to do your best work. From job searching to interviewing, you want to be your very best you. If you're sinking into a bad place, it'll be increasingly difficult to "show up" on a daily basis. Good news is, it's now easier than ever to find some help. And trust me, if the first place you go / the first person you talk to isn't right, don't give up. It might take talking with more than one therapist to find your match. And if you need some medication, it might take trying a few before you find the right one for you. Also, remember, once you're beyond this stage, you may find you no longer need help. Those professionals I referenced who acknowledged their job searches sent them into dark places *all* got back to their old selves once they landed in their new roles and got settled. Remember, there will be ups and downs, highs and lows. Take care of yourself throughout it all.

Share

WE ALL NEED TO SHARE. Sharing is a skill instilled in us at a very young age. When my kids were little, I found myself telling them the same thing my parents told me: "If you don't share, no one will want to play with you." As you know, sharing isn't something only little children need to remain mindful of. In fact, when we are adults, sharing is absolutely still a thing.

I'm a big fan of karma and believe in doing good things because that's what we're supposed to do. I also believe a wonderful by-product of doing good deeds is that good things will happen to you in return. You may be wondering what in the world sharing has to do with job searching and interviewing. Well, it's pretty simple. When professionals find themselves in transition, many become inwardly focused. People think only of themselves and are often either oblivious to or blatantly opt not to help their fellow job searching friends. For example, information about open positions is a simple thing to pass along to others, yet many fail to do so. In addition, making relevant introductions only takes a few minutes and can go such a long way, but many don't take the time to facilitate these.

Another way professionals who are job searching can share is by providing others with useful tips and best practices. Imparting wisdom is always a good thing! I see so many professionals keep information private that could be incredibly advantageous to their peers. To me, this is so strange. Why wouldn't you share information? In my mind, if I share with others, they'll be more likely to share with me. One hand washes the other, right?

Sharing can also mean sharing your time, your empathy, your ear, your hugs. Sometimes people just need a friend to listen and lean on. Thus, sharing your time and giving your ear goes a long way. Being there for others will do good for them, and for you too.

Sitting in my seat for as long as I have, I've repeatedly seen when professionals find themselves "in transition," they tend to come out of the woodwork fast. It's inevitable. One of the first things they will do is quickly reach out to everyone they know to find out who can and will help them. Naturally, those who've previously demonstrated their willingness to help and share their time are the ones who will receive a much warmer reception. They will find that many will gladly go out of their way to be of assistance. I've heard professionals tell me the most wonderful stories about what friends and colleagues have done to aid them in their times of need. On the flip side, there are many professionals who, when all was good in their world and they were gainfully employed, habitually ignored emails and calls from friends, colleagues, and acquaintances who were seeking their assistance. Undoubtedly, when these individuals find themselves sitting on the other side of the desk, they'll face the harsh reality—others may not be overly zealous about sharing their time and helping. Net-net, because we all need the help of others from time to time, my suggestion is to be conscientious about sharing your insights, connections, and time with others. Help people…share!!

That said, I realize I've spent a lot of time talking about how people don't have much free time. So yes, you do need to be protective of your time. No one expects you to share all of your time helping others. But don't completely ignore people when they reach out to you. Respond! Take a few minutes to help. Sharing time, information, contacts, your ear and your friendship is the right thing to do. Bonus is that it will undoubtedly pay off in spades. Don't ignore people because—believe me—the day will come when you'll need someone's assistance and / or guidance. And when that day comes, those who've ignored others will likely find themselves on an island all alone.

Comb Your Hair

GROWING UP, I had really long hair and vividly remember my mom combing it each day. She always used this detangling spray because knots were constantly in my hair, it smelled so good! I remember my mom saying combing hair and brushing teeth were a must before leaving the house each day.

While a lot has changed about me over the years, one thing has remained constant, and that is I look like a total freak when I wake up in the morning. I don't know about you, but my hair is so messed up it looks like I was standing in the midst of a category 5 hurricane for a good hour. I'm not sure exactly what happens while I'm sleeping, but I'm fairly certain I spend a portion of every night having an intense wrestling match with my covers and pillows, and sadly, I don't think I've ever won. Before I leave the house, I assure you, simply combing my hair isn't enough to make me look even slightly decent. Since a baseball hat is usually frowned upon in a business setting, it takes effort and time to look presentable. I'm just not one of those who can roll out of bed and go. My guess is most people know whether or not they've been blessed with the ability to wake up and go. I wasn't.

I think most professionals have heard the news and know that people are partially judged on appearance, right? Like it or not, this is the cold, hard truth. For this reason, isn't it common sense to think about your appearance and try to look your best when walking into an interview? I'm not suggesting you need to be dolled up. But, can you please take a shower, comb your hair, and give yourself enough time so that prior to walking into an interview, you have a minute to check yourself out in a bathroom mirror? If you see your hair looks messed up, fix it! While you're at it, wipe the lipstick off your teeth, clean the mud off your shoes, tuck your shirt in, smooth out wrinkles in your clothes, and try your best to look presentable! If you don't live in the same building where an interview is being held, the chances are fairly high that you've had to go outside in order to get there. Whether you had to walk a great distance or only had to walk across the street, you likely faced some of "the elements." So make sure you don't look like you just walked through a windstorm; straighten yourself up and look professional!

By the way, looking professional does not mean you have to spend a fortune on designer suits, shoes, expensive makeup and / or hairstylists. Just look like you tried. Look like you took a shower. Look like you didn't pull whatever your wearing out of the bottom of your dirty clothes hamper. And, in case you're curious, when people ask me about what proper interview attire is, I always recommend asking the person setting up the interview what their business attire is. Get their opinion on how you should be dressed. It's a simple question: "What is your proper business attire?" Personally, I'd rather be overdressed than underdressed. If the company is more formal, you should wear a suit. If the company is completely casual and you know people wear shorts and T-shirts, unless you are given strict instructions to do so, I would not show up for an interview in that same attire. I'd opt for being in slacks and a nice shirt. That way you aren't too formal, but you're showing a level of respect to their process. If they then tell you, "Wear shorts next time. You don't need to be dressed that nicely." OK, then you can wear shorts to the next meeting. To be clear, though, you better be in some nice, clean, hole-free shorts.

In addition to the clothes you're wearing, let's not forget to give consideration to the shoes you'll be putting on your feet. This is frequently overlooked, and it should not be! You may be thinking…do people really pay attention to your shoes? The answer is: yes they do!

I promise you, plenty of professionals will notice your shoes! Shoe shiners are still in business for a reason, so please wear nice shoes! Keep in mind, nice shoes that are all scuffed up are no longer considered nice. I don't care what you paid for them or who the designer is. If they're past their prime and look beat-up, they're no longer nice!

I remember when I was in my early twenties and finally started to make some real money, when I finally wasn't living paycheck to paycheck. I was so excited and proud to be able to splurge on a gorgeous pair of shoes. I'm telling you, these shoes were amazing. They were so incredibly beautiful…for the first six months. Then they started to look worn. The wear and tear was beating them up! After some time, the fact I had on designer shoes no longer mattered because they no longer looked beautiful and expensive. They just looked ratty and tattered. Worn-out nice things are most notably *worn-out*!

As the saying goes, "You only have one chance to make a first impression." First impressions are critical, and like it or not, your appearance is one of the first things someone notices. Set yourself up for success and make a darn good first impression! When going to an interview, clean yourself up so you can look like the very best, most amazing version of you.

Sit Up Straight

SIT UP STRAIGHT. Stop slouching.

We've all heard this a gazillion times, right? I remember a teacher who often said that to be ready to learn, you had to be sitting up straight in the "ready position". I remember that annoyed the crap out of me. But I digress…

Because it's so easy to slouch, people often develop a terrible habit without even knowing it. We're sitting at desks for much of the day and we're constantly looking down at our phones. Not a good combination for sitting up straight.

As adults, theoretically we know good posture is important on many levels. Physically, it's important to sit up straight so our spines don't start to curve. In the professional world, slouching can make someone seem disengaged, insecure, or even deceptive. Thus, in a job search or interview setting, it's really important to be aware of your posture as I'm sure you don't want to inadvertently send those messages to your audience(s). So, when you're interviewing, be sure to sit up straight! You'll convey a sense of confidence and credibility. Interviewers will perceive you as someone who is taking their process seriously and as someone who has genuine interest in the conversation. Body language speaks volumes.

As an executive recruiter, it's not uncommon for me to receive feedback on a candidate's posture. Believe it or not, this does come up, albeit not often, but it does. In today's incredibly casual world, there are many who likely never give one thought to how they're sitting and how it may appear to others. This nugget of advice does seem to apply more to recent college graduates. That said, I've definitely seen my fair share of people across all age groups who sit in ways I'd deem less than professional.

I've heard it all, and that includes feedback around a candidate's posture. Literally, I've had clients highlight the fact that certain candidates were slouching. One candidate, I was told, appeared as though he was going to slide off the edge of his seat. I've also received feedback regarding professionals who were hunched over, with their elbows on their knees, and appeared to be aggressivelike, as if they were ready to dive forward and attack the interviewer. Yikes!

In addition to making sure you're sitting up straight, it behooves you to be conscious of how you position your legs. For anyone wearing a skirt, please cross your legs! No interviewer wants to have flashbacks to Sharon Stone in *Basic Instinct*. (Yes, I just dated myself!) Trust me, you don't want to have a Britney Spears moment! (I dated myself again! I'm not young!!). Also, because everyone's skirts are short these days, when crossing your legs, be mindful of how high the skirt might be on your thigh. AWKWARD! I've been in situations where someone's butt cheek was sticking out. Not comfortable for any interviewer to see. Also, manspreading is real and it really can offend people. Please pay attention to how you're sitting and just sit in your seat like a professional should.

Sit Still and Keep Your Hands to Yourself

GOT ANTS IN YOUR PANTS?

Did you hear this as a child? In school, I clearly remember teachers telling us to sit still and to keep our hands to ourselves. Even though my kids are no longer toddlers, I still remember how hard it was for them to sit still. And by the way, if you've ever sat in front of a toddler on an airplane, you know kids struggle to sit still. Now, with age should come the ability to sit still. I know it can be hard, especially in certain situations. But it actually seems to be a lot more difficult for adults to sit still than I originally thought.

Watching someone fidget can be a bit nerve-racking. Have you ever watched someone do things like nervously pick at their fingers, bite their nails, repeatedly wring their hands together, click their pen nonstop, incessantly tap their pencil, flip their hair every other second, twirl their hair, or constantly move around in their seat? If you have, you know this can make you feel uncomfortable. For that reason, if you're aware of the fact that you do fidgety things, please try to do whatever you can to stop them. You need to try to sit still. I'm sure you know this, but when someone fidgets during an interview, it can be extremely distracting. Rather than focusing on what the candidate is saying, the interviewer's attention can shift toward whatever the person is doing or fidgeting with, which can undermine the candidate. Not only can the candidate's message get lost, but fidgeting tells the interviewer they're stressed, highly anxious and / or uncomfortable. This can, in turn, make the interviewer uncomfortable. If you're someone who tends to fidget, work on this and do your best to sit comfortably in an interview setting. So, how do you do this? Great question! The first thing is to be aware of what you're doing so you can start to notice how often you do it and then work on changing your behavior. For example, if you pick your fingers, try putting on band-aids whenever you're not in public. Have those around you who you trust tell you to stop picking if they notice you doing it. If you're a hair flipper, pull your hair back so you can't flip it. If you're a pen clicker, don't use pens that click. There are often ways to break yourself of your habits. I used to pick my nails when I was nervous and while it took a lot of time (and band-aids), I did break myself of it.

Please note, we know some people have medical conditions preventing them from being able to control their fidgeting / involuntary movements and I am by no means trying to insult them or minimize their condition(s). For example, I have essential tremor. What this means is I will never be a surgeon. No matter how hard I try, my hands shake (tremor). If I'm holding something—for example, a piece of paper or a glass of water (or wine!)—you will see my hand shake and the liquid might spill over if the glass is full. To those who don't know me, I might appear nervous. I've always been embarrassed by this and do what I can to try to hide it. But it's not my fault, it's neurological. And there's not much I can do to control this. (Interestingly, drinking alcohol helps steady my hands, but we all know it isn't helpful to show up to an interview with alcohol in your system.) So, at times, I've had to state to someone, "Hey, I'm not nervous. My hands shake because I have what's called essential tremor. It's a neurological disorder, and while it doesn't impact my ability to think, don't ask me to thread a needle or do your makeup…" That said, I don't always lead with this because I don't want to call attention to it. But if I can tell it's going to be noticeable, I'll address it so that I don't have to be quite as self-conscious about it. I can assure you my friends and I have had many laughs about this, but in public around people I don't know, it isn't funny to me. It's stressful. So I get how involuntary movement can be difficult to control.

There are other medical conditions that can cause someone to have tics or tremors they can't control, and we need to be empathetic toward those too. So, please know that here, in this chapter, I'm speaking to those who are in bad habits and who are capable of controlling their movements. Therefore, if you don't have any medical reasons for clicking a pen twenty times a minute, try not to do it. Or if flipping your hair is just a bad habit, work on it! Or if chewing / picking your fingers has been a lifelong nervous habit, try to find ways to stop. If you haven't been able to completely change your behavior, do the best you can and know there's always more time to work on it.

Moving forward, let's talk about keeping our hands to ourselves, and no, I'm not referring to physically touching anyone. This is geared toward people who love to talk with their hands (this includes arms too)! I'm sure you've witnessed these people—the ones who are very expressive, to the point that while talking, their arms are sometimes flying around so much they look like they might fly. Or even if it's not that dramatic, there are many who tend to gesture with their hands a lot. There's typically a fine line between what's an acceptable amount and what's too much when using one's hands and arms when speaking. I realize many people like to talk with their hands and often don't realize they're even doing so. In fact, I'm someone who loves to talk with my hands (albeit shaky ones), and at times, I talk with both my hands and arms. I honestly didn't realize just how much I did this until I was videotaped during a sales training class I attended early in my career. During one of the sessions, each participant was asked to do a mock presentation, which was then videotaped and critiqued by the class. What I saw on film was really eye-opening. I always knew I gestured with my hands and arms, but when I saw what I actually looked like doing so, I nearly died of embarrassment.

It was that bad!

From that moment, I quickly began to focus on and practice keeping my hands in my lap. I worked very hard at being aware of what my hands and arms were doing until I made noticeable improvement. By the way, I'm not saying to never use your hands. However, if you're someone who tends to use them a lot, you might want to make sure you're not overdoing it. If you are, ask some trusted people to observe you and provide feedback. If they tell you that your use of hands and / or your arms is a bit distracting, then you need to be sure to tone it down a few notches.

Bottom line—if you're a person who tends to fidget and / or you're someone who uses your hands / arms when speaking, try to ensure it's all done within reason because it can potentially distract your audience which can derail your efforts. Listeners may focus more on what your hands or arms are doing versus what you're saying. You want the attention to be on what you say. Not what you do.

Eat Your Fruits and Vegetables

I WAS REALLY so lucky and so blessed to grow up in the house I did where my parents made sure we ate together as a family and we ate a lot of homecooked and healthy food. My mom always emphasized the importance of eating a balanced meal encompassing all food groups and tried to scare us into believing we wouldn't grow if we didn't eat all our fruits and veggies. Also, getting proper sleep was an important thing in our home. Looking back, my parents probably just wanted us in bed to stop all the chaos and fighting. But, at the time, we were told we wouldn't grow without proper rest and no matter how much we begged, we simply weren't allowed to stay up past our bedtimes.

I'm sure you're wondering what in the world fruits and vegetables and sleep have to do with job searching and / or interviewing. Let me explain…

When you're job searching, you absolutely must prioritize taking good care of yourself. We've covered this before, but it bears repeating. Job searching is incredibly stressful and it isn't easy. Thus, you need to pay close attention to both your physical and your mental health. I've read enough to know that good health starts with both proper nutrition and sleep. We talked about how mentally taxing a job search can potentially be. The stress can cause some professionals to develop anxiety and depression, and for others, it can exacerbate conditions already prevalent. Therefore, we need to do everything in our power to help ourselves stay healthy, and that often starts with making sure you're filling yourself up with good, nutritious foods and you're staying properly hydrated. We all know processed foods are bad for your health. We also know drinks full of sugar, artificial sweeteners, and / or a plethora of caffeine aren't good for you either. In addition to good nutrition, your body needs proper rest, and this means getting ample restorative sleep so that your brain will be operating on all cylinders. A job search is hard! If you feel crappy, you will look crappy and you will think crappy. For the record, "crappy" doesn't typically help you achieve goals. Consider athletes. They fuel their bodies to be able to take on the challenges they face in their sports, and there's a reason they consume what they do. For you to perform at your best, you need to think like an athlete. This is a marathon, not a sprint, and as such, you need to home in on what you're doing every day to keep yourself in the best place possible physically and emotionally. If you let yourself go, you won't perform at your best. And, we all know that it's really easy to develop bad eating and sleep habits, which means you need to focus on this each and every day. I can't tell you how many people have shared the challenges they face on this front, and understandably so.

Think about it...let's say you were just part of a layoff you didn't see coming. This can send many people reeling. In a split second, you go from having some level of structure every single day and week, with your calendar filled with to-dos, meetings, goals, etc., to having it all stripped away from you in the blink of an eye. All the sudden, your normal routine is shaken up. You don't necessarily have to wake up at the time you used to. Or shower, get dressed and race out the door like you always have. All the meetings you had lined up and / or the to-do's on your calendar, they're all gone. Perhaps they shut your email off immediately which means you didn't have a chance to say good bye to your colleagues or send emails to clients, friends, vendors, etc. Suddenly your world got turned completely upside down. The rug literally got pulled out from under you. All of this can and does make even the most stable of people an emotional wreck. People react differently, but one thing I can say with certainty is that in this situation, most don't celebrate.

Now, let's say this happens to you. Whatever your mental state is in the moment this happens and in the moments following, no matter how okay you think you are, you will go through a range of emotions. Even if you know this was not due to your performance, it's still shocking and can be totally and completely devastating. This is often a traumatic experience and can lead some professionals into a serious funk or, worse, a state of deep depression. Sometimes people who are depressed can't eat, they lose their appetite. Others might turn to food as a source of comfort and overeat. Many report challenges with sleep. Some can't fall asleep. Others can't stay asleep. Yet others can't get out of bed and stop sleeping. Any which way, people are clearly struggling and it often is one big vicious cycle. After all, food can affect your ability to sleep and studies show a lack of sleep will affect food cravings. On top of all of this, many struggle with exercise and this is terrible because moving your body does so much good. All of this together affects one's moods and motivation levels. Needless to say, put all this together and it's NOT good!

While I'm not a certified nutritionist, I know how important it is to nourish yourself with vitamin-rich foods. I realize there's a lot at play here, and we can't always control everything that happens to us. But I was always taught, "control what you can control" and I know you can control what you choose to put into your body. You can control whether you get some type of exercise. You have to decide it's important to make healthy choices and be intentional about it. If you decide to put good fuel into your body, I promise you, you will feel better. Your body will start craving healthier foods and the insatiable desire you may have for unhealthy foods will dissipate. Once you start eating healthier options, your body will begin to love them. There are millions of food content creators you can follow who will show you some easy tips and tricks with affordable and healthy foods. Trust me, I absolutely love sweets and if I can learn to satisfy my sweet tooth with healthier versions of certain recipes, I know you can too. Get on your computer and do a little research. It's easy to find a ton of great videos and cookbooks that can help you learn how to create meals you'll love.

Job searching and interviewing can be grueling tasks and require you to be at your best. In order to be at your very best, you need to fill yourself up with good things. Getting proper nutrition, exercise and rest will help you more than you can imagine.

Think Before You Speak

THIS WAS ONE of my mom's mantras. She loved to preach this to us as children. And as I've grown up, it has proven to be a useful tool. I can tell you, in the world of interviewing and job searching, many don't think before they speak and while this makes for incredibly funny stories, it can be the unfortunate reason for so much undue heartache. Have you ever stuck your foot in your mouth? Have you watched someone else do it? Despite having a sophisticated palate, I can assure you that no matter how it's prepared, foot never tastes good.

As discussed, we always encourage candidates to be themselves in interviews because they should want the hiring teams to know who they truly are. Being a fake version of yourself is never good. That said, most people know to be the best version of themselves because interviews are truly auditions. One way to help yourself in an interview is to think about how your answers will sound to the person conducting the interview. Earlier, I highlighted the importance of putting yourself in the other person's shoes and trying to consider how your answer might sound to that person before you say it. Using this perspective will help you as you consider how to answer a question. If you're the hiring manager and hear someone say to you what you're about to say, would it cause you to pause, raise an eyebrow, have red flags, etc.?

If yes, then don't say it.

If the voice inside your head says, "I don't know if I should say this…" then don't say it.

If you are about to say, "I normally wouldn't say this…"—then don't say it.

People, you must think before you speak!

Below are some of the innumerable wacky things candidates have said during interviews—keep in mind that these are all quotes from people with ten or more years of professional experience, all of whom are making well over six figures (in other words, these are not rookies who are just entering the working world):

- "I'm interested in this job because it's close to my house. This commute would be awesome for me."
- "Do you expect people to work from the office? I really prefer to work from home so I can go for a run in the middle of the day. And if I can, I also like to take my kids to school and pick them up after school. It normally doesn't eat up too much time in my day. Well, unless I get stuck talking to the other parents. Then it can be an hour or two. There are some chatty ones there."
- "I've been going through a really awful time in my life, and my confidence is nearly gone. I really need this job and really want you to hire me. No one else will, and I'm running out of options fast."
- "I love sales, but I'm not always good at the prospecting part. I often lose my motivation and start slacking. I'm much better at account management. I'm less likely to slack in a role like that. And, by the way, I'm less likely to shop online during the day as a way to avoid the actual work [insert awkward giggle]."
- This was a message a candidate left on my voice mail: "Hi. Ummmm, this is. I, ummmmm, sent you my résumé about a month ago for, ummmmm, ummmmm, oh, I forget, but I'm interested in any sales or marketing roles you have, and, ummmmm, I need you to call me back. I'm, ummmmmm-mmm, following up, ummmmmm, so call me. I don't know my number, so you can just look on your caller ID and call the number you, ummmm, see. Thanks!"
- "I'm not naturally a happy person."
- "I have anger management issues and am working on them."
- "Ummm, how long is this going to take? I have errands to run and am not too interested in spending a lot of time on this call."
- When I asked a candidate why she'd be open to leaving her current position, she responded with "Because these people are bitches! They're all a bunch of backstabbing bitches, and I'm sick of it."

- When my client was at lunch with a candidate, he asked the candidate what his favorite movie is. The candidate answered by saying, "I have a dark side. I love *Silence of the Lambs*." (OMG—can you say *creeeepy*?!?!)
- When I asked someone to describe his leadership style, he said, "My style is simple. Don't expect me to go the extra mile for you if you won't do it for me."
- "The corporate culture here is totally toxic. I just stay to collect a paycheck. I don't have to work that hard, so I can stomach the craziness for now."
- "My CEO is *insane*. I don't normally admit this, but I *hate* him!"
- "Do you have maternity leave and paternity leave policies and plans? We want a big family, and I can't join a company where I won't be guaranteed a good chunk of time off each time I have a child."
- "If I have to do any work past 5:00 p.m., I can't promise I'll always be available to do it."

I'm hopeful you get the point here. Comments / answers like these undoubtedly give the interviewer reason to pause. And sometimes it is a reason to reject a candidate. I've seen it happen innumerable times. Now, I can appreciate we all say dumb stuff and sometimes things just come out of our mouths because of nerves. In addition, hiring managers do want to know who the candidate truly is. One of the ways to help yourself be at your best in an interview is to think before you speak! Sometimes there's a better way to state what you want to say and if you take a second to hear your answers through the interviewer's ears, you might realize it!

Choose Your Words Wisely

CHOOSING YOUR WORDS WISELY is a lesson I learned the hard way. I was young and according to my mother, I had a big attitude (gasp!). As my mom tells the story, I was mad at her and had some type of meltdown. In fairly typical teen-like behavior, I told her I hated her and I'm not sure what else I said. All I remember is her face. She had shock all over it and tears forming in her eyes. Now my mother didn't cry but she said very quietly and forcefully that my words really stung. I immediately regretted what I said and tried to apologize. My mom ultimately accepted my apology but stressed that I needed to choose my words wisely, that once they're out of the proverbial tube, there's no putting them back in. She stressed how words matter and I needed to be more aware of how much words used can affect another person and / or situation. There was another incident involving a trip to the principal's office when in fourth grade, but I won't elaborate as I'm still totally horrified by the words I chose that landed me in her office. Needless to say, both incidents taught me this valuable life lesson.

Choosing your words wisely is advice that falls into the same vein as thinking before speaking. When we think prior to speaking, we also need to examine the verbiage we choose to ensure we're setting ourselves up for clear and successful communication. One of the things I noticed very early into my professional life as a recruiter is that professionals often sell themselves short and often take away from the magnitude of what they're saying by utilizing what I call "wishy-washy words," as these words are weak. I encourage people to use strong words whenever possible. Let's break this down…

Strong words are words / phrases such as: *confident, know, proven, certain, without a doubt, exceptional, excel, award-winning, top performing, leader* and more.

Wishy-washy words are words / phrases such as: *think, feel, believe, able to, understand, sort of, kind of, competent, proficient, capable, comfortable, adequate, effective, fairly successful, pretty good at*, etc.

Wishy-washy words come with a sense of doubt; they do not convey expertise. Let's say you're in the ER, and a doctor tells you that your appendix is about to rupture and you need emergency surgery. The surgeon walks in the room and says to you, "I'm *proficient* at these procedures" *or* "I'm *competent* at this type of surgery." Does either statement make you feel good about the surgeon and their abilities? What if the surgeon says, "Look, I *understand* these surgeries, and I'm *able to* perform these procedures *effectively*." Does that leave you feeling like you're in the best possible hands? What if the surgeon says, "I *believe* I can do this procedure. I've been *fairly successful* when doing appendectomies."

Well, I don't know about you, but I'd be demanding a new surgeon! Being *proficient* or *competent* doesn't give me the same level of confidence words like *exceptional, excellent,* or *award-winning* do. If someone says they *understand* something or are *able to* do something, that doesn't mean they excel in that arena. I mean, I understand baking and I'm able to bake a cake, but no one is hiring me to make their kid's birthday cake! Hence, *understanding* something and being *able to* do something do not convey expertise.

If someone says they've been *fairly successful*, that implies they haven't been fully successful. So if someone claims to be *fairly successful*, they're also saying they've been *fairly unsuccessful* at the same time...hmmmmmm, don't know about you, but I'm apt to wonder what happened there.

As you can see, our choice of a few select words can completely alter how someone interprets the answer delivered.

Going back to the ER, it's far more comforting when a surgeon walks into the room saying things like "This is a procedure I've been recognized consistently for. I *excel* in these, and you have *nothing* to worry about. I am *absolutely confident* that we'll get you fixed in no time. I'm *extremely* talented in performing appendectomies. You are in *excellent* hands, and I *have no doubt* you'll be just fine. I've been successful in thousands of these procedures."

Let's leave the ER and go into an interview setting...

If an interviewer asks you, "Please tell me about yourself," which response do you like better?

A) "I'm a twenty-plus-year sales professional who *understands* sales and am *able* to sell into companies covering many verticals. I'm quite *competent* at building relationships with new business accounts and am also *proficient* at growing existing accounts via *effective* communication skills."

B) "I'm a *top-performing* sales professional with over twenty years of *proven* success selling into companies covering many verticals. I've consistently been recognized for the *exceptional* relationships I've built with new business accounts. In addition, I'm equally *gifted* at growing existing accounts. I have not only met, but I've continually *exceeded* revenue targets each year for the last eighteen years."

Hopefully you've selected B as the better answer. As you can see, it is a stronger statement and carries a lot more weight. If you picked A—I can't help you!

Yes, you always need to be honest, and thus it really should go without saying, but please only use those strong words when they're appropriate. Don't say something is a key strength of yours if it isn't. Don't say you've been recognized throughout your career for something when you haven't. Whenever you can, though, pick strong words as they make a very real impact and leave a positive impression.

In addition to choosing your words wisely, there are phrases I encourage you to steer clear of. These include phrases such as: *to be honest with you, honestly, I'm going to be really honest, I'm not going to lie, to be transparent, I want to be candid,* etc.

Early in my career, I had a meeting with an executive, and I must have said "to be honest with you" and "honestly" numerous times. At some point, he stopped me and asked me if he could give me some advice. Of course I said yes. He told me when I use a phrase like "to be honest with you," it can imply I haven't been fully honest until right then. His advice stuck with me all these years. The annoying thing is I am so hyper attuned to listening for it still all these years later that I seem to notice whenever others say it. But that's beside the point. My message here is that when you're interviewing, you never want others to think you've been lying or that you've been deceptive in any possible way. Hence, it's a good idea to try to avoid using such verbiage.

When speaking, many people use filler words, such as *um, well, ya know, like, look, listen, so, basically, ya know what I mean, whatchamacallit, whatever, right, okay so*, *blah-blah-blah*, etc. Filler words can be a huge distraction to the listener. Have you ever heard someone repeatedly use a word over and over again? I know someone who says "OK?" at the end of every sentence and sometimes in midsentence too. I know someone who says, "So ya know what?" way too frequently. One of my kids used to start every sentence with, "Basically..."

Filler words often sneak into sentences when we're talking too fast, we're nervous, and / or we're distracted. I find filler words sneak into my sentences when I'm trying to multitask. I've learned two great tips to help you get rid of filler words. Listen up...

First, slow down. Slow the pace of your speech down. You don't have to slow down to a completely awkward cadence. But slow down just a touch. I liken it to eating a bowl of popcorn. If you go too fast, you'll accidentally grab too many pieces and drop some. Whereas if you eat a bit more slowly, you can purposely grab a kernel or two at a time which will help you avoid accidentally dropping some into your lap. And, if you're like me and put a bunch of chili-lime salt onto your popcorn, slowing down will help you avoid dropping pieces and staining your clothes with the chili-lime seasoning. So slow down your tempo just a bit, and this will help you be more mindful of the words you use as you speak which will help you to avoid those filler words from sneaking into your sentences.

Second, you need to focus. When filler words sneak into my sentences, I'm often distracted. Maybe I just said something dumb and I'm thinking, "Why did I just say that?" Or perhaps I just remembered a question I forgot to write down and want to be sure to ask, so I'm running it through my mind. Or maybe I saw a text pop up on my phone from my kid that I know I need to read. Or the doorbell rang and I'm suddenly wondering who is at my door. Whatever the situation is, when I notice filler words are coming out of my mouth, I've learned to refocus my brain, all my thoughts and energy into that very moment in time. I will rid my thoughts of whatever is distracting me. I will center myself into the conversation. And, typically this will enable me to be more thoughtful and deliberate about the words I'm using.

Choosing your words wisely is extremely important in job searching and in interviewing because we don't have endless opportunities, nor do we have endless amounts of time, to communicate and make an impression. Words used can completely affect how what you're trying to say is received...so you better be thoughtful!

Speak Clearly

NOW, BEFORE EVERYONE gets their drawers all wadded up into a bunch, please know—I am by no means directing this chapter toward or talking about individuals with speech impediments and / or hearing impairments. So don't jump all over me and send hate mail. Since interviews involve speaking, and interviews are typically how people get offered jobs, it might be pretty easy to deduce that candidates likely want interviewers to understand what they're saying so they can be evaluated fairly. Have you ever had a conversation with someone you just couldn't understand? It's as if you didn't really have the conversation because you have no idea what was said. For communication to be productive, it's got to be understood.

First I'm going to quickly address fast talkers (pun intended!). I'm going to assume you know this is in reference to people who talk, well, who talk fast. And as you may know, when people are nervous, there's a natural tendency to speak at a more rapid pace. Unfortunately, when people race through whatever they're saying, it's often difficult for the audience to follow along. If you suspect you're talking too fast, you probably are. If someone's actually told you that you talk too fast, you probably do. Listen to them. If someone frequently asks you to repeat what you've just said, could it be due to talking too fast? If you think the answer is yes, slow down. Interviewers want to understand what you're saying. After all, you could be saying brilliant and incredibly impressive things, but if your audience can't register a word you've said, you're going to damage your candidacy. So slow down!

*It's more important to say a few really impressive things slowly than to say a whole lot of impressive things so fast no one can follow.

Now, that doesn't mean you need to speak at a snail's pace. There's a fine line between speaking slowly so what you're saying is understandable versus speaking so slowly that it's painfully awkward. I've interviewed thousands of people, and I can attest to the fact that there are a lot of fast talkers out there. I've had innumerable conversations where I've had to tell someone to slow down (sometimes more than once!) so I can understand them. I've had clients tell me a candidate talked too fast and was so hard to understand they decided not to move the person forward. Keep in mind, in many of the positions I've worked on, communication is a significant part of the job and if a candidate isn't communicating clearly in an interview, that can be reason enough for the hiring team to decide to take a pass, which is obviously a huge bummer!

In addition to your cadence, something you might not think much about is the volume of your voice. And this is paramount! Volume is often overlooked, but I assure you volume matters! If you're a *Seinfeld* fan like me, you may recall the classic episode about the "low talker" and the puffy shirt. Have you talked to someone who speaks so quietly you have to struggle to hear every word they're saying? No matter how close you get, you're unable to make out some or all of the words. For many, this is incredibly frustrating!

In an interview, similar to fast talkers, low talkers can quickly put themselves in harm's way. Obviously, when an interviewer asks a question, actually hearing the entire answer is key. Whether on the phone or in a face-to-face interview, the volume of your voice is something you need to pay attention to. People want to be able to hear one another without having to lean in so closely that they're basically putting their ear to the other person's lips or without having to jam their ear so deeply into the phone that they have a mark on their face for the rest of the day! Let's be real—how frustrating is it when all you can hear is something akin to a breathy whisper? I've interviewed a fair number of low talkers in my day, and it presents an incredibly challenging situation. Of course, I know how to turn the volume up on my phone and sometimes that solves the issue. But I have had plenty of experiences where it doesn't matter if I'm at the max volume level—I still can't hear the person clearly. Most interviewers will start off by politely asking someone to speak up or to repeat their answer. However, this doesn't always resolve the problem, and I'll admit, after asking the candidate a few times, if things don't improve, I've given up. Pay attention: If someone asks you to speak up or to repeat your answer, it could be because you're talking too quietly and need to permanently adjust the volume of your voice for the remainder of the interview. If you fail to do so, you could be setting yourself up for a fast pass to the rejected pile.

In addition to fast talkers and low talkers, there are a whole host of challenging types, including those I respectfully refer to as mumblers, screamers, shouters (also sometimes referred to as loud talkers), sentence droppers, gurglers, question askers, and whiners. Good Lord, in interviewing thousands of people, I've spent a lot of time trying to decipher words people say, and I happen to have decent hearing!

OK, I'm sure some of this is self-explanatory, but let's go through it. Starting with mumblers- do you know someone who mumbles? Similar to low talkers, mumblers are hard to understand. Their words seem to blend all together, and oftentimes it's really hard to make heads or tails out of what's being said. Mumblers can fix their problem by focusing on enunciating better and projecting their voices. Sometimes people who look down when talking end up mumbling. I've also found that people who don't speak into their phones can sound like they're mumbling. In an interview, be sure to enunciate your words. Practice speaking more deliberately so your words don't blend together and sound mumbly. In addition to making it hard for someone to know what you're saying, another downside to mumbling is it can give the listener the impression you either lack confidence or are being less than honest. None of this is helpful when trying to advance in an interview process.

Next are the screamers. These are folks who, while talking, will occasionally let out a scream or high-pitched squeal. This can be in the form of an overly boisterous laugh ("*Ha!*"), an "Oh *my* G-d," or anything that causes this person to basically, well, scream / squeal. It can be painful to be the recipient of their scream(s), and this can often be the catalyst to someone ending a call quickly. Both screaming and squealing can be viewed as unprofessional, possibly a bit juvenile, and all in all, it doesn't reflect positively on the candidate.

Shouters, on the other hand, simply don't know how to speak at a volume that would be characterized in my home as an "inside voice." These people don't talk, they…

…*SHOUT EVERYTHING!!!!*

Not only does it hurt the listener's ears, but it also (ironically) can make it difficult for the listener to understand what's being said. Depending on how loud someone's voice is, shouters can also be loud talkers. Admittedly, I sometimes fall into this category myself and have to make a conscious effort to keep my volume at a reasonable level. I'll sometimes hang up a call and wonder if I was just shouting.

I am a loud talker, but when I cross into shouter territory, that's not good! If you, too, are a shouter, join me in working on it!

Next up—the sentence droppers. These are people who love to start off a sentence with a loud, strong voice but for some strange reason will then dramatically drop their volume to what might be a whisper / mumble as the sentence starts to wrap up. Not sure what that's all about. Regardless of what the reason is, whether it's simply a bad habit someone's formed or something psychologists have a term for, it's not necessarily going to work in your favor. This could prevent you from advancing in the process. Anyone listening to someone who does this might question if the speaker is insecure or perhaps uncertain about what it is they're saying. Neither of which is the kind of positive reaction you're hoping for in an interview setting.

Next, let's address the gurglers out there. These are people who can have strong voices but start making a sound that I'm not sure how to describe other than to say it's "gurgly." Their voice starts to sound cracked and weak. Similar to sentence droppers, these people can sound meek and exude a level of insecurity or inferiority, neither of which serves to elevate one's game. In interviews, you want to convey confidence. Being a gurgler can work against you.

Oh how I love the question askers. These people are great and I put them into two categories. First—there are people who always end their sentences in a tone that sounds as though a question has been posed, yet no question has been asked. These people form complete declarative sentences that include no question and thus if written would end in a period, not in a question mark. Yet their tone makes it sound like they are asking a question and can sometimes sound sing-songy. It's strange and sort of reminds me of the "Valley girl" days (hello, 1980s!). Technically, this is referred to as "upspeak." The smart people who study this stuff say people who upspeak can give their audiences the impression they're insecure or have a sense of inferiority. Other experts argue upspeak is used by those who feel superior. So technically the experts are split on what this can mean about a person. Regardless, it sounds less professional and my advice is, unless you're truly asking a question, say what you want to say with confidence and say it declaratively.

Secondly, there are those who actually ask questions. Can you guess who these people are? Do you think they're people who ask questions? Are you aware that the answer to those questions is yes? (Ha! See what I did there?) These are people who consistently ask questions. Even when answering questions, they ask questions.

Some of the questions are rhetorical in nature. Some are questions the person asks knowing the other individual is going to ask, but rather than wait for that to happen, they beat the person to it by asking the question first. Either way, the question asker asks the question and then answers it without missing a beat. For example, I was working on a senior-level sales position and was interviewing a candidate, Joe. I asked Joe, "Have you ever sold into CPGs?" Joe's response went something like, "Have I ever sold CPGs? No! Can I sell to CPGs? Yes, I certainly can! Do I have contacts in the CPG space? Of course I do. Can I leverage those contacts? You bet! Could I do so today? Yes. But can I guarantee a meeting can be scheduled for next week? No. I can't guarantee anything."

I don't know about you, but I find this to be comical and always crack up when this happens. In this particular interview, Joe basically interviewed himself (and did a great job, I might add!). I didn't need to ask questions. I just listened. Honestly, I was tempted to make popcorn, prop my feet up on my desk, and sit back. Joe did a great job asking all the right questions and didn't need me to run the interview. I always find humor in this style but know it can really get under an interviewer's skin and can cause people to want to end the conversation. An interviewer may assume you could be challenging to work with, or "not a team player," because you don't let people ask questions. A word to the wise—do yourself a favor and let the interviewer ask the questions. That way the interviewer is asking the questions they want to discuss and you're making the best use of your time together.

Lastly, the whiners. Ohhhh, whiners are a special bunch. If you need some help understanding this, pull up some old *SNL Doug and Wendy Whiner* skits. As you will see, these are people who whine when they talk. All I can say is, this is pretty much a nails on the chalkboard situation. Just like we talked about no one liking crybabies, whiners grate on nearly everyone's nerves. Obviously, that can impact your ability to advance in interview processes.

Much of one's success in the professional world is predicated upon the ability to communicate. Candidates need to know how to articulate their thoughts, ideas, and opinions in a sound, succinct manner others understand, and in interviewing, this is paramount. In job searching and interviewing, it's really important to think about speaking clearly, and this is a shout-out (pun!) to all the fast talkers, low talkers, mumblers, screamers, loud talkers, sentence droppers, gurglers, question askers, and whiners. Focus on speaking clearly so others can understand you!

Stop Rambling

MANY PEOPLE RAMBLE when they speak. Ramblers are those who go on and on, venturing off onto one tangent and then to the next, never arriving at their point. Children frequently do this, and while I can't say for sure why they ramble, my best educated guess is that their little, rapidly growing brains are working so quickly, their thoughts move faster than their mouths. As we mature, some learn how to curtail the rambling and deliver more concise and cohesive sentences. Sadly, though, others don't. And in interviewing, rambling can be problematic.

When in a conversation with a rambler, many things can happen. The listener might think the speaker has no idea what they are talking about or that they are either uninformed or misinformed. In addition, when someone is rambling, the listener may disengage from the conversation and start thinking about something else, like the ridiculously long, high-priority to-do list they should tackle ASAP, last night's hot date, the rapidly approaching deadline for a huge project, or the upcoming and dreaded visit to the dentist. Worse yet, the listener may grow frustrated with the speaker. Yes, the list could go on, but clearly, disengaging means someone isn't listening which ultimately can negatively impact the outcome of an interview. Therefore, in an interview setting, it's incredibly important to be succinct, buttoned-up, and brief. Sometimes when rambling, a person will use some / lots of filler words. Remember, these are words such as: like, umm, you know, well, so, mmm, uhhhhhhhh, basically, I mean, look, listen, ya know what, sort of, whatever, and so forth, blah-blah-blah, right (?), etc.. Rambling can really undermine the success of your interview and derail a conversation. If you're speaking and you think you're rambling, if you think you're off topic or you're potentially restating the same thing two or three times, you probably are. Listen to that inner voice and let it guide you. If you can, watch your audience for clues as to whether or not they're engaged and actively listening. If people aren't looking at you, if they're moving around in their seats and fidgeting, if their eyes have glazed over, if people have that blank, eight-thousand-mile stare, if people are checking their phones, those are your clues! Rambling can quickly take what may have started off as a great conversation and turn it into a painful conversation.

An example: We were working on a VP of Marketing search with a health care client of ours. I was tasked with finding a strong all-around marketing generalist who had experience in health care. In addition, it was important for candidates to have strong experience in social media marketing. In the initial interviews, there was a woman whom I was particularly excited about speaking with. On paper, she truly appeared to be a great match. Our conversation started out strong, but it didn't take long for me to realize she might not be as solid as I'd hoped. Throughout our conversation, she wouldn't (or maybe couldn't) stop rambling.

I asked her to walk me through her background starting post graduating from college. She started after college but quickly pivoted, referencing her time as a child and sharing what fueled her interest in brands and brand marketing. It was a good story, so she had me for a few minutes. But one story about *Tony the Tiger* turned into pretty lengthy stories about a couple other brands she adored, all of which I knew and didn't need five-minute dissertations on. All the fluff and extra detail she had provided was totally unnecessary and wasted precious time. Now, I thought maybe she was nervous and hoped that as the conversation continued, she'd get more comfortable which would help her tighten things up. Unfortunately, that didn't happen! From there, I asked about her digital experience, specifically in social media and more specifically around using influencers. I also decided it'd be prudent to remind her I had a hard stop at the top of the hour (she'd already used up half our time). Again, my first question centered on her experience finding and leveraging influencers. Her answer started with how she identified two of the influencers she brought into her current company, which was awesome. But...then... she digressed, discussing some of the other influencers she was considering and how they couldn't come to an agreement with one on financial terms and the fact that brand exclusivity was an issue with another. I was hoping she had a reason for sharing this detail and was going to tie it back to my original question, but she never did. None of this had anything to do with the question I asked about the influencers she was working with. When I could tell she wasn't getting back on track, I guided her back to my original question. She said, "Oh, sorry. I got sidetracked…" From there, she provided what was a solid answer to part of my question but got long-winded on yet another tangent. By the time our hour was up, she had spent the vast majority of the time providing information I didn't ask for or need. She droned on and on about things that were irrelevant and ate up time I wanted to use to evaluate her against what was most important to my client but was unable to do so. It was impossible for me to want to bring her in for a second interview.

We all ramble. We all get long-winded and go on tangents. But in an interview, when there are time constraints, it's really important to pay attention to ensuring you're answering the question that's been asked and you're doing so without rambling. How do you ensure you're actually answering the question? Simple, you ask. In a conversational tone, there are many ways to ask if you've answered the question. Here are a few: You can ask, "Did that answer your question?" You can ask, "Did I give you what you were looking for?" Or you can ask, "Was that enough detail?" Or, "Good?" Again, you want to be conversational and not annoying, so you definitely need to read your audience. I receive this feedback more often than one would think, "Your candidate would not answer my question." Yes, people are nervous. Yes, some interviewers suck at asking questions clearly. But, it's on you to make sure you understand the question, then answer it!

Be Specific; Get to Your Point

LISTENING TO A CHILD tell you something can be a true test of patience. It's amazing how long it can take for some to arrive at what they really want to say. I hate to admit this, but a kid's cuteness can fade fast when it takes them a year and a day to articulate a thought. I'm pretty sure you can surmise how this is relevant when it comes to job searching and / or interviewing successfully, but just in case there's any confusion, let me try to quickly get to my point (ha!).

As previously stated, one of the biggest obstacles to success in interviewing is being able to answer questions concisely and succinctly. In order to communicate successfully, people need to get to the point quickly. This means avoid rambling (as stated in the previous chapter) and refrain from speaking in vague generalities. When it comes to interviewing, there's a delicate balancing act; candidates must get to the point quickly while also being as specific as possible. This is where many professionals struggle. To start with, it's quite common for a professional in an interview to be asked for a quick overview of who they are, what their strengths are, and what they're looking for. Sadly, many tussle with answering those questions. For example, when I've asked professionals to provide me with a quick overview of who they are and what they're looking for, I've received responses like "I'm an *executive* with over twenty years of experience. My strengths include *leadership*, *problem-solving*, and *working with people*. I'm looking for a *growth opportunity* where I can make *strong contributions*" and "I'm a *talented executive* who is known for my *people skills*, *approachable style*, and *collaborative* nature. I have extensive experience with *P&L management*. While I like getting *into the details*, I'm equally strong at *seeing the big picture*."

I don't know about you, but when I read these word salads (or hear them from someone), I'm not clear as to who the person is and what kind of role will best align with them. There's nothing specific for me to get my arms around. Let's examine them more closely.

"I'm an *executive* with over twenty years of experience." OK, let's be honest. Everyone is an executive. Most people refer to themselves as executives. So that didn't help me. What kind of executive are you—marketing, sales, finance, operations, etc.? It's super helpful for me to know that right away.

"My strengths include *leadership, problem-solving,* and *working with people.*" Leadership, problem-solving, and working with people should be strengths of pretty much any professional who has been working for twenty years. Furthermore, how about expanding on what you mean by leadership? Have you led teams, divisions, whole companies? Have you hired entire teams? I need more detail. Problem-solving—well, you better know how to problem-solve because that's a key component to pretty much every single position in any and every company, so that doesn't really impress anyone. What kinds of problems are you solving? Working with people—unless you're in a position where you never, ever have to interact with anyone, you better know how to work with people. Can you define who you're working with? How are you working with them? What are you doing?

"I'm looking for a *growth opportunity* where I can make *strong contributions.*" Looking for a growth opportunity—don't most people say this? I've yet to hear someone say they're looking for a role where they will not have the ability to grow. I've never heard someone say they want to be stuck in the same role for the next twenty-five years. As for making strong contributions—again, this is something *everyone* says. It's vague. It's empty. Please be more specific!

Next, we have "I'm a *talented executive* who is known for my *people skills, approachable style,* and *collaborative* nature." Congratulations!! You're a talented executive! Really…would anyone ever say "mediocre executive"? So basically everyone is a talented executive. OK, we've got that down, but what are you a talented executive *of*? Where exactly are you talented? This begs the question, What functional area are you in? People skills—again, 99.9 percent of jobs require professionals to have solid people skills. Thus, you better have people skills, and you better be approachable. And if in your position you do happen to work with others, being collaborative is a given. Yes? What does this sentence tell the reader about you? Not much, right?

"I have extensive experience with *P&L management*." P&L management of *what*?

"While I like getting into the details, I'm equally strong at *seeing the big picture*." What does this sentence mean? How does this help me get to know who you are and where exactly you might fit in an organization? It's ambiguous...

When I've asked people to tell me what they are looking for in their next role, I've received answers like these:

- "I'm looking for a growing company where I can add value."
- "I'm looking for an executive leadership position."

So what's wrong with these answers? Well, let's start with...they're a bunch of words strung together that are basics. They're givens. They're all incredibly nebulous and leave me with no clue. As someone who works on searches in every functional area, after reading those, I have no better idea of where you fit or what you're looking for in a company.

"I'm looking for a growing company where I can add value." OK, great, so what does this mean? I can't recall a time I heard or read someone say they wanted to work for a shrinking or failing company. Seems pretty standard for someone to say they want to work for a growing company. In addition, most people want to add value. I have yet to hear someone say, "I'm looking for a place where I can do nothing!" Saying you want to add value is rather obvious and doesn't help the reader understand who you are.

"I'm looking for an executive leadership position." OK, doing what, with whom? Give me something to work with. The reader doesn't know what functional area you're wanting to find a role in. Are you a professional in marketing, sales, finance, HR, or something else? What industry or industries are you focused on? Yes, they can read your resume to see where you currently are or have been but some people are trying to switch industries. You don't want people to have to figure it out.

Please remember to be more specific...*a lot* more specific! Tell others who you are and what "bucket" you fall into. Are you a marketing, IT, HR, sales, finance, risk, supply chain, or operations professional? If possible and if applicable, take it a step further and highlight the segments or areas of specialization you may have. In other words, if you are in marketing, does your expertise fall into a specialized category, like social media marketing, digital marketing, or marketing communications, or are you more of a generalist in nature with a fully integrated marketing background?

When asked, "Tell me about you...what are you looking for?" here's a response that has a bit more to it:

"I'm a marketing professional with over ten years of experience working in larger publicly held companies. Within marketing, I've spent the last five years focused on all facets of digital marketing. For the last three years, I've built and led teams ranging from three to five direct reports and have been responsible for managing a budget of $10 million. I've helped companies grow revenues by over 50 percent year over year and have been recognized annually for meeting and exceeding my MBOs. While my experience has mainly been in the industries of education and publishing, my skills are transferable to every industry. I'm seeking senior-level, digital marketing roles in the Chicagoland area. I'm open to remote, hybrid, or in office. I love to lead teams and have an exceptional track record at developing talent. Please know I'm unable to relocate at this time."

As you can see, this all goes back to Jerry Maguire's "Help me help you." If you want people to help you, help them first. Please provide your audience with details. Be specific!

Additionally, here's another way not being specific can be problematic. When professionals use words that have multiple meanings without clarifying what their personal definition of the word is, things can get dicey. For example, *customer* means different things to different people. To some, *customer* can be used interchangeably in reference to a client and / or a prospect. Whereas to others, the word *customer* may indicate a person or company that's currently doing business with you, which is often called a "client." In this situation the word *customer* does not include what would be deemed a "prospect." Many sales professionals use the word *customer* throughout their résumé without realizing it could be confusing the reader. For example, let's say I'm working on a sales position and am looking for someone who has extensive experience selling into new business accounts. In reviewing an applicant's résumé that says, "Extensive focus on growing customer accounts," I may misinterpret this candidate's use of the word *customer* to mean they're working with companies who are current "clients" and may mistakenly assume they're not selling into new business accounts. In that case, I would form the wrong opinion, and in so doing, I'd fail to consider what could be an ideal candidate's background. I'd lose out, and certainly the candidate would lose out too.

Another example—let's say I'm working with a client and am helping them find candidates for an "individual contributor" sales position. Just to be clear, an individual contributor role is one where someone is not responsible for any direct reports. They're solely responsible for their own sales goals and that's it. That said, there are many professionals who have résumés highlighting their "sales leadership" expertise. *Sales leadership* can mean different things to different people. To some, the word *leadership* means they've led teams of sales professionals and have thus held a sales *management* position. To others, *sales leadership* can mean the professional has been a top producer and has in essence "led" sales by closing more business than other sales reps within the same company. In this scenario, the reader might mistakenly assume the professional is someone who leads teams and may pass this person over when focusing on finding candidates for an individual contributor role. As you can see, when you're a candidate, these mistakes can cause you to miss out on many opportunities.

Instead of leaving it up to the reader to figure out exactly what you are saying, please *be specific*; make your point clear so that there is no room for possible misunderstanding.

If You Don't Have Something Nice to Say, Don't Say It

THIS WAS ONE of my mom's mantras, and I must admit, this is one of the most valuable lessons she ever taught me. During the course of my childhood, my mother beat this like a drum into our heads. In fact, every time I hear this come out of someone's mouth, I think of her and smile.

If you've been in the workforce for any period of time, I'm sure you've come across a few difficult people, or perhaps more than just a few. As such, you've probably faced some challenging situations. Since the beginning of time, employees in work settings have had to deal with all sorts of nonsense, from personality conflicts with peers or bosses to poorly run companies to physically challenging work environments to bad products, services, solutions, and so forth.

Well, I hate to be the bearer of bad news, but nirvana does not exist.

It is NOT out there!

Sorry if I just rained on your parade, but we all need to be real. There is no perfect job! There is no perfect company! And there is no perfect person! For those reasons, and about a million more, we need to be sensible and face the truth of the matter, which is that we will undoubtedly face challenges daily. Hopefully most of the challenges are miniscule and can be viewed as good learning experiences that aren't too disruptive. However, many professionals do face challenges one can't classify as tiny, and these tend to impact work lives (and personal lives) to the nth degree. Whatever the case may be, I caution people who are interviewing to be very careful with what information they disclose during any conversation. I'm going to open the vault in a moment and share a few examples…and yes, these really happened!

I interview numerous professionals a day, and on average, at least one person will speak negatively about their current / former situation. Similar to the chapter "No One Likes a Crybaby," speaking negatively about your current or former work situation, be it a peer, a boss, or the company in general, is a really bad idea. Now, this is where I get to quote my mom again, and it's best to heed her warning: "If you don't have something nice to say, don't say it!" This little gem goes a long way! Her advice is incredibly sound, and you'd be wise to listen to her.

When interviewing, there are many ways to articulate any given story, so it's incredibly important to be thoughtful about the verbiage you choose as well as the tone you use. It's completely unprofessional (and, in my opinion, also rather juvenile) to rip on current and / or past employers, colleagues, bosses, etc. Rather than spending time bitching, moaning, and railing on others, take the high road. Speak of the positives. If there are negatives, be extremely cautious in how you frame things. When someone starts ranting about how terrible their situation is or was, interviewers can't help but question what the person may not be revealing, for we all know there are two sides to every story. What part of the story is the candidate strategically leaving out? The listener may wonder if the candidate is the difficult one.

Candidates, think twice about what you want to share and if you are going to share something, how to properly state it so as to not hurt yourself.

You may be thinking that you're not an idiot and would never bad-mouth a former employer in an interview. Well, I've got news for you. There are a lot of people out there kicking themselves for doing this when, deep down, they knew they shouldn't. However, they claim the words just started spilling out of their mouths. I have witnessed firsthand candidates being rejected for speaking poorly about current / prior bosses, coworkers, and / or companies. In one situation, I was working with a candidate who was a senior-level sales leader. He was a VP, managing a team of six people, and reported to the SVP of Sales. During an interview, he was asked why he was looking to make a move. His response, which was delivered in a sort of half-joking, sarcastic manner, was that the SVP he reported to was a "complete moron" and the team he inherited was made up of "mini-morons." (Ummmm, yeah—this is really what he said!) He further stated his frustration was with the executive leadership team and their unwillingness to let him fire the "mini-morons who weren't producing". Yes, referring to colleagues as morons coupled with his tone really didn't sit well with anyone. His interview was pretty much over right then and there. And guess who felt like a moron…

Another example with a candidate whom I really liked, Ted. This guy was good. He was personable, funny, and had a very strong résumé. Every interaction with me was positive. I had no reason to question whether or not he'd represent me and my brand positively. Ted and I had been exploring an individual contributor sales role with a client of mine in the digital media space. My client loved his experience, and throughout the interview process, it seemed everyone had great interactions with him. In his interview with the CEO, though, things didn't go swimmingly. In fact, they went sideways. Ted was asked to walk through his background and explain why he went to the companies he did. (As previously stated—this is a fairly routine question and one every single candidate should be prepared to answer succinctly and articulately. And to date, Ted had answered this question without issue.) Ted started off strong, and according to the CEO, his first impression was great. About halfway through his response was when the wheels came off the track. As Ted had done when asked this same question in prior interviews, he shared why he left a specific company and rather than keeping it more high level and answering as he had every other time, he began to drill down into details never before shared. Not only did he rip on the leadership team, but the examples he shared were questionable in that he potentially revealed proprietary company details. In addition, his tone and choice of verbiage also left the CEO with a bad taste in his mouth. Now, I wasn't in the room and witness to the conversation, but I was told Ted wrapped up by saying something like, "Look, they [meaning the executive leadership at his company] were all a bunch of idiots, and no one should have let them have the keys to the car. I don't care that the CEO went to [insert an Ivy League school]. His Ivy League education was a waste of money because he certainly wasn't smart."

By the time Ted completed the last sentence, the CEO had already decided to move on to other candidates. Ted's language, attitude, and tone were all really bad. And having attended an Ivy League school himself, the CEO disliked the jab made on that front. Needless to say, I was beyond embarrassed. Fortunately for me, the client had previously worked with us successfully on a number of searches and was thrilled with the professionals hired through us. In addition, the fact that many executives who'd previously interviewed Ted and advanced him in their interview process were quick to come to our defense and remind the CEO he hadn't shown any sign of this in previous interviews helped ensure our reputation didn't get tarnished by this one bad experience with a candidate we referred. By the way, Ted knew he blew it from the CEO's body language at the end of the interview. He told me he didn't think the CEO liked him.

Now, you may be wondering how to properly speak to what might be a difficult boss or negative situation. Here are some examples of things people have said:

- "I've had a good experience working here but am ready to take on new challenges and won't have the opportunity to do so quickly. I'd need to be promoted, and that'd mean my boss would need to be promoted or leave. I don't see either happening any time soon. I am not learning and growing in my current role anymore and don't want to remain stagnant. So it's time for me to consider opportunities outside my company."
- "I excel in a culture where all ideas are encouraged and considered. Here, people seem a little less willing to share ideas. I'm not racing out the door, but if there's an exciting opportunity with a company where leadership pushes everyone to contribute ideas, I'd be open to exploring."
- "I completely respect that leadership wants everyone to return to the office full time. That said, I have come to learn that I'm far more productive working from home and thus want to find a company that supports hybrid and / or remote work."
- "I am extremely flexible and completely know my job isn't just 9:00 a.m. to 5:00 p.m. I have no issue taking calls late or working on the weekend when needed. That said, I'm expected to be on call 24-7-365, and it's become challenging for me to have any life outside of work. Having done this for two years, I'm ready to find a home where working over sixty to seventy hours per week isn't the norm. I can absolutely work well beyond forty hours a week, but I do need to prioritize having some semblance of a social life as it's better for me as well as my employer."

- "One of the key reasons I was hired was to build a marketing team. Unfortunately, due to some of the company's economic challenges, I have not yet been able to do so. Now that I'm going into my third year here, it's time for me to think about other opportunities. Leading is a passion of mine and is something I excel at. I want to build a team again and keep those skills sharp. Sadly, I don't think I'll be able to do it here any time soon. For the right opportunity, I'd consider leaving."

As a candidate, sometimes it's hard to know how to position your current or prior situations. This is where the concepts of preparing and practicing are super important. Have professionals you admire and respect help you with this. Preferably find professionals who hire people as they've likely been witness to all types of responses and thus know what works and what doesn't. They can provide you with guidance as to how you can best answer the questions that will inevitably come your way.

The takeaway is…don't bad-mouth. If you don't have something nice to say, don't say it. Know there's always a positive to be found in any negative situation. Any time you've gone through a less-than-desirable situation, you have the power to choose how you position the information. It's up to you. You can choose to not mention the negative aspects by simply leaving them out. Or you can opt to highlight the positives of your experiences while putting the negative(s) in a more "glass-half-full" light.

Negativity is toxic! It fosters negative energy, and we all know how quickly that can spread like a cancer through an organization, crippling success. I think it's safe to say that most companies prefer to avoid bringing negative energy and drama into their four walls. The minute an interviewer starts to question whether or not someone is a negative person, red flags are raised, and this doesn't help to propel someone's candidacy forward. So be positive!

If you don't have something nice to say, don't say it.

It's Not What You Say But How You Say It

HAVE YOU EVER NOTICED how two people can say the exact same thing yet it can come out sounding completely different? As we grow, we learn "it's not what you say but how you say it" that matters. Thus, to be successful in a job search or interview setting, my advice is to be aware of how you say things.

Let's start with tone. Please pay close attention to your tone. I can't tell you how many people my peers and I have interviewed who use tones that are aggressive, defensive, belligerent, abrasive, curt, condescending, demeaning, snotty, and / or completely stoic. We all have bad days, but please take note of how you sound. Your tone matters.

Having been a recruiter for this many years, I've interviewed people with thousands of different personalities and styles. People who sound pissed off, annoyed, rude, gruff, short...let me tell you...those people do not make favorable impressions. My job is to find the right person for the particular position and company. In order to do that, I need to ask questions, many of which I'm confident my client will want answers to. So if I ask you why your two last jobs were short-lived, I'm not doing it to make you feel bad or stupid. And I can assure you my tone will be very casual and matter-of-fact when I ask this. My tone will not be one of "Ha! Now I've cornered you, you lying rat! Why in the world did you only spend a measly thirteen months in your most recent job and prior, only seventeen months at that one? Why? What's wrong with you?"

No, my tone won't be aggressive. I'll say it much more like "Hey, tell me about your most recent job." And then I'll continue to go through someone's background understanding why they joined the companies they did, what they accomplished and why they left.

My tone is always warm and conversational. So when answering me, if you answer in a defensive or aggressive tone, that won't bode well. If you sound completely tweaked, annoyed, or rude, it is highly unlikely I'll want to move you forward. No matter how good your explanation is, your tone can ruin it.

When answers are smooth, concise, and said with confidence, they tend to be received more positively. Conversely, when someone's answer has a lot of filler words like, *ummm* and *ya know* in it, fairly or unfairly, red flags can be raised. So it's important to deliver answers with a tone that conveys confidence, because sounding like you're not quite sure how you want to articulate your thoughts can adversely affect the outcome. Let's say you're being asked why you left your last position without having another job lined up. Which answer do you like better?

A) "Well, ummmmmmmmm, I know it seems odd to, ummmmm, to leave a position when, ummmmm, when, ya know, when the economy is bad. But ya know, I felt like, ummmmm, with my track record of, ummmmmm, success, I'd be able to, ummmm, find a job easily, ya know? I, ummmmm, I sorta wasn't really that worried, ya know?"

B) "That's a great question, and I'm glad you asked. I felt comfortable leaving my previous position because I knew it was the right thing to do. First, as you know, looking for a job when you have a full-time position is extremely challenging. Knowing I was committed to leaving, I felt it was ethically and morally the right thing to do, to be fair not only to my previous employer but to myself as well. I'm glad I made that decision and have no regrets. In addition, I've had an incredible career and have produced exceptional results. I knew my proven track record coupled with my wealth of contacts would enable me to quickly gain traction in my search, and that's proven to be the case."

When someone uses a lot of filler words they can give the impression they either don't know what they want to say or are not confident in what they're saying. We talked about this before—the easiest way to get these filler words out of your sentences is to prepare, practice, slow down your pace just a touch, and make sure your brain is centered in the moment, because thinking ahead or behind can distract you. You can say the most incredible thing, but if filler words are strewn throughout, even the best listener can get distracted and miss your point.

Have you ever heard someone answer a relatively easy question with way too much detail? Does it make you wonder if they're lying? Does it make you think that maybe they don't know exactly what the answer is and so they're talking around it? Regardless, being overly verbose to a relatively simple question can undermine you. We talked about this before. If it takes you an hour to say something you could have said in two minutes, it drives people crazy! You'll lose them.

Have you ever had a conversation with someone who has a completely flat / stoic voice? They have zero inflection? You may wonder if you're boring that person to tears. You may assume they simply aren't interested in the job or the company. You might think they are super low energy. Note: If you're someone who falls into this stoic camp, I know I've said be yourself, and I definitely want you to be yourself, but do your best to have some level of intonation and energy. I had a call with a candidate once who forewarned me at the beginning of our conversation that she fell into this bucket. I don't remember exactly what she said. But it was actually funny and made me totally appreciate her "flat-ish" tone. It helped me not jump to any possible conclusions about her before giving her a fair shake. Also important to note—some people start off flat and then as they get comfy, become more animated and lively in a conversation. I know it is not easy to do, but if you know you're like this, try your best to get there quickly so people see and / or hear more of "that you."

Have you ever had a conversation with someone who nods a lot and actually doesn't finish their sentences because they assume you know what they're getting at with their nodding? For example, I was on a Zoom with a candidate and was asking about the challenges their company was facing. The woman's response was "I know...things are crazy here [lots of head nodding]...I'm sure you've read about our funding... [lots more head nodding]." I said, "No, actually I haven't read about it. What's up?" Her response: "Well, let's just say the CEO isn't happy...[head nodding]." I said, "I'm sorry—I really don't know what you mean. Why isn't the CEO happy?" She said, "Have you seen the news about the state of health tech? That tells you what you need to know...[head nodding]." At this point, I got tired of this game of "fill in the blanks" and stopped asking questions. If she wasn't going to spell things out a bit more clearly, I wasn't going to press further. Technically, there was nothing wrong with what she was saying, but it was how she was saying it—all the head nods and lack of complete thoughts caused me to lose interest. And going back to how important being able to communicate is, the fact she wasn't speaking in complete sentences told me she's not the best communicator.

    How you say something matters. When your tone is one of annoyance, frustration, or anger, the listener might not be drawn to you and what you're saying. When you say things in more of an open and engaging tone, you create an easier flow within a conversation. When you say something with confidence, when you get rid of filler words, when you're concise and articulate, when you speak in complete sentences, your odds of success increase.

Look at Me When I'm Speaking to You

MY HUSBAND AND I used to say this to our kids at least ten times a day. When they were really young, they had the attention span of fleas. As preteens, they had the attention span of cats. As teens, it's better but not perfect. It's still hard to get them to focus for a long period of time. When their eyes start to wander, I know they're thinking about something else. Probably about how annoying their parents are…

While I didn't graduate with a degree in reading body language, over the years I've heard many experts tout the importance of good eye contact. Many have highlighted how failure to maintain eye contact can indicate someone is lying or being deceptive (which I'm pretty sure means the same thing as lying). Furthermore, lack of eye contact can also indicate someone is insecure.

Please note, there are medical conditions that make it very difficult (if not impossible) for some to keep eye contact, and I am not at all speaking to these people. Severe social anxiety, autism, visual impairments are some of the medical conditions that can impact one's ability to have good eye contact. As interviewers, we don't always know whether someone has an actual medical condition, which makes this a tricky topic. However, knowing decision makers have referenced poor eye contact in their feedback of candidates, I felt it important to cover.

If you've ever had a conversation with someone who won't look you in the eye, you know it can be a bit awkward and uncomfortable. You might be talking and looking at them, and they're looking at the ground or to the side. If they're on video, you may not know what they're looking at. If in person, you may be able to see they're not actually looking at anything in particular. They're just not looking at you.

Have you ever had a conversation with a group of people in which there's someone who, when they speak, will only look at one person and not any of the others? Talk about uncomfortable...I was just in that situation at a party where there were three of us standing together, my dear friend Missy and Barb. Barb was someone we just met for the first time. (She was the new girlfriend of someone at the party.) Being in the line of work I am, I'm pretty good at getting conversations started, so I asked Barb a few questions, and every time she answered, Barb only looked at me, leaving Missy just standing there. In an effort to make it less awkward, I made sure to direct my comments and eye contact to both women. But, even when Missy asked Barb a question, Barb only looked at me when she answered.

With regards to eye contact, there's most certainly a happy medium. Staring someone down can be as uncomfortable as no eye contact. So, we need to be mindful of holding good eye contact but also not burning holes in the other person's retinas. In an interview setting, holding good eye contact tells someone you're being truthful and that you're a confident person / professional. Hiring managers are looking for people whom they can trust.

If you know you struggle with holding eye contact, you can work on this, and with effort, you can get better on this front. Candidly, I'm someone who has had to work on this and sometimes still do. Since I coach people on this, I'm more in tune to it and know when I'm failing on this front. All that said, if you do have a medical condition that causes you to have issues with holding eye contact, it's a real thing, and I don't at all mean to poke fun at or minimize your challenges.

Couple quick things. In group interviews, please be sure to make eye contact with everyone in the room. That means as you're answering questions, try to look at each person when you're speaking. Depending on how long your answer is, that might not be possible. But, share the love, as I like to say. Give eye contact to everyone and it may be that the next answer is one where you look at those you weren't able to earlier. I've had candidates go through group interviews where the feedback was that the person only focused on one person every time they spoke. So, people do notice. Make a conscious effort to look at each person.

In video interviews, this can be really tricky. Many people look at their screen into the eyes of the person talking. And when they speak, they keep their eyes on the other person's eyes rather than looking into the camera. What I do is try to look at the camera. Inevitably my eyes will shift and I'll mentally realize it and look up at the camera again. Also, I often have notes taped up on the wall behind my laptop which force me to look up.

Looking someone in the eyes isn't always easy. Job searching is hard and many people lose some confidence when they face rejection and / or when things just aren't going swimmingly. When in a low confidence zone, I do a few things. First, I am a big fan of the "fake it till you make it" school of thought and will force myself to do better on the eye contact front. In addition, some other things that help me get myself hyped up are, playing music I love, thinking about all the successes I've had and what I'm grateful for and sometimes I'll do power poses as those do make a difference. Might seem corny, but it's true. Reality is, sometimes we need to talk ourselves into finding confidence. Have you heard of "imposter syndrome"? It is real! And knowing (almost) every single person on the planet has been in this situation, should give you comfort and make it easier to look people in the eye.

Don't Interrupt

WITH TEENAGERS, I say, "Shhhhhh—don't interrupt me. I'm speaking" all the time. When I used to drive carpools, I remember telling all the kids to stop interrupting and stop talking over each other constantly. While interrupting seems to be prevalent among kids, it's something adults do all the time too. Learning to wait your turn to speak so you don't interrupt others isn't easy. While we've all been guilty of interrupting, there are some who consistently and blatantly interrupt others, oftentimes in a dismissive and downright disrespectful way. Others will catch themselves and apologize for accidentally doing so. Some are great at paying attention to whether or not they're interrupters and others simply don't care.

I'm hopeful you already know this, but interrupting someone can be rude and disrespectful, especially if done numerous times. Yes, we all do it from time to time. I'm certainly guilty of interrupting and make a conscious effort to try to avoid doing so. When I interrupt, I try to quickly catch myself, apologize, acknowledge I just interrupted, and ask the person to resume what they were saying. During the many interviews I conduct, I come across those guilty of being chronic interrupters. Surprisingly (or not!), there are a lot of these people out there! I try to respectfully provide this feedback to a candidate, especially if I intend to move them forward. My intent is to help them work on this bad habit prior to any possible interviews with my client (and just in general). Unfortunately, it doesn't always seem to matter because "interrupting too much" is feedback I receive and a reason many candidates don't get asked back. So please trust me when I tell you this is a horrible habit many have and one that needs to be broken. To be fair, in an interview, candidates know they have a limited amount of time and are often excited to share certain details. Inevitably, this can lead to interrupting. In addition, some people get a heightened level of nervous energy in interviews, causing them to be overzealous and do things they don't normally do, interrupting being one of them. Even though this can be understandable, some hiring managers / interviewers will assume this is their standard behavior and view it negatively.

Here's the rub—it's incredibly frustrating to be interrupted by someone…especially when someone does it repeatedly. Now, I know I am not alone when I say this, but I really don't appreciate it when people won't let me finish my thoughts. Even worse than that is when people try to finish my sentences for me. Call me crazy, but isn't it awfully bold to finish someone's sentence for them? Especially in an interview setting! It's one thing to do it with a friend or family member. But in an interview?! Shockingly, this happens a lot, and I can assure you, hiring managers do not look at this behavior kindly. In addition to sentence finishers, there are also sentence assumers, and these folks can be rather annoying too. These are people who interrupt and assume they know how the speaker is going to finish the sentence or thought. Once they interrupt, they take off running in that direction, and their assumptions aren't always right. Have you ever been in a conversation where halfway through a sentence, you're sure the speaker thinks one thing, and then as they keep talking, you're totally surprised that they think something different? Sentence assumers, especially when they assume incorrectly, can really hurt their opportunities.

When I find myself interviewing a serial interrupter, I'll eventually just stop talking. Some people realize what's going on. However, there are many who will just blab on and on without any clue. Interrupting is both disruptive and highly unproductive. Doing it once is not a big deal. If you're someone who can't wait your turn, though, I strongly—I emphatically—encourage you to work on this and fix it! Otherwise, you'll quickly sabotage your chances of advancing in an interview process to the offer stage. If you can't let others speak in an interview, hiring managers can only imagine what you'll be like once you're hired. They'll have visions of you in meetings and will assume no one else in the room will ever get a word in. Don't interrupt others when they're speaking!

Shhhhh, Stop Talking

GROWING UP, my brothers told me to shut up countless times a day. We weren't supposed to say "Shut up," but anytime my parents weren't around, that's what they said and I really don't blame them! I literally drove them crazy with my relentless yapping.

When I was young, I wasn't comfortable with silence. Ironically, now I can't get enough quiet…funny how things change! Seriously, though, do you think people who talk too much know that they do? Do you think they have any clue that others can't get a word in? The definition of *conversation* is "oral communications between persons." So conversations involve persons—notice that's a plural word, as in more than one. In an interview situation, a surefire way to tick off the person conducting the interview is to talk incessantly. Honest to G-d, there are few things more frustrating than trying to interview someone who will not stop talking.

Here are some pointers: When in an interview, first and foremost, your answers need to stay on point. Second, they need to be succinct and crisp. (Of course, one should provide a level of detail, but delivering a soliloquy is going overboard.) Some of us have a little voice inside our heads telling us when we're talking too much and / or if we're on a tangent and no longer on point. If you have that voice in your head, and if it's telling you this, then do yourself a favor and listen to that voice, because it's typically right! Another way to tell if you're talking too much is to think about how much time you've been speaking versus how much time they've talked. If you're dominating significantly, you need to stop! Also, look at your audience. Try to read the body language of those you're speaking with to see if there are obvious signs of boredom. If someone is yawning, fidgeting, looking down, looking away, or looking at a phone, or their eyes are glazed over, those are telltale signs you've lost the listeners' attention. When that happens, you might as well be speaking a foreign language, because nothing you're saying is being heard.

It's like the teacher from *Charlie Brown* talking…"*Wa waa waa wa wa waa…*" No one is registering what you're saying!

In addition to frustrating the interviewer, another negative aspect of interminable chatter is the more you talk, the less information you (the candidate) can gather. The more an interviewer talks, the more information you'll be able to receive about what's most important to those hiring for the position being discussed. This information is gold! This can and will help you determine if the role is truly a good fit. If you do in fact align with the role, any information gleaned will help you better position yourself as an ideal candidate. Or, conversely, you may quickly realize this isn't an opportunity that aligns and you'll be able to prevent yourself from wasting valuable time.

I have received feedback innumerable times about candidates who simply would not stop talking. I hear this a lot! So, bottom line, talking too much does not give you points in the "hire this candidate" column. Be sure to work on keeping your answers brief and to the point, and for Pete's sake, come up for air and let someone else speak! If you think to yourself, "Gosh, I'm doing most of the talking," you more than likely are! So in the words of the late and great Chris Farley, "Shut your big yapper!"

Listen

"SHHHHHHHHHH—STOP TALKING—JUST LISTEN!" I think I heard my parents say this a million times as a kid. I know I said it repeatedly to my own kids! In fact, I think I still say it to them. What is it with kids thinking their parents know nothing and never wanting to listen?

Over the years, you have hopefully learned what an incredibly important skill listening is. You've probably heard the saying that goes something like, "G-d gave us two ears and one mouth, so listen twice as much as you talk." One of the great things about listening is when we listen, we learn. In fact, we can learn a whole lot! In the world of sales, professionals are often taught the importance of not only listening but also making sure they're using "active listening" skills. According to *Sources.com* the definition of active listening is:

> Active listening is a communication technique that requires the listener to understand, interpret, and evaluate what they hear. The ability to listen actively can improve personal relationships through reducing conflicts, strengthening cooperation, and fostering understanding. When interacting, people often are not listening attentively. They may be distracted, thinking about other things, or thinking about what they are going to say next (the latter case is particularly true in conflict situations or disagreements). Active listening is a structured way of listening and responding to others, focusing attention on the speaker. Suspending one's own frame of reference, suspending judgment, and avoiding other internal mental activities are important to fully attend to the speaker.

Sales professionals are typically trained in this area and know that by actively listening to the prospect and / or client, they will dramatically increase their closing ratio. To be clear, in sales, closing business is a good thing!

Have you noticed good listening is a skill many people fail to possess? I see this daily! Trying to have a productive conversation with someone who won't listen is really exhausting, isn't it? When you don't listen, you don't learn.

In a job search process, and more specifically in an interview setting, listening is an essential skill candidates need to demonstrate mastery of. Admittedly, it's often difficult to actively listen during an interview because there's a lot going on. At any given moment, minds are racing. People are taking in their surroundings, observing the characteristics of those in the room, thinking about the answer they just delivered to a question, contemplating which question to ask next, focusing on something that was said, panicking that the interviewer saw the tiny amount of saliva fly out of their mouth across the table…and so much more. That being said, it's incredibly important for candidates to focus and use active listening skills! While interviewing, professionals need to remain truly present in the conversation.

Information imparted during an interview is invaluable!

Therefore, candidates need to fully hear, absorb, and interpret what's being said. Doing so will dramatically improve the odds of having a successful interview, which is obviously the goal, right? Think about it—as a candidate, if you're actively listening, you'll be better able to evaluate whether or not the position is potentially a fit technically / skill-wise as well as whether or not the company seems to be a good fit for you on a personal level. Information imparted during an interview often helps candidates learn what's most important to the particular interviewer. For example, many interviewers will describe the qualities and characteristics of an ideal candidate. Additionally, interviewers will often articulate the goals set forth for the position and company. Each interviewer may have slightly different priorities around what they're looking for in a candidate and they may have slightly different goals. You won't know if you don't listen. When armed with this information, astute candidates can better position themselves in alignment with those stated priorities. (Or they can realize it's not a fit and cut bait.)

Here's an example: During the start of any interview, I provide candidates with a detailed overview of the specific position we're going to discuss. Recently, I was working with a great client of mine. I was helping them find a senior-level sales professional for an individual contributor position they had open in Chicago. During interviews with umpteen candidates, I followed my normal process of explaining, in tremendous detail, the specifications of the role. I clearly stated the position was an individual contributor sales role and stressed the importance of knowing this role would remain an individual contributor position for the foreseeable future. I further highlighted that if the candidate was seeking a sales management position, this would not be the right opportunity to pursue. Just like I do in every search I work on, after going through a lengthy description of the position, I then conducted a thorough interview of the candidate. While doing so, I always ask the candidate questions around what they are looking for in their next opportunity. During this particular search, it was not atypical for candidates to state their desire was to find a sales leadership role!

Whaaaaaaaaaaaaaaaaaaaaaaaat?????

Ummmmm—did these people not hear what I just said? (Where are those active listening skills, I wondered?) After candidates made such an admission, I'd step in and restate the fact this role was an individual contributor sales role without a career path to management, at which point professionals would double back, changing their tune(s). Many would stress why they'd be fine with an individual contributor position and how management wasn't actually that important…backpedal, backpedal. Meanwhile, for decision makers like me, it was often too late. At that point, the toothpaste was out of the tube. The candidates had already shot themselves in the foot. In this example, it was pretty obvious many didn't actively listen to the overview I delivered. For if they had been listening, you'd think they'd have been smart enough to steer clear of highlighting a desire to move into a leadership role. Now, if a candidate truly had zero interest in an individual contributor sales position, it was certainly good for decision-makers to know this as soon as possible. Obviously, there was no need to waste time interviewing for the job. But if a professional had a sincere interest in pursuing the particular position and wanted to stay "in the game," they should have refrained from highlighting their desire to only consider opportunities that were sales leadership positions. This is obvious, right?

Moral of the story—you will find that you'll have a lot more success in interviewing if you truly pay attention and really hear the words someone is saying.

Listen!

It's a Small World

"IT'S A SMALL WORLD" isn't simply a favorite ride at Disney. (I mean, really, who doesn't love to go on that ride? It's a classic! Or maybe you don't love it. Whatever…just work with me!) As we grow up and move forward in our careers, many of us realize our world is indeed a very small one. Quite early in my executive search days, I learned how true this is. Everyone knows everyone! It's nuts!! The longer you stay in any one particular industry, the smaller it becomes. What this means is…you always need to protect your reputation. Reputations are hard to earn yet easy to ruin.

As professionals, we need to be mindful of a very key point:

Anything and everything you do *can* and *will* be held against you. Not just in a court of law, but in the boardroom too!

I've worked on many searches where candidates were rejected based on information gathered behind the scenes. Whether you like it or not, whether you think it's fair or not, it is reality! Reference checking doesn't only happen formally at the conclusion of an interview process. So be careful. We all know how negative information seems to magically pop up when you least want it to…Murphy's Law at its best! Unfortunately, past situations can rear their ugly head at any time, so make sure you do whatever you can to repair relationships and your reputation. Always treat people with respect, apologize if you've done something wrong, and try to be nice as you go about each and every day.

Not only do people in every industry know each other, but technology has also made our world even smaller. Social media sites enable people to see inside one another's lives. While I don't consider myself a prude, I must admit that various pictures and / or posts on social media sites frequently give me reason to pause. In fact, I often find myself wondering what someone's thinking. In this day and age, pretty much any Neanderthal can figure out how to use social networking tools to check people out. Pictures and posts can (and often do) come back to haunt someone. This is especially true in a job search setting. For this very basic reason, it's best to be extremely cautious about what you put out into cyberspace. Not only have I read an endless number of articles about this, but I've also seen this play out in real life numerous times. Who hasn't heard about professionals being rejected from various opportunities for posting questionable pictures and comments? This has and will continue to happen. It's not going to change. As we've discussed, everything you do is a representation of who you are, and most companies don't get too excited about hiring someone who appears to lack good judgement. Most don't get excited about hiring professionals who have: an issue with wearing enough clothes, a drinking or drug problem, a fascination with lap dances, an obsession with dark topics, incredibly strong political opinions, an aggressive style and sharp tongue, a sailor's mouth, and so on.

Please note—I will be the first to admit that I wholeheartedly enjoy using colorful language. I realize dropping an "f-bomb" or any select four-letter word here or there can be quite cathartic. But in a job search / interview setting, you must use common sense and discretion. Please be smart and always represent yourself in a positive and professional light.

Before you post something, anything, the barometer I suggest using is this: Ask yourself if you would be mortified if your post was on the front page of the *Wall Street Journal* or *New York Times*. Ask yourself if you'd be embarrassed if your parents or in-laws saw it. Now, if you have crazy parents like me, for whom pretty much anything goes, you may want to up the ante and ask yourself if you'd want the CEO of the company you work for to see it or if you'd be okay with your kids seeing it. If you're not sure, or the answer is no, then don't post it!

Again, it's a small, small world, and we always need to remember that people know one another and people talk. It isn't hard for others to learn things about you. So be careful!

You Don't Know Everything

GROWING UP, I remember saying I would never be like my mom. Not that my mom wasn't amazing. But we all undoubtedly had someone we thought nagged at us, right? One of my mom's favorite sayings was "You don't know as much as you think you do." I'm sure I was a teenager when she used that one with frequency. I totally thought I knew everything. What teen doesn't?! At the ripe age of twenty-one, upon graduating from college and entering "the real world," I quickly learned I didn't know much of anything. There was so much I needed to learn! And twenty-five (ahem) years later, there still is! And now, I have that full-circle moment numerous times a day (called "payback"), when it dawns on me that I sound exactly like my mother, and I'm actually quite proud of it. True to form, my kids frequently act like they know everything! I'm constantly having to remind them, in the words of Matt Foley (a.k.a. Chris Farley), they don't know "jack squat" and they need to stop and listen. Anyone with kids or anyone who's been around kids knows the *last* person kids want to listen to is their parents.

No matter what stage of life you're in, the truth is you (still) don't know everything! In job searching and interviewing, it's amazing to me how many people don't set themselves up for success by both seeking out as well as accepting the help being offered. What do I mean by this?

First, there are a million resources with tips on these topics. In prepping people for interviews, it's blatantly obvious many professionals don't seek out any information regarding job searching and / or interviewing. Why wouldn't you do a bit of research and get yourself some invaluable information? (Now, you're obviously reading this, so you've taken a solid step toward learning how to improve your job search and / or interview outcomes. Yay!) That said, if you just graduated from college and had to take a class about interviewing and where there was perhaps a book you had to read, do not think you're all set and couldn't possibly use more information. Don't assume you know everything. If you've done really well in your career and landed in your current job by sailing through their interview process, don't assume you know everything. Just because you were successful in interviewing there, doesn't mean you'll be successful interviewing elsewhere. If you're not actively looking but were contacted about a cool job opportunity you figure you'll explore but know you won't be devastated if it doesn't work out, don't assume you're good to go. You may get into a process and realize you're in love with the opportunity and suddenly you care a whole lot more than before. So, no matter what the situation is, know that we all need to bone up on our skills. In today's world, it's not hard to gather some great information to better yourself because, guess what…you don't know everything!

Second, aside from doing your own research around how to best conduct a job search and / or how to successfully interview, if you're working with a recruiter or someone like me: Please take our advice and our support to heart. Listen to us. We have information and insights you don't, and I think it's safe to say that people like me won't risk our own reputations by doling out bad advice to purposely sabotage you. There are so many stories with great examples I can give you to illustrate how, I'll generously say, not smart it is to ignore someone like me.

As I mentioned before, in prepping a candidate for interviews, 99.5 percent of professionals love what I cover and then about 0.5 percent don't. The ones who don't will often cut me off and say they already know everything there is to know, that what I'm covering isn't new info to them and thus they don't need the help. Here's the deal—I'm not going to insist on doing the prep. It's a chunk of time for me to give to the person, and for those who don't value my expertise, I will wrap up the call. Unfortunately, while I haven't tracked it perfectly, I can tell you that many of those candidates got cut from an interview process for things the prep covers! Ugh! Had they just taken the time to listen, they likely could have avoided whatever it was they did wrong. But no, they thought they knew everything and it turned out they actually didn't. Listen to a recruiter's advice. We eat, breathe, sleep this stuff 24-7-365. This is our area of expertise. We have great insights. Not just about the company, the job, the hiring team, etc., but we also have great insights around how to be successful in interviews. Most of us can't and / or won't give you the answers to the test because we do not want to rig the system. The right people won't end up in the right jobs if we did. However, we still have valuable advice that could make or break how things go for you.

A quick example: I did my normal prep for a candidate, Jane. She was interviewing with a great client and was so excited about the opportunity. She was really perfect for them and vice versa. In the prep, I highlighted the importance of writing and sending thank-you notes. Jane mentioned she'd read somewhere that, in today's world, crafting / sending thank-you notes wasn't necessary. I said I'm old school and while some professionals state thank-you notes aren't important, I stressed they remain important and should not be disregarded. I left it at that. My point of view was clearly stated. I did not tell her that this particular client puts a ton of stock into thank-you notes because I wanted Jane to make her own decisions. Fast forward a few days later. Her interview went great. She was even more excited about the opportunity. I said that's wonderful and indicated I'd follow up with the client the next day to get feedback. The next day the client said they were really excited about her but they hadn't received a thank-you note yet and thus wouldn't commit to moving forward. Now, I could have hung up and immediately called her to say she needed to get a note in if she wanted to move forward. But, I had already told her it was important and it was up to her to decide if she was going to listen to me. Afterall, I made it very clear in my experience thank-you notes were extremely important. Well…she didn't write the note and got cut. When I followed up with her, I asked her if she'd written a note. She said no. I asked why. She said she discussed it with her husband subsequent to our conversation and he reiterated her position. He told her they were no longer necessary. I asked her what her husband does for a living. She said he's a Director of Supply Chain for a manufacturer. I asked her if he had ever been a recruiter. She said no. I then politely explained she should have listened to me because she was getting passed over due to not writing a thank-you note. Now, you can blame it on my client and claim they're ridiculous for expecting a thank you. But that'd be really dumb to do. Knowing the role was a client facing role where they'd expect thank-you notes to be written, they considered this a representation of someone's follow-up skills. Jane failed to impress them. Other candidates did. They moved forward with the others. End of story. Jane regretted not listening to me. She agreed it was stupid to listen to her husband in this situation because not only wasn't he an expert in interviewing like a recruiter is, but he also didn't know the client and I did. He didn't know everything!

Moral of the story: If a recruiter offers you insight, if a member of the hiring team offers you insight, if a current employee offers you insight, listen to it! And I mean really, truly listen (like we discussed in a prior chapter). Hear what they're saying. And take it to heart. These people know things about the process, about the company, the people, and more. Their intel is priceless and will be extremely useful to you, ideally leading to better outcomes. You don't know everything!

Everything Has a Consequence

AT A YOUNG AGE, we're taught a very important lesson—there are consequences for all of our actions. Every single thing we do, whether positive or negative, has a consequence.

I'll forewarn you that part of this has already been covered. However, since these are all important points, they bear repeating. We'll move quickly, I promise.

While some of you are from my generation and remember life preinternet (yikes!), I'd like to think everyone is aware of how the World Wide Web can both help and hurt you in a job search or interview setting. As mentioned, the internet makes our world a much smaller place. We can quickly connect with people—friends, colleagues, former classmates, professionals, or someone we've never officially met but want to meet. It doesn't matter where someone lives; the internet brings us all together. Technology has clearly helped people and professionals in countless ways, but boy oh boy, is this a double-edged sword! For all the positives, there are countless dangers lurking, and you best beware!

Email: Can you imagine life without it? I can. Yes, I remember! I remember life before email, before cell phones, before answering machines, and even before microwaves…but no need to make myself feel old, so I'll stop here. Back to email—in the push of a button, we can connect with people from every corner of the globe. In today's world, email is a necessary tool for job searching. Companies and candidates often connect via email first, and thus we all need to have a personal email address. Here's the deal with email addresses—you absolutely must have a professional email address for any and all correspondence related to your professional life. Let me repeat myself—you must have a professional email address to communicate from.

Email addresses like partyanimal@, dancingfool@, catlover@, boozehound@, ballerinagirl@, jessesgirl@, fuzzywuzzy@, dogrescuer@, shaker666@, beerchugger@, lovergirl@, hoozierfan@, cabbagepatchdollsrock@, etc., are absolute no-nos! For the most part, you can clearly see how very not professional (dare I say ridiculous) these are. If you want to use an email address like those with friends, that's fine (albeit dorky). However, in your professional life, you absolutely must use a professional email address. Period. End of story! Email addresses like the aforementioned ones give off such a poor first impression that you might be rejected before your actual email even gets read. In case you'd like a few examples of what constitutes a good / professional email address, here are a few: Juliesmith99@, Juliehsmith@, JHSmith2@, SmithJ2@, SmithJH2@, SJH2@. If you're not sure, ask a few friends to help you. If you have a common name, it can be hard to use your first and last name. But there are plenty of options out there to enable you to keep it professional. Believe it or not, your email address is often the first impression you make.

<u>Social Media</u>: While we've already homed in on the internet and the importance of using technology to network, I can't express strongly enough the negative consequences technology can have. Social media is a huge part of our everyday existence. This has provided people with a portal into one another's lives, which means recruiters and hiring managers / companies can check up on you and snoop all around to learn more about who you are and the decisions you make. No matter what level the job, before extending an offer to a candidate, many companies will browse around to see what they can uncover. Many mistakenly think this concern around social media is more applicable to college graduates. After all, a lot of us who went to college likely had a few wild times. However, I've been left speechless more times than I care to count by the tasteless pictures I've seen of various professionals, at all levels, on many sites. I'm sure you, too, have seen crazy pictures. While researching candidates, I've seen pictures of people who were hunting and had their kill draped over their shoulders. Ick! Whether you agree with hunting or not, most don't want to see something dead draped around your shoulders. This can call into question your judgment. I've seen pictures of people dressed in clothes that leave little to the imagination. I've seen pics posted of men who look, shall I politely say, a bit tipsy, with arms draped all around a bevy of blondes (all

very scantily clad). I've seen people with bongs in their hands. I've seen pictures of someone surrounded by dolls. (Like the kind of dolls I had in my room when I was a little girl. Cute at age four. Not so cute at thirty-four. Also can be super creepy!) In addition, I've seen pictures of clowns (scary!), cartoon characters doing weird things, pictures of skulls and crossbones, pictures of Jack Nicholson from *The Shining*...this list could go on and on for a very long time!

Equally as bad—some people post comments that are rude, aggressive, lewd, and / or funny but not so funny because they're not OK for the public to see. These can be very inappropriate and highly unprofessional. You have to think before you put anything online. Nothing truly disappears. You have to know that by now, right? You may not be a tech whiz, but you should know that every social media site has security settings you can use to prevent the general public from being able to see photos / comments. It's essential to protect what's posted and make sure you know what is visible to the masses and what's only visible to specific people. There are many great candidates out there who've been passed over due to postings, pictures, and / or comments made on various sites. Don't put yourself in that situation. Oh, and not to make you too paranoid, but be sure to pay attention to photos others may have posted of you too. The stakes are high, and the consequences can be dire.

OK, so you may be reading this and thinking you should just get rid of all of your social media and have zero footprint out there. Not so fast! This isn't necessarily a good idea. I've had candidates whom I've tried to find on LinkedIn who didn't have a profile. This raises eyebrows in today's world, not just for me but for my clients too. If you are in a highly specialized field that's very niche, it might be OK to not be on LinkedIn. But for most, it's truly important to have a profile. What about the other sites, like Facebook, Instagram, Twitter (X) etc.? Is it acceptable to not be on any of those sites? The answer really depends on what field you're in and what functional area you're in. If you're in the technology sector and you're in marketing, it might be odd to the hiring team and negatively impact you. If you're in IT and set up payroll systems, it might not matter quite as much. When I want to find someone and have trouble doing so, I'll simply ask the candidate if they have a profile, and if they don't, I'll ask why not. If their answer seems legit, I move on without much thought. If something makes me suspicious, I might dig deeper or pass that person over for someone else.

<u>Treat People Well</u>: Everything does have a consequence, and this includes when you mistreat people. Remember the saying "What goes around comes around"? Well, when people are rude, disrespectful, cold, or simply not helpful, karma has a way of coming back to bite offenders in the ass. If you mistreat people, you can and should expect a negative consequence. That being said, it is simply so much easier to be kind to those around you. While being courteous and respectful should be a given, it's also important to keep in mind that anyone and everyone you come into contact with can be a potential link to a future position or business.

So…treat people the way you want to be treated!!

Make sure you're polite and helpful to others. The consequences of positive actions are bound to be good. You never know who can help you get your next job, so don't be an ass!

<u>Don't Rush</u>: The consequences of rushing and being hasty can be devastating! We talked about this. While proofreading your work, being thoughtful and more strategic, tailoring any and all of your communications, etc. will take additional time, you will reap the rewards! When people rush, there are consequences. Mistakes happen, and those can quickly lead to rejections.

There are a million things I can speak to in this chapter because, truly, everything has a consequence! If you're slow to respond to a company's or recruiter's outreach, you might miss out on a great opportunity. If you don't give something your best effort, you might not get the best outcome. If you walk into something feeling as though you're not good enough or that you won't succeed, you probably won't do well. If you aren't careful on social media, it can be the reason you don't get a job offer. If you don't help others, they won't help you. If you move hastily, mistakes can happen. If you don't proof your work, you might have mistakes. I could go on and on and on. Just remember, good or bad, there are always consequences to our actions.

You Can Be Anything You Want to Be—ish

I THINK WE ALL LOVE TO ASK KIDS, "What do you want to be when you grow up?" Hearing a child's response to this question is so fascinating. Kids have wild and vivid imaginations; their thoughts, hopes, and dreams often reveal they have very lofty goals, often with no restraint. After all, kids are frequently told, "You can be anything you want to be."

Ummm—no, you can't. Pop! I just burst your bubble. Sorry.

One of the many hard lessons we learn over the years is you can't always be anything you want to be. There are certain skills and abilities each person excels at. Conversely, there are certain things people—to put it bluntly—are either not as talented at or, worse yet, simply suck at. Most people cannot truly excel in every single thing they do. (Yes, people can absolutely work hard to gain skills, improve upon them, etc. But that's not what we're talking about here.) This is known as recognizing one's strengths and weaknesses. Perfect example—I wanted to be a professional gymnast. Problem was, no matter how hard I tried, I was only so good. Never good enough. Another—as shared earlier, my hands shake. No matter how hard I try, I can't wish it away, concentrate it away, learn it away, or practice it away. It's a neurological issue and won't ever change. Thus, I could never, ever be a surgeon. If that was a dream of mine (good news—it wasn't!), there was simply nothing I could have done to achieve it. I know my inability to have steady hands is a weakness of mine, and it limits me, not only in the medical field but also in other fields that require precision with hands. (Not that you would, but don't ask me to be on your Jenga team or to do your makeup for a big event!)

In a job search or interview setting, professionals are told to highlight their strengths and minimize their weaknesses. This certainly makes sense. However, in an effort to not get overlooked in a competitive job market, professionals often portray themselves as experts in virtually every possible area. Knowing that on average hiring managers spend less than a minute scanning most résumés and knowing many companies may be leveraging AI technology to scan résumés looking for select key words, professionals will pepper their résumés full of every buzzword or phrase out there with the hope of not being weeded out. For example, I've seen résumés with summaries reading something like this: "Exceptional in areas including but not limited to business development, operations, human resource management, project management, marketing, social media, account management, sales, analytics, product development, event planning, strategy, market research, planning and strategic execution, leadership, problem-solving, customer service, call center oversight, thoracic surgery, and puppy training."

Really??? You're exceptional in all of those areas?

Perhaps you should also add "able to cure cancer and achieve world peace!" and then run for president, because you sound f*cking great!

Seriously, though, we all know someone can't possibly be remarkable in so many areas. Unfortunately, professionals who try to present themselves in this way (even if their summary isn't quite as overstated as the one above) are doing themselves an enormous disservice. I'm sure you've heard the saying "jack-of-all-trades, master of none." It's virtually impossible for any human being to be the best in every possible facet of work and life. It's far better to identify your key strengths and home in on them. I understand the logic behind trying to be all things, but candidly, the idea stinks! When taking this approach, you're wasting your time and lessening your chances of receiving an interview. By the way, this isn't just something people do on their résumés. I also see LinkedIn profiles where professionals position themselves in a similar fashion so as to ensure their profile pops up in more searches. While I'm not a betting type of gal, I'm so utterly confident this strategy backfires that I'd be willing to put my 401(k) on it! Here's the deal—when you do this, one of two things will happen. Either the reader will assume you're full of shit and decide not to interview you for that very reason. Or they'll wrongly assume you are, in fact, extremely talented in areas you truly are not. And this, my friends, can lead you down a dangerous path. If you don't have product management expertise, do you really want people reaching out to you about positions within product management? If you're hired into a product management role where they expect a certain level of experience you actually don't have, do you think you can just wing it and achieve the expectations set forth?

Undoubtedly, every person has strengths. So be honest with yourself and state what really stands out as your core / key strengths. We can't be all things to all people, so highlight your strengths and position those in the best possible way. Presenting yourself as a "jack-of-all-trades, master of none" will not help you as you go through your job search!

The exception to this is if you're looking for your very first "professional" job. If that's the case, you aren't going to claim expertise in many areas because you don't have true work experience. If you've had relevant internships, then you should use those to highlight experience. Otherwise, you need to determine what path you're trying to pursue, and if there are any synergies you can bring forward to show tangential experience, great. However, it's often challenging.

Bottom line is—know your strengths and use those as guides. With hard work, grit, determination and time, you can absolutely achieve great things. I was always taught, anything in life that's good is never easy. When you work really hard, when you dedicate time to learning and growing, good things will happen. If a path you choose doesn't seem to be panning out, pivot. Many people have experienced this. (Many successful startups evolve into businesses that are different from the original plan.) While the sky might not actually be the limit, no one can stop you from working extremely hard. And if you do that, you'll be able to be anything you want to be…"ish."

Memory Is a Tough Game

DID YOU EVER play the game Memory while growing up? I absolutely loved this game and was thrilled my kids loved it too. They spent hours upon hours playing, and like me, they found so much joy in turning the right cards over when they knew there was a match.

I often wonder why we as adults tend to lose the keen sense of memory we used to have. (Save the blonde jokes!) The explanation I tend to prefer goes something like this: the older we get, the more stuff we have to remember. Eventually this stuff starts to fill up all of our memory compartments. I like to picture an actual storage room that gets filled with boxes stacked floor to ceiling, one row after another. At some point, there's no room left. With the storage room filled to capacity, it becomes increasingly difficult to locate a specific box quickly. Similarly, when our memory compartments keep filling up, eventually the storage room is filled and retrieving the "box" packed with the details we're seeking is just not so easy. Thus, with age, we fill lots of boxes and accessing information becomes more and more challenging. If you have a junk drawer like mine, you know exactly what I'm talking about. Our junk drawer is filled with stuff that's been randomly tossed in there, and with everything jumbled together, it can be quite a daunting task to find whatever it is I'm in search of. (Yesterday it was a book of stamps…took almost five minutes to find.)

So where am I going with this? How does the game of Memory relate to job searching and interviewing? Actually, in more ways than you might remember—ha!! Sorry! Had to do it!

OK, first and foremost, while we've covered this already, I can't stress enough the importance of getting yourself organized before launching a search. Meaning, you need to have some type of tool to keep yourself organized so you know the following:

- Whom you reached out to (name, title, company, relationship to the person)
- When you reached out to them (date)
- How you reached out to them (phone, email, text, social media)
- What happened when you did all this, which means you need to take notes (if you had a conversation- when, how, what happened, next steps)
- Which job(s) you applied to (name of position, job #, company name)
  - Track what happened and when it happened, and have details you can easily access at a moment's notice. I've reached out to numerous professionals who, when I've shared the name of the company I'm working with, simply couldn't remember if they'd already reached out to the company directly. The name may sound familiar to the candidate, but they had no way to determine whether or not they'd already reached out to the company, applied to a job, and / or possibly had a conversation. Or they may know for sure that they'd had a conversation with the company but can't remember when the conversation happened and / or whom they spoke with, all because they didn't track any of their activity. In such situations, I've encouraged the person to do a search on their computer, but often that proved fruitless and they weren't able to answer any of the important questions I asked. Now, not only is this a bad look to someone like me, but imagine if an internal talent acquisition person reaches out and the professional can't recall whether or not they'd had a prior conversation. Keep in mind, it could have been months earlier and thus the details easily get lost in someone's brain. How does it make the person look bad? For starters, if it comes to light that the candidate previously engaged with them in some way and that point wasn't disclosed, the hiring team may question this person's honesty. They may wonder if the professional was trying to hide that fact for any reason. In addition, the company may wonder if the professional is buttoned-up and organized. All of those questions can negatively impact that person's candidacy.

Don't rely on memory because in any job search or interview setting, there's a lot that happens and it's easy for things to get confusing fast! Being able to quickly put the pieces of the puzzle together is helpful. For example, let's say you've interviewed with a company three times and the last interview was two weeks ago and you suddenly get a call from the admin, Jeff, who has been coordinating your interviews. Jeff may want to schedule you for a couple more interviews. What if Jeff asks you if you've already met with / interviewed with John Smith. It really doesn't look good if you can't respond with confidence as to whether or not you have. And trust me…if you're interviewing with a number of companies, it isn't always easy to keep everyone straight. Or perhaps you're only interviewing with this particular company, but in your current job, you meet with lots of different companies and thus names get a bit mixed up in your head. What if a VP of HR from one of the three companies you're interviewing with calls you and asks you what you thought of your conversation with the head of client services? It's certainly helpful to have notes handy so you can quickly refresh your memory about that conversation. Or perhaps you were told nine months ago the position you were interviewing for with ABC company was put on hold but you'd hear from them the minute the search was resumed. And suddenly you receive a call asking you if you'd like to revisit the process because they're relaunching the search. It's a million times more stressful when you can't easily find notes and refresh your memory on all that took place nine long months ago. Being organized so you don't have to rely on your memory is critical and will enable you to be far more successful in your efforts.

"Don't rely on memory" also means not everyone will remember you. This means it's your job to remind people who you are, especially if you haven't been in regular communication for a while. We covered this before, but as a reminder, if you're reaching out to someone (via any form of communication), here are the things you should always do:

1. Quickly state who you are.
    a. Provide a brief summary of your professional background.
    b. If you've "met" before, be sure to state where and how you two met. Was it via email after an introduction from Bill Smith? Or was it face-to-face at the ABC Trade Show two years ago when Nancy Thompson introduced you to each other?

  c. Refresh the person's memory by sharing details, pertinent details. Something like "We were introduced by Nancy Thompson at the ABC Trade Show, and we laughed about the juggling clown who walked by us. You shared how you were a clown in a skit you did for a talent show. We then discussed the possible marketing position your team may have opening up in the fall. So I'm following up with you to see if that role is in fact going to be available soon…"

2. Clearly state why you're reaching back out to the person. Define what your objective is and provide any additional information that will best help the person *help* you. For example, "We were introduced by Nancy Thompson at the ABC Trade Show, and we laughed about the juggling clown who walked by us. You shared how you were a clown in a skit you did for a talent show. We then discussed the possible marketing position your team may have opening up in the fall. So I'm following up with you to see if that role is in fact going to be available soon because I'm about to launch a new job search and would love to explore such a role with your company…"

  If you are sending someone an email, I'm well aware it might take a few extra minutes to put this overview together, but it's far more productive than sending someone an email that simply says something like, "Hi. Just checking back in with you. Wanted to know if you have a marketing role open now or if one will be in the future."

  I'm really lucky to have incredible friends, many of whom are married to wonderful people. A lot of my closest friends are ones I've known for well over ten years, some for over thirty years (oh jeez, time goes fast!). Theoretically, I should absolutely know what all of my friends and their husbands do professionally. However, I can honestly say I can't tell you *exactly* what everyone does for a living. To make matters worse, I can't clearly articulate to you what a select few extended family members do professionally. (Now don't go judging me…I can tell you roughly what these people do, but I certainly can't be eloquent about it.) And I assure you I'm not alone in this. Many people struggle with accurately summarizing in detail what people they know do in their careers. So what does this mean? Simply put—you can't assume people remember / know things about you, and this includes those you consider closest to you. For this reason, you need to make it easy for people by reminding them what you do professionally, what your goals and aspirations are, and anything else that will help them help you. Even if the person you're reaching out to is a good friend, it's better to err on the side of caution and provide a brief recap of the specifics. Most people do not have time to read an email from you and then go research your background, pull up your résumé, look you up on LinkedIn, etc.

To give you an idea of what I'm talking about, here are some examples of the types of emails I frequently receive:

- "Hi, Nicki, you and I connected a while back. Just wanted to let you know I am still looking. Please keep me in mind."
- "Hi, Nicki. Just checkin' in. What's new?"
- "Hi, Nicki—wondering if anything interesting has crossed your desk. Please keep me in mind."

As you can see, the senders didn't include any additional information to remind me who they are and what they're looking for. And oftentimes, the sender doesn't attach their résumé.

Now, I truly wish I could remember each and every person I've talked with, but unfortunately, I simply can't. Of course, there are many I do remember. But being an executive recruiter, I interview *a lot* of people each day, five to seven days a week, which adds up to a lot of interviews very quickly. When a recruiter receives an email such as the ones above, without relevant detail around who the professional is and what they're looking for, it's hard to quickly identify if my firm has any active or future searches that might be a fit. Keep in mind, in most professions, people are bombarded with emails and calls daily. Thus, even if the professional you're reaching out to isn't an executive recruiter, it's incumbent upon you to remind the person who you are, what you're looking for, and why you're reaching out. Like we've discussed at nauseum, help them help you. This isn't a game. It's real life. So don't rely on anyone's memory!

People Aren't Mind Readers

GUESS WHAT I'M THINKING. You can't. Why? Because people aren't mind readers. If they were, a lot of people would lose a lot of friends. Lucky for all of us, we don't always know what others are thinking. As adults, many of us learn, especially in relationships, that open and honest communication is key because you can not know what your significant other is thinking at all times. Admittedly, for some of us, this isn't an easy lesson to learn. But that's a different book...

Connecting the dots to job searching and interviewing, this means that as a candidate, if you want something to happen, you need to speak up and clearly tell someone. Don't mince words and beat around the bush. Say what you want to say, and say it with confidence (politely, of course!). Don't assume interviewers can read your mind by assessing your facial expressions or body language. Don't assume decision-makers will reach the right conclusions about you on their own. Speak up and tell your audience what you want them to know. Anytime you leave things in the hands of the other person, you're playing a dangerous game of chance. Anytime you leave things unsaid and hope the other person can figure it out on their own by reading your mind, you're rolling the dice, and you might not like the results. Candidates must know others can not read their minds.

I've interviewed many candidates who are challenging to read. Some professionals clam up a bit during an interview, becoming pretty stoic, which is often the result of nerves. This presents quite a challenge for the interviewer, because when a candidate is stoic, it isn't always obvious what a candidate's level of interest is. So do yourself a favor. If you're interested in a job, you have to say it! Don't make interviewers try to read your mind and guess. People aren't necessarily familiar enough with your facial expressions and tones to know if you're interested when you aren't spelling it out. It's also important to note—many interviewers are looking for someone who is passionate about a particular position and will opt to pass over candidates who don't seem genuinely excited about the opportunity. Don't misunderstand me…I'm not telling you to fake your enthusiasm. However, two candidates being equal, the majority of hiring managers will make the offer to the person they know wants the job. So speak up; don't make someone read your mind. Don't make someone guess.

During interview processes, candidates often want to come across as extremely flexible and total team players. What can happen, though, is that when presented with questions, many of those professionals won't answer with full honesty because they fear putting their own candidacy at risk. For example, if hiring manager Fred was interviewing candidate Bob and asked something such as "Bob—if given the choice, would you rather work from our downtown office, our suburban office, or home?" Bob may have said, "Gee, Fred, I am completely fine with any option. I am just so excited about joining this company and being able to contribute quickly. I have no preference" when in reality, Bob strongly preferred to work from home. But Fred can't read minds and doesn't know this. Bob clearly said he was flexible. Unfortunately, when Bob got an offer, he was disappointed to learn he would be working from an office, not home. He found out that the team he was assigned to works from the corporate office in the city and had recently changed their hybrid work policy. They just asked everyone to return to the office full time. During the interview process, they didn't tell Bob about the change because he said he was flexible, that he didn't have a preference of where he'd be working from. The fact Bob was going to have to work from an office could have caused Bob to decline the offer. Or if he decided to join the company, he might not have been happy and might have resigned fairly quickly. Moral of the story is Bob should have been honest and said what he really preferred when asked the question.

This is an example of what to do: I was working on a CFO search for a startup company and the hiring manager, who happened to be the CEO, said that this hire would not lead a team for the foreseeable future. They would be an independent, one-person finance team. The CEO said, based on the growth of the company, the CFO would eventually be able to build a team but the CEO didn't know how quickly that would happen. When I interviewed CFO candidates, I had numerous people who said they were OK with not having direct reports (a team) immediately upon hire, but that they'd only be okay with this for a short period of time. Not being able to read their minds, I asked them to articulate what a short period of time meant... we all know the definition can vary from person to person. I sincerely appreciated their honesty and ultimately decided not to move forward with any of them. They told me what they were thinking, and it helped us determine the CFO position being discuss did not align all that well with their career goals and preferences.

In every interview process, I ask candidates what their compensation requirements / expectations are. I explain that I need to clearly understand what they need to see compensation wise to ensure a role is worth their time and consideration so we don't waste time discussing a role that's misaligned. Quite often candidates feel stressed about answering this because they don't want to create a situation where they get a lower offer than they could have or potentially say a dollar amount that's too high and knocks them out of contention. This is a tricky topic and a question I always recommend answering directly so you don't waste your time. There are many ways to handle this. One is, before you answer, you can ask the interviewer what the compensation range is first and see if they'll provide the information to you. If they are willing to give you the range, you'll then be able to determine if the role is in a range amenable to you. Another option is to respond saying something such as, "I'm flexible. Before I waste your time, though, I'm assuming the range for this role is north of xxxx." Here you will state a dollar amount you believe the role is within the range of and actually state a range. Make sure whatever you as a candidate need compensation wise is in that range. See their response. If the role seems to be below that dollar amount, you can bow out of the process. And yet another option is you can answer this question with your range. Just put it out there. "I am looking for an opportunity with a base salary between $90,000 and $110,000 and a bonus on top of this. Does this align? Is the role in that range?" Based on their response, you can further qualify your expectations by finding out more about their benefits. If a company covers the entire cost of benefits, this can be substantial money added to your paycheck. Bottom line is that a company / hiring team needs to know your expectations. They can't read your mind. If you want to ensure you're not wasting your time pursuing roles that aren't in your range, have the conversation. I've heard too many stories about people getting completely ridiculous offers they'd never accept at the end of extremely lengthy interview processes, which is never fun. It's a total waste of time and energy.

I know it can be very tricky when interviewing and job searching. Professionals want to do everything they can to protect their interests but sometimes this can backfire. Always remember that people can't read minds, and if you don't make your thoughts known, you might end up with things you don't want.

Follow Directions

BACK WHEN I WAS GROWING UP, the importance of following directions was drilled into our heads. We learned consequences of failing to do so were often harsh. In school, you could get sent to the principal. In sports, you could get penalties and lose games. Labs in science class were dicey when directions weren't followed. Bottom line, we knew failing to follow directions could land us in very hot water. The consequences were never and are never fun.

In a job search and / or interview setting, following directions is paramount. Companies and search firms have certain procedures applicants are expected to follow, and failing to do so can often result in a candidate's rejection. There are many ways this applies. Here a few examples…

When candidates reach out to me to introduce themselves, hoping I might be working on a position that could potentially align with their backgrounds, I often ask them to fill out a pretty simple questionnaire. This takes most people less than fifteen minutes to complete and, by the way, this is much more general in nature compared to the candidate profile questionnaire used for specific searches. I explain how this helps my firm best understand who they are and what type(s) of positions might match up. What we do is not unique. In fact, this is standard practice for many search firms. For that reason, you can imagine how blown away I am by the professionals who send this document back to me half-filled-out, with no explanation around why certain questions were left unanswered. You know my mantra (cue *Jerry Maguire*): "Help me help you."

Seriously, this is important.
Read closely.
If you want people to help you, then you need to help them help you.

If you want my help, follow my directions. It's annoying as well as a bit rude and disrespectful to send back a document with half the questions left blank. Alternatively, some choose to respond with "see résumé" as an answer to one or more questions. This response really irks me! Of course I know I can look at your résumé and possibly find the answers to some of the questions. Anyone can look at your résumé! However, I asked you to fill out a document, and you can either follow my directions and do what I've asked, or you can roll the dice and possibly tick me off, ultimately jeopardizing whether or not I'll help you. Since I'm typically the gatekeeper who can get you in to or keep you out of opportunities, you might want to follow my directions.

Another example: When hiring managers ask candidates to do certain things like apply to a position in a specific way, fix a résumé in a particular way, work on a project, bring specific items to an interview, etc., please be sure to do so. I can't tell you how many candidates fail to do what's been asked of them. This does not give a favorable impression! You need to pay attention and follow the directions given to you! Why so many people mess this up, I'll never know.

While working with candidates, I always review their résumés, and whenever possible, I'll provide feedback and offer suggestions on ways to potentially make improvements. Without exception, I provide the disclaimer that I'm not a professional résumé writer and would never demand they make the changes. I emphasize I can't and won't make any changes to their résumés for them. When providing suggestions, I note how and why suggestions could be beneficial for them in general and if there's an actual position we're exploring together, how it helps them specifically there. Now, I haven't done a formal study but as previously discussed, I'd guesstimate about 85% of the résumés I review have a typo and / or inconsistencies worth cleaning up. And I'm not kidding you when I tell you about 10% of the time, professionals don't implement any recommended changes. They'll claim they forgot or didn't have time. Really?? You don't need to hear me slam folks for this, but you can imagine how thrilled I am to hear people say they just didn't have time to make the suggested changes to their résumés after I took the time to review it and then offer the suggestions. News flash—if you want others to take the time to review your résumé and offer you suggestions, suggestions that will help you move closer to job offers, but then claim you don't have the time to make those suggested changes, you're not going to win friends! Those people helping you by offering the suggestions might think you're a total jackass.

When working on a particular position with executive recruiters, I know it can be extremely frustrating when you aren't getting any feedback as to what the client thinks of your candidacy. As a recruiter, I can assure you a lack of feedback isn't always the recruiters' fault. Sometimes it's due to the client not providing feedback to the recruiter. Many companies are simply not great at giving timely feedback. While many in the recruiting field do the best we can to provide updates to candidates letting them know we're still waiting to receive feedback, some people get so frustrated, they decide to take matters into their own hands. They'll bypass the recruiter and go straight to the hiring manager to see if they can find out where they stand in the process. As a classically trained salesperson, I completely understand what someone is doing and why. In many ways, I can't blame them. However, I know this is rather risky and can ultimately backfire, which I've seen happen firsthand numerous times, and it isn't pretty. For example, I'm extremely fortunate to have many long-term clients. I've worked with these companies extensively for numerous years, and they look at me as a true partner, a valuable extension of their business. Clients like these are the best; we've built an incredible bond and have limitless respect and admiration for each other.

While working with these clients, there have been situations where the feedback was slow coming. A couple of professionals lost patience and likely didn't trust that I truly hadn't received feedback. So those professionals went around me, contacting hiring managers directly. While this hasn't happened often, when it did, certain clients saw this behavior as disrespectful toward me and toward their process in general, ultimately opting to take a pass on those professionals. Again, I completely understand how frustrating the whole process can be for a candidate, but please be careful. If a recruiter asks you to sit tight and wait on their feedback, you need to follow directions.

A few more examples: When hiring teams post roles, there may be instructions around how to apply. For example, sometimes you'll see they state they want résumés provided in a PDF format along with a paragraph sharing why the candidate thinks they're a fit for the job. If you fail to do one or both of these things, your candidacy can blow up instantly. Sending your resume via Word rather than PDF could be a non-starter. When scheduling an interview with a company, if you've been asked to bring something with you, like a portfolio of your work, yet you show up on the big day empty-handed, that could be a catastrophic mistake. If a job posting says to apply via email and explicitly states "no calls please" but you decide to call, you're rolling the dice and likely not going to get yourself into consideration.

Following directions isn't always easy, but in a job search and interview setting, failing to do so can lead to lengthier searches with a lot more disappointments. Slow down and pay attention to what's being asked of you. If you're being given specific directions, be sure to follow them!

The World Doesn't Revolve All Around You

IF MY MEMORY of a child psych class serves me correctly, there's a phase in the development of children where youngsters learn the world does not truly revolve all around them. Aren't those who never come to that realization called narcissists? "It's not all about you" is a favorite phrase in our house.

When my kids were younger and wanted something, they wanted it immediately! I remember them wanting to play certain games or with certain toys when they wanted to. I remember them wanting the television to be tuned to something they wanted to watch. I remember they always wanted to pick the restaurant when we went out to eat. They wanted to start and stop things on their terms. In case you didn't figure this out, that stuff didn't fly in our house. From a young age forward they learned they're not in charge and the world does not revolve all around them. (Truth—even though they're older, we still haven't mastered this concept.)

To tie this back to the topic at hand, the sooner those job searching realize an interview process does not revolve all around them, the better. What do I mean by this? Well, first, we all need to acknowledge that a hiring process is actually a very selfish process. Let me explain. At the beginning of any interview process, the company doing the hiring really only cares about what you can do for them. They tend to not be overly concerned about, or focused on, what their company or position can offer to you, the candidate. This means companies typically don't hire someone out of the goodness of their heart(s) to help the professional build upon certain skills, round out their résumé, take the next step in their career, reduce their commute, enable them to work from home, give them a job because they're unemployed, etc. For the most part, companies are looking to hire people who can fill a need they have and who can and will deliver results helping them to meet and / or exceed their goals. During an interview process, hiring managers often ask questions like these:

- "Why are you interested in this position?"
- "Tell me, why should we hire you?"
- "Why are you a good candidate?"
- "Why are you here?"

There are many flavors these types of questions come in, and if you're a candidate being asked such a question, you must remember this oh-so-important fact: hiring is selfish. Companies hire you based on what *you* can do for *them*. Thus, your answer must speak to what *you* bring to *them*. Be sure to answer from the angle of *what's in it for the company* versus *what's in it for you*. As honest as these answers are below, they're all about what's in it for you, the candidate and don't help the interviewer assess what's in it for them (what you bring to the table):

- "This job is exactly what I've been looking for. It is the next step in my career and will really help me advance my skills."
- "I really need a job. I'm unemployed right now and can't pay the bills."
- "I'm tired of commuting an hour each day, and this would be great because your office is five minutes from my house."
- "I really need to diversify my résumé. Your company is in a different industry from where I've spent the last eight years, which will really help me."
- "Are you kidding? Who wouldn't want to work here? You guys are the talk of Boston. Plus, you give free lunches every day."
- "Working for early stage start-ups, my life has been a bit too chaotic over the last few years. As you know, the last two lost funding, which resulted in me getting laid off. Being an established company, this gives me some much-needed stability."
- "My boss is psycho. I totally need to get out of there."
- "I don't know enough yet to answer that. You tell me…why should I want to work here?"

You probably get the gist of what I'm trying to highlight here. While all of those real-life candidate responses may have been truthful, none are helpful because they all highlight what is "in it" for the professional versus what's "in it" for the company. Of course, once a company falls in love with a particular candidate, they'll take into account what the potential employee might be looking for. However, companies do not hire you to help you! They will only hire you if they believe you can meet and exceed the expectations of the position they're trying to fill (regardless of whether there's a learning curve). Therefore, when you are asked, "Why are you interested in this position / our company?" your answer needs to first highlight what you bring to the table for them. Remember, your needs are important…to you! And if you're working with a recruiter, they should be well aware of what your needs are, too, so the two of you can focus behind the scenes on how opportunities align with those. (This is a great reminder—make sure you know what your priorities are as you evaluate companies and positions. Far too many professionals fail to give this consideration until they're far down an interview path. This can waste your valuable time! Take the time to put pen to paper and write out what your priorities and goals are. And yes, put them in order of importance. As you assess opportunities, this should be used as a checklist and guide.)

Back to the bigger point, though: In the early stages of an interviewing process, make sure you start off by underscoring what you can do for the company, and keep in mind that the world doesn't revolve around you! I never tell anyone what they should say because you need to be you. But remember, when you're asked questions like, "Why are you here?" you should think of it like a commercial on TV. Companies advertising a product don't come out and say "Buy our stuff so we can make more money and increase shareholder value." We all know that's the point of the ad. They want to get you to buy. And, to do so, they tell and show you what's in it for you, the consumer. Remember, companies are hiring based on what's in it for them.

Whether we like it or not, hiring is truly selfish. Think about it: You don't hire someone to be your dentist because that doctor needs more business. You do it because you want to take care of your teeth. You don't hire someone to sell your home for you simply because the person is just getting into real estate and needs a few clients. You want an expert who can sell your home quickly and get you the most money. You don't hire someone to remodel your kitchen because they're nice. You hire them because they do amazing work and can hopefully accomplish the remodel as painlessly as possible. Point is, you hire these people because you (hopefully!) feel confident they are going to help you with the strengths and skills they have. You're hiring them selfishly because you have a need and you want someone great to meet the task. Similarly, companies hire people based on what they bring to the company.

As a candidate who is interviewing for a job, you need to remember the world doesn't revolve around you. What you want, what you're looking for...as important as it is, companies care most about what you can do for them. So, in job searching and in interviewing, highlighting what you bring to them will enable you to stand out from other candidates and be more seriously considered (that is, assuming you bring much of what they're needing!).

Use Your Head

GROWING UP, my brothers and I were idiots. Not unlike most kids, we did some really dumb things. When my parents would find one of us jumping from the top of a flight of stairs, thirteen stairs up, we'd hear, "Use your head! You're going to break a leg—or your neck!" Or when they'd see us outside building various ramps to ride bikes, Big Wheels, and skateboards over, they'd quickly notice these were not well-engineered works of art, but were more like death traps, we'd hear, "Use your head! You're going to get hurt!" Or when we decided not to reveal a bad grade or share the news of a visit to the principal's office, we'd hear, "Use your head! Did you think I wouldn't find out about this?"

My dad was famous for saying, "Use your head! You gotta think!"

While everyone may not fully master "using your head" in grade school, hopefully as we age, we learn to be more thoughtful in everything we do.

At this point, we've spent time on many topics that can parallel "using your head." For example, we've talked about thinking before speaking. But let's take that one step further and include thinking before doing *anything*! Using your head is really important as it can save you from being a total idiot. While we've already laid out many of these points, let's briefly run through them and add a few more into the mix. Use your head means:

- Don't send a résumé titled "MJ resume v38 2020" to someone. Take the time to title it in a way that won't make the reader think either you've been looking for a job since 2020 or you had to create thirty-eight versions before someone possibly showed interest in you. As you can imagine, this can give the recipient a reason to pause. Readers might think you've been looking for a job since the Mesozoic era and fear there's some fatal flaw preventing you from being hirable. So, what should you do? Great question. A good option is to retitle your résumé every time you send it out with your name (first and last) and, if needed, put the month and year at the end of that title. Again, just be sure to constantly update it whenever you send it to someone—for example, "Nicki Perchik Resume July 2023." Note, you're ideally tailoring your résumé to every opportunity which should make this easier to do. Use your head!

- Don't get all pissy with recruiters or hiring managers. I know everyone has a lot to deal with in life, but you don't know what the other person is dealing with either. If someone is rude to you, try to be the better person and don't give attitude back. I've witnessed some people get completely bent out of shape with those who are extremely nice to them, and it's absolutely unacceptable. Not to mention this won't help advance your candidacy in any way. Every person matters and has influence. Be nice.
- Don't apply to a position by accidentally sending cover letters or résumés you've addressed to someone else. When ABC company receives a résumé you previously sent to (and still have addressed to) Jeff at XYZ company, that's a senseless mistake many won't and don't overlook.
- Don't send résumés / cover letters that make zero sense for the particular role. I realize we all make mistakes, but be sure you're sending correspondence you've tailored to each position and company. If you're applying to a sales position requiring over ten years of sales experience, sending a résumé that clearly shows you've been in marketing your whole career and thus do not have the requisite ten years (plus) of sales experience is typically a waste of time.
- Don't mass apply to every single job possible. The "spraying and praying" approach is a huge waste of time. If a recruiter recognizes you as someone who does this, they won't pay attention to your résumé at all. Be selective about what you're applying to and thoughtful in your approach.
- Don't send correspondence or résumés that aren't professional in nature. Again, if your work looks like something a grade-schooler could have created in tech class, don't use it! I often ask people, "On a scale of one to ten, one being awful and ten being exceptional, how do you rate your own

résumé?" It's amazing how many people give themselves a ranking below eight. I really don't expect a lot of people to give themselves a ten, but if you're sending a résumé out into the market you rate at a seven or below, that doesn't seem too smart, right?

- Keep your emotions in check—if you know you're likely to cry in an interview if asked why you're open to considering a new job, you're not ready to have an interview. If you know that you're likely to yell at an interviewer because you just can't keep your emotions regulated, then you shouldn't do the interview. If you can't answer questions without sounding bitter when you speak, you're not ready to interview. These behaviors can be disastrous for candidates. Keep your emotions in check! By the way, this is where practice really helps, because if you can get used to saying things in more of a routine way where they roll off your tongue, you have a better chance of being less emotional about whatever you're saying.
- If a hiring manager sends you an email requesting you answer a few questions, responding by saying "see my résumé" or "this is on my résumé" or "already discussed" is absolutely ridiculous. Yes, it can be quite annoying to have to retype or cut / paste some information already on your résumé, but if you want to be considered for a position, sometimes you have to take a little time to answer a few questions. Deal with it. Suck it up! Use your head! Think of it this way…if you're in the ER with chest pains and a doctor asks you what was going on, I highly doubt you'd just say, "See my chart. I answered that question with the triage nurse already." I'm fairly confident you'd answer the question the doctor posed to you with more substance and less attitude.
- Don't reach out to someone and say, "Please review my LinkedIn profile to see if I fit anything you're working on." We talked about this. Help people help you. Do not expect people to take their precious time to figure out who you are and guess what you might be interested in. They do not work for you.
- Don't post stupid stuff online; this includes rude / obnoxious comments as well as questionable pictures. I've belabored this one…but I gotta tell you, I see stuff on a daily basis that stops me in my tracks and makes me think, "What a f*cking idiot!!" If you're struggling to get a job and you're

someone who spends a lot of time on social media—Twitter, Instagram, Snapchat, Facebook, TikTok, or other sites—you might want to think long and hard about your social media behavior. And don't kid yourself: people see and / or can find just about anything! Think twice about every single picture, every single comment, every single video before posting. This stuff sticks with you and can be detrimental to a job search. (And when employed, it can affect your current position.) Be smart!

- Use a professional email address. Most people will be turned off by emails like "Poledancer69@..." or "Doghater1@..." or "kittenmommy2@..." As discussed previously, a professional email can be as simple as your first name and your last name at _____. Or first and last initials along with a number. Keep it professional.

- If you have a picture on LinkedIn, make sure it falls into the category of "professional." No, you don't have to go out and have a fancy photographer take your headshot (although those tend to look nice and be worth the investment). If the picture looks like a police mug shot, don't use it. If you're not smiling and you look angry, that might turn people off, especially if in a people facing role. If you're in HR and look unapproachable, that can be an issue. If you look drunk—not good. If you have a cartoon character, it might not be great…again, this depends on your functional area. Just remember, LinkedIn isn't Instagram; it's a professional site. So my advice is if you want people to look at you seriously, put a photo up that presents you in such a fashion. Use your head(shot)!

- Speaking of LinkedIn—have a complete LinkedIn profile! This is still the number one place hiring managers and talent acquisition people go to find great talent. People sometimes wonder why they can't gain traction when job searching, and oftentimes there are some rather easy things being overlooked. Having a complete LinkedIn profile is certainly an obvious one. This is your online résumé, and as such, it needs good content.

  Word of caution—there's a fine line between providing helpful detail and overloading your profile with so much gobbledygook that it's impossible to determine who you are. Now, I realize some people fear updating their profile as they're worried their boss may find out and then think they're looking for a new job. I remind people (a) you can set your profile up so your network isn't notified every time you make a change, (b) the odds are great your boss is pretty busy and isn't monitoring who is updating LinkedIn all day, and (c) having a good LinkedIn profile is important for credibility in your current position. Since many of the positions we work on are in client-facing roles, the reality is it's extremely important to have a strong LinkedIn profile because external people will do research on the company and on you. A strong profile gives you and your company more credibility. Think about it…when Joe Blow calls into ABC Manufacturing and gets a meeting, where do you think people from ABC go to find out about Joe Blow in advance of their meeting? Yep, you guessed it…they go to LinkedIn to research Joe Blow. If Joe has a robust profile, this will put him and his company in a stronger position than if he has a weak profile. In fact, Joe's profile may be a big reason why he got the meeting in the first place. Having a complete LinkedIn profile is important.

- Interviewers, no matter how cool they are, are not your best friends. Many people have had an interview with someone they instantly hit it off with. You know what I'm talking about. This is the interview you walk out of thinking it felt nothing like an interview. In fact, these meetings feel an awful lot like you're out for a drink with a good friend. You have instant rapport, and there is an ease about the conversation; it feels completely natural and totally normal. Here's the deal—do NOT forget—you are on an interview! As much as you think this person is going to be your next best friend, you better remind yourself that you're on an interview. Think before you speak. Use your head!! What happens when people get too comfortable? Well, they often share things they shouldn't. Many interviewers have a disarming style, and while this takes the pressure off by putting people quickly at ease, it can be a double-edged sword! An interview is not the place to talk about your dating life, your psycho boss, your awful divorce, your drug-addicted sister, your issue with bourbon, what a hard time you've had since you've been laid off, how incredibly disappointing this job search has been, how messed up your middle child is, the mental issues your mother has, how jealous you are of people who have easy jobs, how you like to be very involved at your kids' school, everything your parents did wrong when raising you, your challenging in-laws, or anything else that has absolutely nothing to do with how you are going to add value to both the position you're interviewing for and the company as a whole. You're on an interview and everything is being evaluated.

- You know everyone's phone has caller ID, right? So why in G-d's name would someone call another person relentlessly without leaving a message or sending a text? The only time that's legit is if you're in jail. In that situation, we know you only get one call and obviously you don't want to waste it talking into someone's voice mail. In a job search setting, please do not be a stalker and call hiring managers or recruiters eighty-five times in one day. (Creepy!) Doing this is completely unprofessional and super annoying and makes you appear desperate. If you need to get ahold of someone, leave a voice mail and / or send a text. Additionally, you can send an email, but make sure to acknowledge the multiple approaches, too, so someone doesn't find you to be overly aggressive. Then be patient and assume the person will receive your message(s). You need to give them ample time to get back to you. You aren't always the first call someone is going to return. So it may take a little time.

- Any number you provide as your contact number must have a professional greeting on the voice mail. While job searching, please don't have your children, grandchildren, or any children for that matter say the greeting on your voice mail. I've called many cell phones and have heard, "Hi. You've reached my mommy's phone. She can't answer. Please leave a message." I understand your cell is a personal phone, but if you give out this number when job searching, assume it is now a business phone, and thus it's best to stick with a standard, classic greeting. I'm sure your kids are adorable! They sure sound super cute on those greetings! But when you're job searching, don't have them on your greeting.

    I've also called professionals who've had greetings where they're saying things like, "Yo, wassssssupppppp? Leave me a message! I said...leave me a message!" Here's one I found amusing: "Why are you calling me? [long pause]...oh, it better be good." There are people who opt to use a movie clip as their greeting. I've heard funny clips from *South Park* shout-out to the people who've used clips from a Jerky Boys call (Google it if you have zero clue who the Jerky Boys are!). I have a whole slew of examples I could share, but I'll spare you.

Bottom line here is…I've witnessed, firsthand, hiring managers who've questioned the judgment of professionals with greetings that are, shall we say, lacking a certain level of professionalism. By the way, make sure your voice mail is set up to receive messages. It doesn't happen often, but from time to time, I'll call a number that's listed on someone's contact info and after a number of rings, I'll hear that standard message about the voice mail box not being set up. If you want people to reach out to you, be reachable!

- In the same vein, whenever you answer your phone, do so in a professional manner. I've called people who've answered their phones by saying things like, "Yes?" or "*Go!*" or "What do you want?" or "What?" or "Dude!" or "Wassup, beeeeaaaaatch?" Clearly, these folks didn't expect me to be on the other end and were quite embarrassed when they realized their mistake. The lesson here is, you always need to be ready. Answer the phone professionally. And while we're at it…please make it a habit to answer your phone saying your name. For example, I will answer by saying, "Hello, this is Nicki." In today's global economy, there are many people with names quite challenging to pronounce, and it is so helpful when you answer it by stating your name for the caller. Regardless of whether or not you say your name, just be professional.
- This always cracks me up—when leaving a message with your phone number, why do people speed up and say the numbers so fast? Do people not realize it's extremely hard to follow? It's seriously funny. Pay attention next time you listen to a message. People will leave these nice long messages delivered at a normal pace. Yet when it's time to state a phone number, people hit the gas pedal and race as quickly as possible through their number, making it virtually impossible to catch what was said. I don't get it. It's as if there's some unwritten law somewhere that you're supposed to say your number as fast as humanly possible. Look, if you want people to return your calls, please state your number clearly and slowly. And for safe measure, go ahead and state your number twice, just to be sure it's heard clearly and someone has a chance to write it down. Similar to the Verizon

commercials where phones drop calls right at the very moment someone is saying something incredibly important, it never fails—when people are leaving their numbers, cell signals like to go bad, making it incredibly hard to decipher what someone is saying. Thus, stating your number twice (at a normal pace) is super helpful. You want people to call you back, right? If yes, say your number slowly enough that someone can write it down. Help them help you.

- Speaking of phone numbers, when you call someone and get their voice mail, please remember to actually leave your phone number in the message. Even if you believe the person has your number, leave it. You might be thinking, "Nicki—didn't you just say everyone has caller ID? Thus, wouldn't the recipient of my call see my number on their caller ID?" Well, yes, smarty-pants! Theoretically, your number should appear on a caller ID. But sometimes people get a lot of calls throughout the day. Do you really want them to have to figure out which number is yours? Sometimes caller ID is blocked and / or the person keeps their number private. Some people still have landlines, and if they're out of the office calling in for messages, they won't be able to see the caller ID log tied to that phone. Keep in mind not everyone syncs their cell phone and laptop, which means some might not be able to retrieve your number without getting back to their computers or seeing the caller ID from the landline. Hence, if you want someone to call you back, just leave your phone number every time you leave a message. And if you want to argue with me about this thinking it's stupid, a pain, or ridiculous, just think about whether or not you actually want your call returned. If you do, then just shut it and clearly state your phone number as part of the message you leave. It's pretty simple.

Using your head encompasses so much more, but in an effort to not drive you crazy, we'll stop here. Bottom line, getting a job that you want is really important. If you want to get that job, you need to use your head every step of the way.

You Are in Control of Your Own Actions

"IF SOMEONE TOLD YOU to jump off a bridge, would you do it?"

I'd be shocked if you didn't hear that one at some point during your childhood. In grade school, most children begin to comprehend this important life lesson: you are in control of your own actions. Flash-forward to adulting—when navigating your way through a job search or interview process, this is extremely important to keep in mind as it applies in many ways:

- Job searching is hard work, it's up to you to do all of it; no one can do it for you. As with all hard work, you'll get out of it what you put into it. So if you choose to spend only a few hours a day in front of your computer, during which time you surf a few job sites, apply to a number of postings, do an hour or more of online shopping, and then log off to hit the gym for a few hours, don't whine when you're not seeing overwhelmingly positive results. A few hours of sending some applications does not constitute "hard work." And spending however many hours simply sitting in front of your computer doesn't matter if it's not productive…just doing "things" isn't going to cut it. Job searching is a full-time-plus job. And for those who opt to treat it more like a part-time position or hobby…well…you're likely to have a lengthier job search ahead of you. You are in control of how you spend your time.
- Your reaction to your situation is your choice. If you're annoyed at the world and you decide to act like a royal jerk to others, that's your choice.

Yes, there are enormous injustices in this world, and sometimes we can get dealt a crappy hand. And that can really suck! But if you want to play the victim, that's your choice. Just know that your negativity isn't going to aid you in your plight to land a job. Don't go blaming everyone else for everything that's happened to you! At some point, you need to recognize your accountability, and you need to decide to make the right changes to help get yourself into a better place. If you choose to be negative, that will absolutely impact your job search and make things a whole heck of a lot more frustrating and upsetting. Choose to change your attitude and how you react, and good things will start to happen. You're in control!

- When in an interview process, it's up to you to get all the information about the opportunity and company. You can't expect the recruiter, the talent acquisition person, the hiring manager, or anyone else you come across to know every single thing about an opportunity—the position, the hiring manager, and the company as a whole. Now, a recruiter who's good at their job should be able to provide you with a wealth of insight, but it is still *your* job to peel back the onion so you can truly explore and investigate an opportunity. Just because someone told you the corporate culture is great and the hiring manager rocks doesn't mean you are going to feel the exact same way. In fact, your opinion may be completely different. Just like we all have our own unique perspectives on taste, beauty, love, music, and so forth, you must realize you can't just take someone's word as gospel that an opportunity is great. If, G-d forbid, you accept a position and things don't work out the way you thought they would, you can't always point the blame toward everyone else for the situation you find yourself in. You have personal accountability in the matter, and you need to take ownership. For example, I've heard professionals describe why a certain position they accepted didn't work out. They'll berate the recruiter who placed them into a position, saying they did not give them enough information about the company, their leadership team, and / or the hiring manager. Perhaps the candidate is right. Maybe the recruiter didn't have much information to share. However, it's still the candidate's job to find out the information they need in order to determine, for themselves, if the job and the company are a fit. Keep in mind, the candidate's views could be very different from the recruiter's.

On the other hand, professionals have said the recruiter / hiring manager provided an incredible amount of detail but it was wrong; they either knowingly or unknowingly misrepresented the corporate culture and the leadership's style. Again, as a candidate, you absolutely must take ownership of the process and inspect every aspect of a company and opportunity for yourself. One person's opinion / perspective may not be similar to yours. Plus, you have to keep in mind, if you're working with a recruiter, that person may not be an actual employee of the company you're interviewing with, which means the recruiter can't possibly know exactly what it's like day in and day out inside the particular company. Now, for fun, let's say the recruiter does in fact work for the company...unless you're interviewing for an inside recruiter role, the interviewer will not know exactly what it's like to be in the position you're interviewing for. They don't report to the marketing department, the finance department, the IT department, etc., so they don't know firsthand what it's like to be in that exact job, on that exact team, in that particular function at that company. Therefore, it is up to you, the candidate, to do your due diligence and thoroughly assess each and every aspect of an opportunity for yourself. Do not simply take someone else's word for it. There are many professionals out there who've shared stories with me of feeling burned by the recruiter, and I'm certainly sympathetic to them. In every situation, though, the candidate did not solely interview with the recruiter and get the job. In every case, the candidate had multiple interviews and ample time to dig into the details. And by the way, as a candidate, if you don't feel you have enough detail and / or you haven't met with certain people you'd like to speak with prior to accepting an offer, it's totally within your right to request the details, conversations, and meetings. If a company is unwilling to accommodate your requests, then I'd take a hard look at whether or not this is an opportunity even worth your consideration. You should always be afforded ample time to ask key questions to numerous people within a company, so you can fully assess the role, the company, and the leadership team. I know some of you are going to come back at this and say the recruiter or hiring manager still totally misrepresented the opportunity. Unfortunately, there are shitty recruiters and hiring managers out there who may be misrepresenting a company, an opportunity and / or dismissing candidates' concerns, which is totally lame. However, the professional needs to put it upon themselves to vet the opportunity from every possible angle. You are in control of getting the information you need to make a smart decision, and you need to find out "the good, the bad, the ugly" for yourself.

So how do you find out about a company aside from the obvious things like going on a company's website and looking at their company page on LinkedIn? Should you look at Glassdoor ratings? Yes. That said, in my humble opinion, I would never put all my eggs in that basket because ratings aren't always a full and accurate picture of what a company is like. Ratings can be "off" regardless of if their rating is high or low. We all know it's more common for people who aren't happy to leave reviews. So there's that issue. In addition, everyone's opinion of a specific job and company is unique to the individual person. I often joke that I absolutely loved my first career. Loved it! But for every Nicki, there were probably two people who hated the same job. My experience was amazing. Not everyone had the same experience. Those like me don't often give reviews. It's those who dislike something who voice their opinions. So, my advice is to take note of the rating, read all the reviews you can, and ask questions during the interview process. If there's a low rating, ask them to speak to it. If there's a consistent theme among those who gave less-than-stellar reviews, ask about that specifically. And I encourage you to see if you know anyone who has or is currently working at that company and / or if you have a mutual connection to someone who's worked there. Reach out to those people and pick their brains. If you hear bad things and you fully believe in what the person is saying, then perhaps that's your indication to bow out of the process. If you're hearing mixed reviews, use that intel to better formulate questions. Dig deeper. Do your own due diligence to find out what you can about a company in other ways too: Google searches, checking out the Better Business Bureau, etc.

Let's go beyond the interview process—once someone is hired, there's a lot that happens. People onboard, they transition into their roles, and settle in. Sometimes things don't work out as planned. And if they don't, you need to look in the mirror and truly inspect every aspect of your time spent at the company and in the position. Yes, the hiring manager might have a lot of culpability here. But merely pointing blame at everyone else isn't going to help you going forward. You need to be introspective and evaluate your performance. Did you come into the position like a bull in a china shop? Did you rub people the wrong way? Were you abrasive? Did you take feedback well, or were you defensive? Did you insist on doing things your way and your way only? Were you constantly late arriving to work? Did you consistently leave early? Were you late for meetings? Did you have a clear picture of what you were being evaluated on in the first 30/60/90/180/365 days? Did you regularly speak with your boss to make sure you were on track? Did you meet the goals set forth for you during the time you were there? Were you reliable? Did you drop the ball on something? If in sales, did you get the kinds of meetings they wanted with the results they desired? When in those meetings, how did you do? Were your presentation skills good? Did you demonstrate great follow-up skills? Did you add value? Were you quick to complain? Did you say, "That's not my job!" or "That wasn't in my job description!" Did you give your boss any reason to doubt your level of commitment? Did you frequently bad-mouth coworkers? Did you get busted online shopping? Did you call in sick only to be spotted on the jumbotron at the Cubs home opener? I could go on and on for days…

The bottom line is this: you need to recognize you are in control of your own actions and if things didn't work out, there's a good chance you had some degree of culpability. For that reason, it's important to remember that during an interview process, it is your job to fully assess an opportunity. Do not accept what others tell you, be it a hiring manager, a recruiter, a friend, or a colleague, without exploring for yourself. You're the one who has to decide if a position, the company, and the management team are right for you. No one should make that decision for you. And once onboard, you have a significant role in how well you do. You are in charge of how you react to every single thing; your actions are in your control.

Practice Makes Perfect

AN OLDIE BUT A GOODIE, RIGHT? Practice does make perfect! While we learn this early in life, it's a valuable nugget at any age, in pretty much any arena. Think about it. As kids, we practice most everything—writing the letters of the alphabet, doing multiplication tables, reading out loud, playing sports, playing instruments, practicing our lines in a play or in a choir, etc. As adults, we recognize the importance of practicing doesn't fade with age. For example, professional basketball players practice their free throws every day. Baseball players have batting practice all the time. Gymnasts go through their routines umpteen times before they perform them in competition. Musicians and actors have rehearsals. Golfers practice their swings. People in corporate America often practice their pitches and presentations before big meetings. Before an important speech, most will rehearse a few times. And the list can go on and on…

So what does this have to do with job searching? Well, one of the biggest challenges in job searching as we talked about earlier is interviewing! Interviewing is not easy, and I tell people all the time that the biggest obstacle to being successful in an interview is simply being articulate. We went through this already, but as a reminder, many people struggle with providing answers to questions that are succinct, eloquent, and stay on point. Often, people are way too verbose, way too choppy, and way too rambly.

Why do people struggle so much in interviews? Well, for starters, I think many people underestimate how difficult interviewing can be because many assume "the interview is about me, and I know myself better than anyone else." Yeah, you may know yourself better than others, but trust me, that doesn't make it easy. I can't even begin to tell you how many impressive, articulate, and accomplished people end up fumbling and stumbling their way through some or all of an interview. Yes, it's true.

Even those who are extremely articulate and accomplished can struggle to answer interview questions. So what can you do to avoid that? Easy—you need to practice interviewing before you get to the real one. Why? Because practice makes perfect!! Here are some things you can do:

- Spend time thinking of typical interview questions. You can do a quick Google search of "most commonly asked interview questions." I also suggest researching "toughest interview questions." It's mind-boggling how many executives are not prepared to answer basics, such as "Why do you want to work here?" or "What are your goals?" or "Why / how did you pick this career path?" or "What are your strengths / weaknesses?" or "What about you can frustrate those who work with you?" or "If I were to call your boss, what would they say is their favorite thing about you as well as least favorite thing about you?" These are just some of the many "basic interview questions" you need to be prepared to answer. As such, you need to practice your answers to as many common questions as you can come up with so that you're as sharp as you can possibly be.
- I'd also research "behavioral interview questions" and see examples of those types of questions. Since behavioral interview questions are situational, many candidates seem to struggle. While you can't predict what you'll be asked, practicing will certainly help you be better at thinking on your feet. I liken it to doing crossword puzzles. The more you do them, the better you get at them.
- Look at the position you're interviewing for and think of what types of questions you'd ask someone if you were hiring for this role. If there's a job spec, a great place to start is by turning the bullets detailed there into questions and then formulating your answers. Practice, practice, practice!
- Anticipate the concerns and objections the company you're interviewing with might have about you. It's always helpful to look at your résumé through the hiring manager's eyes. Where might they find issues with your candidacy? How are they going to view your background? Are there any points on the job spec you don't align with? Do you fall short in any way?

Anticipating possible objections a hiring team might have about you and your candidacy will help you determine how best to address these points should they come up. For example, look at your background…have you switched jobs every year or two? If yes, someone might be uncomfortable with all those moves. How will you explain this? If you've spent ten years with your current employer, is it possible for someone to view this as a shortcoming? How do you handle that? What will you say? Have you spent the last five years in a different industry from the one the position you're interviewing for is in? Have you only been in marketing for eight years yet the job spec requires over ten years? Have you been with your current employer for only six short months? Why would you possibly be looking this soon after joining? Have you been out of work for eight months? Why? What have you been doing? Do you have experience leading direct reports? If that's a requirement and you don't have the necessary experience to easily check that box, why should they consider you anyway? You get the point…

Anticipating possible concerns and practicing how you'll speak to them will undoubtedly help you be more articulate when in the moment. And by the way, some obvious objections might be best addressed with you proactively by bringing them up earlier in your conversation versus waiting for the hiring company to possibly raise these concerns. As a classically trained consultative salesperson, I was taught the importance of anticipating objections and controlling the conversation by speaking to certain objections first.

Practice does indeed make perfect. But please note, you do not want to sound overly scripted. So yes, practice, but don't memorize a script. You want to sound natural and conversational. Not robotic. Spending some time gathering your thoughts and practicing answers will enable you to more easily retrieve the right words and deliver fluent, meaningful answers with confidence.

Perfection Doesn't Exist

MY MOM ALWAYS joked she was perfect but no one else was. That only worked for a while, though. My brothers and I quickly realized she was full of it and far from perfect (sorry, Mom!). Not sure what exactly made us come to that conclusion. Was it when she forgot to pick us up after school one day and we ended up in the office having the school admin track her down? Or was it when she burned an important dinner and the fire alarm went off? Or was it when she backed her car up into another car after dropping us off at school and literally half the school saw / heard the "incident"? Clearly, she wasn't perfect and made mistakes. Although, I'll admit while not perfect, she's pretty darn good. That said, I am not exactly sure how I learned perfection as a whole doesn't exist. I remember teachers and coaches using encouraging phrases like "No one is perfect" and "Nothing is perfect." As an adult, I often think about and frequently reference the Wayne Gretzky quote I read forever ago: "You miss 100 percent of the shots you don't take." I've probably said this to my kids a thousand times. Both tried almost every sport, and whether in soccer, basketball, baseball, or hockey, the advice always held up. Like many baseball players, my son has had many batting slumps, and I've heard both coaches and his father tell him you can't always wait for the perfect pitch. I could go on and on, but let's bring this back to job searching and interviewing…

When I was twenty-one and interviewing for my first "real" professional job, the world was a bit different. Cable TV existed, but there weren't a million different ways to get television content. There was no streaming. There were only a few main channels whereas today we have hundreds of options. Back then, CBS, NBC, and ABC were the three powerhouses, and I had it in my head that I wanted to work for one of those stations selling advertising space. In every interview, I was told I needed a year or two of real sales experience and once I had that under my belt, I should come back and interview again. So I moved off of TV and thought the next best thing would be to work for one of the major radio stations. That sales experience would surely be valuable and enable me to come back to the TV stations in a year or two. Well, they said the same thing: get some real sales experience and then come back and interview again. So frustrating! It seemed every place I wanted to work told me I needed good sales experience before they'd consider me. I interviewed with a lot of places and got rejected a ton! At the same time, though, I avoided a number of opportunities thinking they weren't exactly what I wanted. I refused to compromise. After many months of not making money and not getting offers, I realized beggars couldn't be choosers. I wanted to move out of my parents' house and into the city with my friends, and I had to come to terms with the fact that I wasn't going to get my dream job. I needed to give up on finding the perfect job and just needed to find any "good-enough" job. So I ended up taking a job I really wasn't excited about…at all. I knew I'd get really good sales training and sales experience there, though, and thus thought I'd simply plug my nose and suck it up. I figured I could stick it out for a year or two and then use that to pursue what I really wanted, to be in advertising sales at one of the major stations. I was convinced the job I'd accepted was going to basically suck. And guess what?!?

It did not suck at all!

I actually completely loved it!

What I thought was going to be a torturous year or two ended up being ten amazing years of incredible and invaluable experience, not to mention lifelong friendships. During my tenure there, I saw a lot of people leave for greener pastures only to return later and share that the proverbial grass wasn't always greener. Over the course of those ten years, I worked for some good bosses, some great bosses, and (ahem)… well, fill in the blank. Throughout all that time, I learned so much more than I ever could have imagined, and one of the very best, most important lessons I learned is that nothing is perfect—no company, no person, no solution, no process, no boss, no client, no employer, no employee, no nothing. Perfection does not exist. It doesn't!

In my position today, I'm constantly hearing professionals' career overviews. Many will share stories of leaving certain companies / jobs for this reason or that only to find their next home was no better. Sometimes they were worse. I've worked with some people who decided to pass over certain amazing opportunities for a reason that really should not have been "the reason" to pull the plug. When I put my "career coach" hat on, time and again I've had to advise professionals to think twice before turning down what's really a great opportunity because something unimportant, in the grand scheme of things, was missing. We can't seek perfection. It doesn't exist!

Similarly, I can't begin to tell you how many hiring managers have wanted to pass on someone who is truly a phenomenal candidate because they were missing something that could be learned. It is critical for companies to recognize perfect candidates on paper are 99.9 percent of the time flawed in some way. Perfection doesn't exist!

Yes, we all want to make smart decisions about the companies we consider, the jobs we consider, the candidates we consider…but we also need to know that perfection doesn't exist and we risk missing something great in our search for perfect. As the saying goes, "Perfect is the enemy of good."

When You Fall Down, Get Back Up and Brush Yourself Off

WHEN YOU LOOK AT PICTURES of yourself as a kid, did your legs always have a ton of bruises? Were your knees constantly skinned? If you watch kids, they fall a lot! Especially little ones. I'm sure you have memories of some big tumbles. I remember a horrible doozy I did flying off my bicycle. I was lucky I wasn't seriously injured; there was a lot of gravel that needed to be removed from my leg, which hurt like hell. However, nothing broke. That was one of those moments where my life flashed before my eyes. As I went over the handlebars, I thought that was it. Scary stuff. Anyway…

What did we learn when taking those spills? (This is rhetorical.)

We learned to get back up and brush ourselves off, right? Kids quickly learn falling is a part of life and they seem to get used to it rather quickly. Somewhere along the way, though, many forget this important life lesson. In the professional world, we all get knocked down, some more than others. Whether you've recently been fired or laid off, had a horrible meeting, did particularly lousy in an interview, or thought you crushed it in an interview only to be told you were not advancing in the process, it happens. When things like this take place, of course it is easy to get down. It's human nature to get bummed out and even a bit depressed. It's completely understandable that one might lose some confidence. However, after a short period of time, many adults are able to put things into perspective and bounce back. Sadly, though, there are some professionals who just can't seem to shake it off. They get knocked down and struggle to get back up, sometimes finding themselves completely stuck.

One of the best lessons I learned early in my career is if you fall down, you absolutely should stop to reflect on what's taken place and then get the f*ck off your butt and get up. Get back in the game!

What I'm talking about when I say you need to reflect on what's happened is that you must try to objectively assess the situation from all angles and ask yourself what you could have done differently. Are there areas you need to focus on and improve? Are there skills you're lacking? Are there personality traits you need to try to adjust? None of us are perfect, and we all have areas we can work on. Now is a good time to take stock and reassess. As I like to say, we're all a work in progress. So, spend time reflecting. Get feedback from others if you can. Ask friends, former colleagues, and former bosses to provide you with some honest feedback so you can learn more about what people view as areas we might label as flaws or areas we need to work on. Don't get mad at them for being honest. What they're doing is a gift. Thank them. And then make a game plan of how you're going to help yourself going forward. And while you're allowed to feel whatever emotions you have in your challenging situation, within a reasonable amount of time, you need to pick yourself up, suck it up, and move forward! Get going! MOVE!!!

I'm just going to throw it out there and state the obvious-—getting fired usually isn't much fun. In fact, it typically sucks! However, it happens, and more often than one would think and to more people than you'd guess. While it isn't something to necessarily boast about, people need to recognize how common this is and that many professionals have either been fired or pushed out of a position / company. People may say they quit. But truth be told, they could have been given the "quit or we will fire you" ultimatum. Now, if someone hasn't personally been fired or pushed out of a job, they likely know others who have, especially if they've been in the workforce for a while. And by the way, in case you didn't know, getting fired doesn't only happen to those who commit gross offenses (stealing, purposely blowing up a $10 million project, ramming your car into the company's office building because you're mad about your title, telling your boss to f*ck off, flipping off the CFO at a stop light, etc.). Thus, if you find yourself a member of the "I've been fired club," you don't have to wear it as a scarlet letter forever.

Being fired doesn't have to mean your career is over.

Being fired doesn't mean your life is done.

Keep in mind that many impressive executives have either been fired or pushed out of at least one job during the course of their careers (hello, Steve Jobs!). After all, success isn't easy, and isn't always pretty...it comes with steps forward, backward, sideways, up, down, and all around. There are hiccups, monkey wrenches, failures, and successes along the way. There's a saying about success not being a straight line for a reason! Therefore, it's important to recognize one bad experience shouldn't and doesn't have to define an entire career. I see far too many professionals beat themselves up for insane amounts of time, and this only serves to be the ball and chain holding them captive. At some point, you have to quit lamenting, get yourself together, and commit to moving forward.

What I'm talking about is grit.

It's resilience.

I know it isn't always easy to "just move forward," but it must be done. After you've given yourself a little bit of time to process your situation and work through the emotions, start by figuring out what you need to do to right the situation.

If you've done something wrong, how do you fix it? Atone for it? What can you do to make things better for the present moment in time? Plus, what can you do to make things better in the future? If you've actually done something, you need to hold yourself accountable and fix it. In addition, you need to figure out how to best position your situation. If you aren't sure, ask experts, friends, or confidants and work on wordsmithing this so you'll present your situation in the best light possible. That said, please remember the importance of being honest...never lie or misrepresent what's happened. You have to own it; you can't conveniently omit disclosing this. Figure out how to best articulate your situation, and get moving. You'd be surprised how many people will appreciate your honesty and transparency. If you know what you did wrong and can work to improve it, others might respect you more than you'd assume.

And by the way, you'll be happy to know I often hear people tell me, looking back, getting fired was one of the best things that ever happened to them. While it might not feel that way at the time, getting fired might be a gift in disguise! Look at the positives, learn from what's happened, and then pick yourself up and brush yourself off!

Now, maybe you didn't get fired. Maybe you just had a shitty thing happen.

Maybe you prepared for an important interview for an insane amount of time and you completely messed up the interview. Maybe you worked really hard on a project and then totally bombed. Maybe you had to deliver a presentation to your leadership team and everything that could go wrong did. Whatever it may be, we all have had situations where we've taken that proverbial "fall" and we've needed to get back up and brush it off. As we've talked about before, don't start with blaming everyone else. Don't drone on and on about how unfair life is. That's a waste of a whole lot of energy. Get up, brush yourself off, figure out what you could have done better, and go make it happen. Positive self-talk is really helpful in these situations. Often, you are who you think you are. If you think you're a loser who will never amount to anything, you're likely to be a big ole loser. If you think you're a winner, and work like winners do, you will become a winner. None of us are perfect, and all of us fall down. Those who relentlessly get back up and try again are the ones who succeed. Everyone has bad stuff happen at times. Some is justified. Some isn't. Regardless, don't wallow. Get up and brush it off.

Don't Be a Quitter

I WAS ALWAYS TAUGHT to never be a quitter. Does "losers quit and quitters lose" sound familiar? My parents always said we couldn't quit something we started. As parents, my husband and I agree. If our kids signed up to play on a team only to decide later that they either didn't like the team or the sport, guess what? They had to play through to the end. We always say, if you make a commitment, you honor it.

In your professional life and in your work life, it's the same thing. You keep your word. You honor your commitments. You can't just quit. Well, I mean, you can. But it's often not a great idea. We talked about this earlier—like it or not, hiring managers tend to have a bias against those who are unemployed, and many don't easily buy the story of "I didn't feel it was right to look for a job while employed by another company. It felt a little like I was cheating." Now, truth be told, I can completely sympathize with this and actually appreciate when someone recognizes they're inevitably eating into some of their work hours when job searching and those work hours are being paid for by the employer they're leaving. However, not every hiring manager is willing to accept this at face value and some may still question this further.

What about before you get to the point of knowing you want to quit? What can you do when things aren't going great and you're starting to contemplate whether it's time to pull the cord and move on? Sometimes professionals don't succeed in their roles because they haven't been given the right training or tools. Sometimes people just need a little help to get over a hump. Now, this isn't always the case, and I'm certainly not advocating for staying in a place where you're miserable and your health is possibly being negatively affected. If things are truly that bad, then you do need to move on. Toxic environments can take a big toll, and life's too short. But there are times when situations can be turned around and it might make the most sense to give it a go. If you're someone with a recent short stint already on your résumé and leaving this position will give you two short stints in a row, you could be viewed as a job hopper. Or perhaps you have only stayed at your last three jobs for two years or less; you could be viewed as a job hopper. And as many of us know, some hiring managers get nervous about candidates with one or more shorter stints on their résumé. Hiring managers may unfairly assume you're one or more of the following: difficult to work with (you got fired or pushed out), not good at your job (you got fired or pushed out), fickle (you get bored easily or do a lousy job assessing opportunities for fit), or you're easily lured away (you'll listen to other opportunities pretty much right from the time you start a new job, and any new "bright and shiny" opportunity can quickly catch your fancy). Perhaps none of these are accurate, but if the assumption is made, it can be very difficult to overcome. So before you quickly quit a job, think twice. Give new(ish) jobs ample time. Onboarding can take some people six to twelve months. Change is hard for many people.

"Don't be a quitter" can also mean...don't bail out if you're the runner-up. If you're in consideration for a role but you find out they've made an offer to someone else, you're essentially the runner-up. This can be extremely disappointing. After all, you likely put a lot of time and energy into the process. If possible, try to obtain feedback; ask what caused them to go with the other person. In my experience, the "difference maker" is often nothing major. And I've had many clients tell me they could absolutely go with the runner-up if something doesn't work out with the person getting the offer. Now, depending on how long it's going to take for the offer to be accepted, background checks, the person resigning, etc., I may stall in an effort to avoid telling candidate #2 that they're the runner-up. I know some people don't love being the silver medalist. After finding out they didn't get the gold, they'll get ticked off and have a bad taste in their mouth about the company. The reality is the silver medalist can get the gold more often than you may think, and thus it behooves people to try to refrain from immediately ruling out the company. In my experience, rarely does the hiring team rule out all the other candidates in the final round. Often, there is a silver medalist and that professional isn't viewed as someone they'd be settling for if things don't work out with the gold medalist. So this means the silver medalist candidate needs to know they're not the leftovers…they're not viewed as "less than" the gold medalist. And I can't tell you how many times I've seen the silver medalist end up getting the job and the hiring team later stating how happy they are that things didn't work out with gold medal candidate because they're thrilled with silver medal candidate.

So the moral of the story is, try not to be a quitter. You never know. You might end up in the job. Some offers don't get accepted, some candidates try to resign and take counteroffers (bad idea!), some background checks reveal a disqualifier, some candidates are recognized as a bad fit for whatever reason within a few months of onboarding, and more. The company might come back to you, and this could be an amazing opportunity you should not miss simply because your ego got bruised.

Also, "when the tough gets going, the going gets tough", right? This means, despite a job search being hard, you cannot quit. There are ups and downs, but if you do the right things every day, good things will happen. Like we've talked about, even the best athletes go through ruts. Sometimes the ruts last longer than anticipated but we've all seen them come out of their "down times" and this shows us that if we stay focused, work hard and stick with it (aka-don't quit), things get better. Job searches can take a LOT longer than anticipated and this can really weigh on someone. I've witnessed many exceptional professionals lose all confidence and faith. You have got to dig your way out of those holes! If you believe things will get better, and you work hard, they will. If you quit, though, you'll never know. I always encourage people to reflect on a time in their life when things felt impossible; totally bleak and yet, they came through it. Go back to it, see it and feel it. And use that to fuel you as you move forward and face your current challenge(s). Whatever you do, don't quit. You can take a little break. But don't quit!

Finally, this also means you should not accept an offer and then rescind your acceptance (or quit before you even start). Sometimes when people have multiple opportunities they're exploring, they'll say yes to the first offer knowing they may rescind their acceptance if another opportunity they're more excited about results in an offer too. This is a terrible idea! Do not accept an offer knowing you might end up backing out of it. As discussed, every industry is small and this is a very quick way to ruin your reputation. I have seen so many professionals wear scarlett letters for doing this and it ends up being an anchor weighing them down. For some, it caused them to have to switch industries to try to rid themselves of the ball and chain. Your word is often everything. And when you say yes to an offer, it needs to be a solid yes. Not a "maybe". If you're not sure whether or not you truly want to accept an offer, then you need to figure out how to buy time OR you need to say no. It's that simple. And never, EVER, play the game of getting an offer in the hopes of getting a counter-offer from your employer. If you want a raise or a promotion, you need to have that conversation with your leadership team. But, do not play your company by going out and getting an offer just to pressure your current employer. Doing this is a terrible idea. What if your current employer doesn't give you a counter offer? Even if they do, know that studies show those who accept counter offers are often gone from the company within twelve months. Employers have claimed they felt played and didn't appreciate the professionals putting them into the position of feeling like they had to make a counter offer. No employer or hiring manager likes to feel as though someone is playing games. Bottom line, being a quitter before you even start can derail your career. Don't do it!

Things Break

THINGS BREAK. And why does it seem like everything breaks all at once? You know what I'm talking about. One day your car is driving fine, and the next, there are lights flashing across your dashboard and you can't get the engine started. By the time you get that under control, your dishwasher starts making some crazy noise. Oh, good grief, the ice maker stops working, and your laptop is doing weird things. Didn't you just buy a new vacuum? Why's this one not picking anything up? Ugh! Things break (in bunches), and it's so frustrating!

Looking back, do you have memories of your favorite toy breaking? I know I do, and one in particular stands out. I had this remote-controlled dog that walked, and if memory serves me right, it flipped. This dog looked like a stuffed animal with a leash, and the control was at the end of the leash. Anyway, I loved that toy, and one day, it just stopped. It was as if my own real live pet had died. I was devastated! Why oh why was it always your favorite toy that broke? Is it because your favorite toy was used and abused more than the others? Is it a karma thing? Is it because the universe wanted you to be nicer to the other toys and pay attention to them too? Who knows…

It's a tough pill to swallow, but kids learn that things break. So what does this have to do with job searching, you ask? Well, I'm taking the liberty of tying this to technology and will start with cell phones, because it seems many view their cell phones as toys, and these things break! They drop calls, batteries die, voices break up, and complete thoughts can't be heard when someone's reception is poor. In addition, one of my favorites—cell phones can have echoes on one or both ends, which is always super frustrating. Cells misbehave and, at times (the worst times), create undue havoc in our lives. (Don't even get me started on misplacing your cell phone…when the ringer is on silent.)

I'm pretty sure it's safe to say most people have opted to forgo their landlines and now live in a world where the only phone they have is a cell phone. When it comes to job searching and / or interviewing, this can create unique challenges. I have had countless interviews with people on cell phones, and there were inevitably all sorts of issues, including but not limited to those just mentioned. Not only can this be incredibly distracting and irritating, but it can also potentially impact your candidacy. I've gone through interviews where someone's cell dropped the call four times. Trust me, by the fourth time, I was at my wit's end. I've had more than my fair share of interviews where I couldn't understand the candidate because the signal was so poor. During those calls, I spent more time saying, "I'm sorry, I can't understand what you said. Can you please repeat that?" than I did asking valuable questions. For these reasons and more, when you're interviewing, I strongly encourage you to make sure you're somewhere with a strong signal. And, try to refrain from standing in a wind tunnel.

Aside from cell phones, the pandemic gave everyone a taste of using video technology to conduct meetings, and many now use video for interviews in addition to normal business meetings. Video technology can also pose various challenges. So make sure you have someone's cell number just in case the video jams up, drops the feed, etc. You want to have a "plan B" for when things "break."

By the way, if using a video tool you're not used to, practice with a friend to ensure you know what you need to do to enter a conversation (or meeting), where the mute button is, and how to turn on and off the video / speaker. This way you can feel more confident on the day of the interview and focus on what you're saying versus navigating the technology. Also, many of us have experienced logging onto a platform only to receive a message stating the program is performing an update. And naturally, the universe loves to make sure the update takes forever on days where we have no time to waste. The stress of watching the update move at a sloth's pace is insane. So, logging on the night before your interview, you'll typically get the update done and be ready to go when it's show time. Bottom line, you want to minimize the odds of something going wrong because things do "break"!

Technology in general is a necessity. In today's world, there's no way around it. And while something might not fully break by literally falling apart into a million pieces, things can "break" by failing to operate properly. For example, firewalls can mess up email exchanges. So please pay attention to your "junk folder" as important emails can sometimes be routed there (for no good reason), and you most certainly don't want to miss important ones. Make it a habit to check a junk or spam folder with frequency. I can't tell you how many candidates have admitted to not checking their junk folder. And sometimes they've found important emails waiting for them there. And, unfortunately, at times it was too late.

Another example to consider—documents can reformat depending on the type of computer you create the document on. As you may know, if you use a Mac and then send a document to someone with a PC, sometimes it can look different on their screen than it did on yours. The spacing might get messed up. Or margins might be goofy. I always recommend creating a PDF to avoid that issue.

Another example of things breaking:

We rarely do work on entry-level positions. But once in a while, a client will ask for our help, and we will oblige. A while back, we accepted a search and quickly found a number of seemingly strong candidates. The location was a major city, and it was mid-January. For those who live in climates with harsh winters, you know how brutal it can be in the dead of winter living with snow and ice. The night before two of our candidates were scheduled for interviews, this city had a massive snowstorm. I'm talking three feet of snow. It was predicted and thus was not a surprise to anyone. If you've lived in a city with snow, you know that traffic is going to be awful the next day. Traffic is always terrible after a significant snowfall. In addition, common sense should tell you that if you have a car and it's parked outside, there's a 99.9 percent chance you're going to be digging it out of a major snow pile and will need to allocate ample time to do so. Because you'll be shoveling, you should know and be anticipating how sweaty this task is. It's a workout! Lastly, most people also know, with brutal cold, you have to make sure you have enough gas in your car (over a quarter tank) so it doesn't freeze when temps plummet. If gas freezes in your tank, it makes your car inoperable. Now with all that said, when preparing each candidate, I stated quite clearly that if there were any issues and / or concerns about making the interview on time, they should call me. Then, if they don't reach me to call the client next. If they get client's voicemail, leave a message and then email the client directly, with me cc'd on the note. Well, shocker of shocks, neither candidate made it to the interview, and neither followed my directions. Did I get a call? Nope! Did my client? Nahhh! Did I get cc'd on an email to my client explaining the situation? No! How'd I find out? Well, I got a call from my client telling me the candidates were no-shows. (If you are assuming the client was tweaked by this, you're right!) When I called the candidates to find out what happened, here are the excuses I heard (none of which were on my bingo card!):

One claimed he couldn't get his car out from under so much snow. He explained how he went to his car about fifteen minutes earlier than he would have in normal weather conditions. But due to the aforementioned snow, there was just too much to shovel and he couldn't get it out in time. (Ummmm...first of all, have you heard of Uber or Lyft???? Second, are you kidding me that you thought fifteen minutes was enough time to dig your car out? Not to mention, did you also think shoveling that much snow, while in your interview attire no less, would be similar to a workout? That you might get sweaty and be a skosh less presentable?)

The other said she hadn't filled up her tank in a while and unfortunately, she just couldn't get her car started. She said her engine must have been broken. (Again, hellooooo, *Uber and Lyft*, anyone?!?!) Ugh! I explained to her the importance of filling up your tank if it's below a quarter full when in winter months so as to ensure your engine can start. I told her that her car wasn't broken. Her plan was. She told me she tried to call her dad to help her, but he was busy. I said, adulting is hard. Problem solving is a skill we all need to bone up on. She told me her dad is nice. I said I'm sure he is.

Needless to say, both candidates dropped the ball. I was incredibly frustrated, as was my client. Not surprisingly, the client chose not to reschedule interviews with the candidates and opted to move forward with others.

Things break. Plans break. Gadgets break. You need to learn to deal with it professionally, especially in job search and interview settings. It really is a "plan B world" and thus we always need to be ready for when things go wrong.

People Are Busy

WHEN YOU WERE A CHILD, didn't it seem like adults were always rushing around complaining about how busy they were? Did adults repeatedly tell you the older you get, the faster time goes by? I know I heard it all the time. In fact, as an adult, I'm now totally convinced they were onto something. It seems like with each passing year, the earth rotates faster than it did the year before and either scientists know this but haven't disclosed it or they haven't made this realization just yet. Time goes way too fast and there aren't enough hours in the day!

We can all agree people are busy, and as stated numerous times already, no one has time to spare. For this reason, when you're job searching please remember, people are very protective of their time. Thus, if you're trying to schedule coffees or informational meetings, know that people might be reluctant to accept your invitation. In fact, any time you ask someone for more than five minutes, your odds of getting something scheduled go down considerably. Therefore, it's best to state up front you understand their time is limited and make it clear you'll be flexible by accommodating their availability. If you don't know the person(s) you're reaching out to, you should ask for only a few minutes of their time via phone (not in person). If you ask for a few minutes and get the meeting, people will typically give you more time if they find the conversation to be compelling and of value. However, people are quick to say no to meeting requests when they fear you'll be eating up their precious time. So make it easy for someone to say yes by clearly stating up front that you're only asking for a couple minutes. And by the way, you absolutely must be flexible and accommodate their schedule. There are few things more frustrating than someone asking for a meeting and then being completely inflexible with their calendar. And PS: If you're the one requesting a meeting, please do not ask the other person to send you a calendar invite. This happens to me all the time, and I honestly don't get it. If you've asked me for my time, then you need to send the calendar invite to me. Don't ask me to do it. It's rude, unprofessional, and lazy. And it drives me totally bonkers (in case you couldn't tell!).

Networking is a key part of a successful job search. Your network is your most valuable tool and one you should leverage from day one. To get the most out of these people, though, you have to make it as easy as possible to get their time and attention by not asking for too much time and not inconveniencing them. People are busy!

Once you do get their attention, don't be a dumbass and renege on your promise of keeping things brief. If you ask for five minutes, take only five minutes. Once you overstay your welcome, you're seriously jeopardizing any chance of getting help from the person not only now but in the future too. And as discussed, this is indeed a small world, and you never know who is talking to whom and when your name could come up. Might sound like something you'd roll your eyes at and think, "No way—that won't happen." But I can assure you, this happens all the time.

In addition to being respectful of keeping the conversation / meeting to a short period of time, you better darn well make the best use of every single second with that person. This leads us back to prior chapters. You need to diligently and strategically prepare for your time with this person. Know what your objectives and goals are for the time together. Know what you want to say. Have a sense of how you can offer to help them in return as a thank-you for their willingness to carve out time for you. Do your research and be ready for your moment. You have one shot at this. Get it right. People are busy and aren't likely to give you more time if you swing and miss the first time you're up to the plate. And this is no surprise, but send a thank-you email after every interaction, no matter how brief. It makes a difference!

If You Did It, Admit It

WHILE I WAS GROWING UP, my parents always said, "If you did it, just admit it. If you lie about it, we'll figure it out, and you'll be in a lot more trouble than if you just admit it now." And, boy, did my brothers and I learn this lesson the hard way…and stupidly, more than once! I still don't know how they found out about certain, shall we say, "things", but they always did!

Bringing this back to the subject at hand—When companies give an offer, they're typically subject to a thorough background check. As stated previously, I'm not a lawyer, and no, I do not play one on TV. So this is by no means legal counsel. However, in my experience, if there's anything in your background that could be problematic, it's best to address this in advance of getting to the final stage of an interview process. If you were fired, if you have a DUI, if you've declared bankruptcy, if you stole something and it's on your record, etc., my advice is to fess up and speak to this sooner rather than later. There are many people who are empathetic and understanding of others making mistakes. I'm sure this isn't always the case, but on the rare occasion we've had candidates with blemishes on their background checks, disclosing earlier has resulted in better outcomes.

If a candidate proactively shares any "issues" that could come to light in a background check, a company / hiring manager will be more apt to fairly assess them versus finding out bad news once the results of a background check are returned. After having been in this profession for more years than I care to count, I (mistakenly) thought I'd pretty much seen and heard it all. Boy, was I wrong! This one's a doozy: I was asked to help a client find a new Head of HR. I was relatively early in the search and had just presented a candidate whom they were excited about and whom I totally loved. They quickly scheduled an initial interview with this person, and they, too, completely fell in love immediately! I'm talking, they thought this person was the one! Naturally, I was ecstatic! Not only could this mean I might wrap up the search quickly and be able to take on another ($$), but it could selfishly make me look really good in my client's eyes.

Can anything ever be easy?!?!

Nope!

(Cue the ominous music...)

So I was driving my son to baseball practice, and I received two calls, one right after the other. Caller ID flashed on my dashboard. Both times it was my client. The same client. Being paranoid, I of course assumed that was a bad sign. Quickly after the calls, the dreaded text "bing" went off, and I again saw the client's name on my dashboard. I always try to avoid doing business with others in the car, so I waited until my son was out before doing anything. Rather than peeling out of the parking lot and racing home, I pulled into a spot and looked at my text. It said, "Listen to my voice mail." (Oh dear Lord—my gut told me this was bad.) I listened to the voice mail, and essentially, my client said something to the effect of "I just emailed you. Take a look. I'm assuming you didn't know this. But Joe Schmo [a top exec at the company] was researching HR candidate Bob and found Bob has a record...a criminal record. Call me right away to discuss."

(Me: I'm sorry—whaaaaaaat?!?!?!?! A record? Like an arrest record??)

I checked my email (after having a massive coronary), and sure enough, my client had forwarded me the email from Joe Schmo, which said something like, "Hey. I don't know if Nicki's team shared this with you or not, but see these links. Bob appears to have had some issues with the law. Granted these arrests were quite some time ago, and I'm not saying this is a deal-breaker. People grow up and change. But it's something for us to consider. Let me know if you knew about this."

My client asked me if I in fact knew about the two times this person was arrested. Uh, yeah—two arrests. Not one. But, two. And by the way, these were both felony charges. One case was settled. And in the other, the charges were dropped. But whatever...my candidate, Bob, was arrested twice! And both arrests were made when Bob was in his twenties. (Holy shit!) And no, I had zero clue!

OK, so, first of all, you're all undoubtedly (and rightfully) wondering why I didn't know this. A quick Google search by my client unearthed this info, and it's absolutely fair to ask me why the heck I didn't Google this person myself and uncover it first.

Valid point! My explanation—after doing hundreds of Google searches that netted me the same information I was finding out in conversations and on résumés, bios, websites, etc., I got complacent. I stopped doing them. In addition, because all my clients do thorough background checks, I trusted candidates to disclose if anything shady would be discovered. (By the way, once I know someone is a viable candidate and they're interested in moving forward in my interview process, I make it very clear that thorough background checks will be done by the client at offer stage. I stress to each and every candidate that if there's anything, anything at all, I should know about in advance of said thorough background check, they should please let me know.) Needless to say, Bob did not accept my invitation to fess up when I went through my spiel about background checks. And I got burned! Now, lucky for me, my client could not have been nicer about this situation and, in fact, was really struggling with whether or not to cut ties with the candidate. They were being extremely open-minded about Bob's bad judgment. Ultimately, though, because HR touches some of a company's most sensitive information, they decided they couldn't proceed. The leadership team needed to know without any hesitation the hire could be trusted. Because Bob wasn't forthright with his "record," it felt a bit deceptive. We all fully empathized with the fact that a person wasn't going to typically start an interview process with "Before we get going, I want to let you know I was arrested twice, and here are the stories…" At the same time, though, Bob had spent a great deal of time with me prior to getting in front of my client and chose to withhold the information. I truly believe Bob's a good person, but this falls into the "if you did it, admit it" category. Had Bob addressed this earlier in the process, there's a very good chance the client would have proceeded with him. Substantial time had passed since the two run-ins with the law, and they did say they believe in giving second chances. But alas…we'll never know.

Here are some other examples:

If you messed up the time of an interview and missed it, don't just disappear and ghost the company (or recruiter). Fess up. Don't assume you're out of contention. If you own it and apologize, you might have a chance to stay in the process. People goof up. People miss interviews. Many hiring managers will give you one free pass. You can salvage your opportunity…if you admit your mistake.

If you were fired from a position, own it. Admit it. We've talked about this before. It's never fun to have to say you were fired. But most people are forgiving and open to learning more about the situation before immediately making a judgment call. In an interview process, if someone asks you about a failure or a regret, have an actual answer. You can't go through life without a failure. We've all had them. Not to sound cliché, but I love failures (OK, maybe not all failures…), and I know a lot of execs who do too. Failures lead to successes. If you did something to help cause the failure, own it. Admit it. Share what you learned from it. Many of my clients in the start-up arena love to hire people who've been in similar-sized companies and who had failures because it often means they know what not to do; they know where some of the land mines are hiding.

If you did it and you admit it, this helps those interviewing you feel confident you're an honest person. Honesty and integrity are two characteristics lauded by most companies. If you give decision-makers any reason to question your honesty and / or your integrity, you will likely get knocked out of a process quickly.

Owning it and admitting it also help people know your ego is in check. We've all met the person who has done no wrong, the person who always has someone they point to and put the blame on. They never seem to look in the mirror. Ever. You know who I'm talking about, and that person totally sucks! Don't be that person. If you did it, admit it!

You're NOT the Boss

WHEN YOU WERE A KID, did you have that friend who insisted on everyone doing everything their way? You know this kid…they're the one who pouted if they didn't get to be in charge and make every single decision. The kid who took their ball and left the park if they didn't like how the game was going. I don't know about you, but I found "that kid" to be super annoying. Therefore, I did everything in my power to ensure when my kids were young, they weren't "that kid." It's tricky, though, because you don't want to discourage them from developing leadership skills. And, truth be told, it was rather funny watching them play with friends and hearing someone say, "You're not the boss of me!" It always made me laugh.

At some point in your youth, you probably had a job of some kind. Whether it was mowing lawns, watering plants, babysitting, reffing, umping, dog walking, working in a restaurant, being a camp counselor, etc., you learned what it was like to have a superior, someone who had the ability to call the shots whom you "reported to." In other words, you learned what it's like to have an employer / a boss who gets to tell you when to come and go, what you need to do to keep your job, and how to respect authority. Some of us learned the hard way what happens when we don't fall in line, when we ruffle feathers. Now, I'm sure you'll be shocked to learn, I am a total rule follower. I was always scared of getting in trouble. I wouldn't dare talk back or disobey authority.

Back when I was a candidate interviewing for jobs (yes, it was a long time ago!), I would have never ever challenged or disrespected authority. I was always so thankful to have the opportunity and if I was there, I wanted that job. I would never have dreamt of making bold requests as I knew full well that stating my must-haves up front would likely not bode well. I knew how fortunate I was to get the interview and if I started declaring my expectations, I'd be immediately passed over, resulting in no job for moi, which in turn meant no money too!

In today's post-pandemic world, employees / candidates seem to be far more comfortable making their list of demands known to current and / or future employers. For example, because remote work was the norm during the height of COVID, people got comfortable working from home and many simply refused to go back to the office when their employers began implementing "return to office" mandates. As a recruiter, I continue to see innumerable professionals flat out refuse opportunities that aren't fully remote or hybrid. Now, you may be thinking there's nothing wrong with making such demands or having such expectations. And in an extremely robust job market (often referred to as a "candidate's market"), you'd have a valid point! However, in a tough job market where opportunities are more scarce, being open to opportunities that might not fully fit what you want is critical. Someday, when you're the boss, you can make decisions. I can promise you a longer job search makes it increasingly more difficult to land a job, especially earlier in your career. (The more senior you are in your role, the fewer open positions you'll find and thus job searches often take longer.)

By the way, if you're currently employed, please note that bashing your employer for mandating a return to office policy is not smart. You don't hold the cards. They do. And, they have every right to make such a decision.

As an employee, if you disagree, what you can do is quit. But what you can't do is act out and / or threaten your employer for their decisions. You are not the boss. If you dislike decisions at the top, then don't work there. No one has handcuffed you to the job. As a small business owner myself, I see up close the sacrifices people who start companies make not only financially but personally too. There is a tremendous amount of risk tied to starting a business and the amount of blood, sweat, and tears that go into trying to get a business off the ground and then, ideally, making it thrive is enormous. If you want to call the shots, then you go do your own thing. Start a company yourself. Be an independent consultant. Do whatever you want, and then you get to be the boss. Until you're willing to do that, though, you need to know you're not the boss and you are not making the decisions. So fall in line or get out. Period. But seriously—quit bitching, whining, complaining, moaning, and groaning. It's exhausting! Bottom line is, as an employee and / or a candidate—you don't get to call the shots.

Every Story Has an Ending

AT SOME POINT, we're taught every story has a beginning, a middle, and an end. While I could go on and on for hundreds more pages, at the risk of getting too repetitive, it's time to bring this to a close. I'm hopeful you've enjoyed this journey. We've covered a lot of ground!

Please remember to use common sense along with the basics we all learned while growing up. If you do, you'll find more success in less time while job searching and / or interviewing. Whether you're a college graduate searching for your first job or you're a seasoned professional, know we are all a work in progress and it's "normal" to lose sight of some of the fundamentals we covered throughout this book. By revisiting them, we can avoid many of those common missteps and realize far more success.

You should be so proud of yourself as you've already done such a great thing by investing in yourself here! So…

Once upon a time, there was a wonderful person who didn't have a miserable time with their job search because they read a book that helped them avoid some of the mistakes many make which often lead to disappointing outcomes. They got an amazing job, and their career continued to flourish and soar. They achieved all they set out to. And they lived happily ever after. The end!

And for you too—I wish you all the best and a very happy ending!

www.ingramcontent.com/pod-product-compliance
Lightning Source LLC
Chambersburg PA
CBHW032101090426
42743CB00007B/197